# UNCOUTH NATION

The Public Square/Princeton University Press

*Series Editor*
Ruth O'Brien

*Uncouth Nation* by Andrei Markovits

# UNCOUTH NATION

----------------------------------------------------------------

## Why Europe Dislikes America

Andrei S. Markovits

PRINCETON UNIVERSITY PRESS

PRINCETON AND OXFORD

Requests for permission to reproduce material from this work should be sent to Permissions, Princeton University Press

Published by Princeton University Press, 41 William Street, Princeton, New Jersey 08540
In the United Kingdom: Princeton University Press, 3 Market Place, Woodstock, Oxfordshire OX20 1SY

*Library of Congress Cataloging-in-Publication Data*

Markovits, Andrei S.
Uncouth Nation : why Europe dislikes America / Andrei S. Markovits.
p.   cm.
Includes bibliographical references and index.
ISBN-13: 978-0-691-12287-8 (alk. paper)
ISBN-10: 0-691-12287-3 (alk. paper)
1. Anti-Americaism—Europe. 2. Europe—Relations—United States. 3. United States—Relations—Europe. 4. Europe—Civilization—American influences. I. Title.
D1065.U5M37 2007
303.48′24073—dc22
2006009790

British Library Cataloging-in-Publication Data is available

This book has been composed in Janson with Flood Std. and Memphis display.

pup.princeton.edu

Printed in the United States of America

10   9   8   7   6   5   4   3

# CONTENTS

------------------------------------------------------------

I sat on our green-striped sofa, alone, midmorning, the day after President George W. Bush's reelection. The *Times* lay unopened in my lap. Hearing my Dutch mother-in-law come down the stairs, I thought she was headed for the kitchen, when she surprised me. Coming up from behind the sofa, she poked my right shoulder. "See!" she said—as if I were a member of the Republican electorate. Startled, I turned my head to look at her. But before I could reply, she had disappeared into the kitchen.

Any other day, I would have followed her. I would have tried to hold my own. But that morning I didn't. I couldn't blame her. I was the only American she knew. And I was sitting before her. Still, her jab left me feeling affronted, misunderstood. What hurt most was the realization that her response wasn't just about the election. She'd always felt this way about the United States. The election results merely gave her a chance to poke me.

Andrei Markovits' fine book captures my mother-in-law's opinion as well as that of many other Europeans. As he so astutely observes, it's not my mother-in-law's Dutch identity that explains her behavior. Although she's a proper Dutch housewife who wears sensible leather shoes, what makes her European is her anti-Americanism. To Markovits, anti-Americanism is now "common fare." It has become "proper etiquette," even for housewives. It exists in the "right, left, and center, in economics, politics, culture, the social world, and almost every realm." It is "lingua-franca" for both the counterculture youth and the cultural elite. Anti-Americanism unites Europeans of all ages and backgrounds. My mother-in-law's voice constitutes only a tiny part of this glee club.

What made her jab so poignant is that it accentuates a long-existing prejudice that the Bush administration has only heightened and made worse. As Markovits explains, fears about Americanness are as old as the earliest phase of European expansion into the New World. Martin Heidegger's portrayal of the United States as a "soulless, greedy, inauthentic force" that undermined Europe is nothing new.

What does make the current anti-Americanism distinctive as well as different from other prejudices, Markovits rightfully points out, is the "question of power." Whereas discrimination against peoples considered weak and helpless is viewed as abhorrent behavior, this isn't. Anti-Americanism is regarded as a form of fighting back. It's battling against an eight-hundred-pound gorilla, which Markovits characterizes as "threatening, powerful, clumsy, yet also inferior." Anti-Americanism is the cry of resistance of those virtuous Westerners who defend the underdog by standing tall against a new global empire.

So, too, Markovits shows us how a new form of anti-Semitism has become one of the anti-American refrains. While the old anti-Semitism portrayed Jews as feeble victims, the new anti-Semitism views Israeli Jews as powerful agents taking charge. Israel is a new bully in an old land. Worse, the Israelis are the new Nazis. In a move certain to ignite discussion, Markovits illustrates how anti-Americanism has led to the expression of a new type of anti-Semitism in which Israel represents the "collective Jew." Like anti-Americanism, anti-Semitism has no country-specific differences and is antonymous. Europeans see Israel and the United States as "too strong and too weak; too rich and too poor; too radical and too conservative; too assimilated and universalistic, but too sectarian and clubby and particularistic." What is most telling for Markovits is that the Europeans' hostility toward Israel does not translate into any support for Muslims or disadvantaged Arabs on the Gaza strip. It is simply a blank bias or prejudice.

It is just this type of provocation that makes Markovits' book perfect for the Public Square. This new series features public intellectuals writing on politics, broadly cast. Writing to get us thinking, to get us talking, and to get us arguing, Markovits will undoubtedly fulfill the Public Square's mission. Not only does he show us how "substance and debates matter because they create 'frames' that influence political behavior and contribute to enduring elements of political culture," but his book offers its own frame. By tracing the shifts in language and unpacking the "new codes for old ideas" about anti-Americanism and anti-Semitism, Markovits is "writing politics."

Ruth O'Brien
The CUNY Graduate Center
New York, New York

---------------------------------------------------

When my father and I arrived in the United States as immigrants from Romania—by way of Vienna—in the summer of 1960, we spent a number of weeks living with American families in the greater New York area. Some were Jews, like us; most were not. But all spoke some German because our English was virtually nonexistent at the time. What impressed me no end and will always remain with me was how all these people adored my Viennese-accented German, how they reveled in it, found it elegant, charming, and above all oh-so-cultured. For business and family reasons, my father had to return to Vienna where I attended the Theresianische Akademie, one of Austria's leading gymnasia. The welcome accorded to me in this environment was much colder and more distant than it had been in the United States, but not by dint of my being a "Tschusch" and a "Zuagraster," an interloper from the disdained eastern areas of Europe, but by virtue of having become a quasi American. From the get-go until my graduation from this school many years later, I was always admonished by my English teachers in their heavily accented, Viennese-inflected English not to speak this abomination of an "American dialect" or "American slang" and never to use "American spelling" with its simplifications that testified prima facie to the uncultured and simpleton nature of Americans. Of course, any of my transgressions, be it chatting in class or playing soccer in the hallways, was met with an admonition of "Markovits, we are not in the Wild West, we are not in Texas. Behave yourself." Viennese-accented German—wonderful; American-accented English—awful. The pattern still pertains nearly fifty years later just like it pertained fifty years before.

European-American comparisons, as well as the perception of one continent's culture by the other and vice versa, have remained central to virtually all aspects of my personal and professional life. Thus, for example, my previous book published by Princeton University Press (*Offside: Soccer and American Exceptionalism*) analyzed America's sports culture in a direct comparison with its European counterpart. Since 1980 I have regularly published a number of academic and journalistic articles in the United States and Europe on the topic of anti-Americanism. In my studies of German-Jewish relations, I have come to learn a bit about anti-Semitism and anti-Zionism in Germany and beyond, which has led to articles on these related topics in scholarly as well as journalistic venues over the past twenty-five years on both sides of the Atlantic. Even though I have expressed myself on these related issues in many fora virtually since the beginning of my academic career, I had never published a book on any of these subjects, either separately or jointly.

That is reason enough to make this volume very special for me. But there is yet another that needs mention. The specific origins of this book date back to an inaugural lecture I delivered on September 24, 2003, upon becoming the Karl W. Deutsch Collegiate Professor of Comparative Politics and German Studies at the University of Michigan. According to this fine university's rules and customs, anyone awarded a "collegiate professorship" may name her or his chair after a former (or even current) person associated with the University of Michigan's faculty or staff. I had the singularly good fortune of being able to name "my" chair after my mentor and friend Karl W. Deutsch. Not only had he received an honorary doctorate from the University of Michigan; for years, he had also cooperated closely with colleagues at Michigan, and he had been a guest professor there in the fall of 1977.

In our close relationship as academics and (above all) friends, which we cultivated intensely for years on both sides of the Atlantic (mainly in Cambridge, Massachusetts, and Berlin), Karl Deutsch and I were constantly posing comparisons between Europe and America. Be it political science or theater, education or leisure time activities, economics or literature, there was not a single subject that we had not touched upon. Although Karl had left his native Prague for the United States as long ago as 1938 and was thirty-six years older than I, there was a great deal of common experience—in the Old World and in the New—that bound us together. We also spoke, of course, many times about anti-Americanism as a normative and empirical construct that deserves attention and study. I therefore thought it appropriate to dedicate my inaugural lecture, in Karl's honor, to the subject of anti-Americanism. In front of a very large public that included—most important and loveliest of all—the late Ruth Deutsch, Karl's then ninety-two-year-old widow and a dear friend to me in her own right, I gave a lecture with the title "European Anti-Americanism: Past and Present of a Pedigreed Prejudice." This was—and certainly shall remain—the greatest and most moving experience of my academic career.

Bespeaking the Zeitgeist, I subsequently delivered nearly forty lectures in the next three years on this topic at universities and other venues in the United States, Canada, Germany, Austria, Hungary, and Israel. A number of scholarly articles appeared in German and English on both sides of the Atlantic. In October 2004 I published my first book written in German: *Amerika, dich hasst sich's besser. Antiamerikanismus und Antisemitismus in Europa* (Hamburg: Konkret-Literatur Verlag). To my great delight and even greater surprise, that book met with critical acclaim in both Germany and Austria and is now in its third edition. The book at hand owes much to all these precursors but represents very much an endeavor all its own.

Lastly, there is yet another personal dimension informing this book and project. It pertains to my life-long affinity with the democratic left in Europe and the United States. There can be no doubt that anti-Americanism has become a kind of litmus test for progressive thinking and identity in Europe and the world (including the United States itself). Just as any self-respecting progressive and leftist in Europe or America, regardless of which political shade, simply *had* to be on the side of the Spanish Republic in the 1930s, anti-Americanism and anti-Zionism have become *the* requisite proof of possessing a progressive conviction today. In making this comparison I am not trying to equate the morality of these two tests of progressive character. On the contrary, the high moral legitimacy that support for the Spanish Republic enjoyed on the part of the European and American Left at that time is something that in my view neither anti-Zionism nor anti-Americanism can claim. This example of the interwar era Spanish Republic merely serves to illustrate the similarly potent and almost universal mobilizing power of anti-Americanism and anti-Zionism for today's Left. In the 1930s it was impossible to be regarded as any kind of leftist without having supported the Spanish Republic (with the exception—briefly and after the fact—of those Stalinists during the Hitler-Stalin pact who toed the Comintern line, chastising anti-Franco activists as "premature antifascists"); today it is hard to be accepted as a leftist by other leftists without anti-Americanism and anti-Zionism. Over the last thirty-five years, a steady anti-Americanism and an uncompromising anti-Zionism, which occasionally borders on the anti-Semitic, have become key characteristics that both divide and determine political identity absolutely. They are "wedge issues"—clear articles of faith or "deal breakers"—whose importance overshadows, and even negates, many related components of the "clusters" that characterize such an identity.

I can explain this using myself as an illustration: I am an advocate of affirmative action in all realms of public life; a supporter for decades of numerous civil rights organizations, in favor of complete equality for women and discriminated ethnic groups, especially blacks, in the United States; an opponent of the death penalty. I favor legally recognized marriages for gays and lesbians; support the right of all women to complete and exclusive autonomy over their bodies, in other words, the right to an abortion; support unrestricted stem cell research, an issue on which the European Left incidentally shares views that are far closer to those of the much-hated George W. Bush than they are to mine; and favor the Kyoto Climate Protocol, the International Criminal Court, the Ottawa Conventions on the ban of land mines, and the International Biological Weapons Convention. I do not want prayers in public schools and oppose charter schools; I favor strict gun control laws and—as an animal benefit activist— oppose hunting for sport. I have always supported trade unions in their difficult struggles, always favor increases in the minimum wage, have never broken a strike or crossed a picket line, even when I did not agree with the striking union's demands; I welcome the legalization of marijuana, advocate a more just and socially conscious health care system, and desire progressive taxation and a much greater role for the public sector in economic matters. I am a decisive opponent of subsidies for rich American (and European) farmers, deride the exclusivity and price gouging of the pharmaceutical industry, oppose trafficking in women and exploitation of children, and am appalled by the erosion of civil liberties in the United States as well as by the shameful, completely illegal situation in Guantanamo and the outrageous abuses in Abu Ghraib prison. I have been a committed supporter of American and German labor and a student and partial, if often critical, admirer of European social democracy and its Green offspring.

In terms of the Israeli–Palestinian conflict, I have always supported the creation of a sovereign Palestinian state and have held views that have been akin to the Israeli peace camp's. I have regularly condemned and opposed certain measures of American foreign policy, regardless of which party needed to be held responsible (whether the Vietnam policy of Democrat Lyndon B. Johnson or the Iraq policy of Republican George W. Bush), and I have therefore—as should be obvious from the above list—positioned myself quite clearly on the left side of the political spectrum in America (and Europe as well). Yet I am increasingly avoided by leftists on both sides of the Atlantic owing solely to the two wedge issues mentioned above. As a reaction against this, I find myself having withdrawn from the established American and European lefts in whose presence I feel increasingly misplaced. I am not writing this to elicit sympathy for my increasing political marginalization but rather to make a point of how central anti-Americanism and anti-Zionism have become to virtually all lefts on both sides of the Atlantic and beyond.

I am greatly indebted to so many people whose help in one way or another proved indispensable to the creation of this book that I cannot list them all in this limited space. But a few will be named nonetheless. Peter Katzenstein and Robert Keohane, who are in the process of publishing their own path-breaking work on anti-Americanism in a number of venues, proved to be more influential on my thinking and writing on this difficult issue than I cared to admit to them in person. I have known and admired Peter's prodigious work on so many topics for nearly forty years, perhaps—I admit it—not least because he, too, shares a particular bond with Karl Deutsch, having been Karl's doctoral student at Harvard. Our many e-mails about anti-Americanism attest to the emotional charge of this sensitive topic and our disagreements about aspects of its importance and nature. But the correspondence also bespeaks a mutual admiration, collegiality, and friendship that I share with Peter and that I will always cherish, no matter the differences in our opinions and interpretations. I do not know Bob as well as I do Peter. But I am grateful to Bob's analytic acuity, his conceptual rigor, and his well-founded criticisms that he expressed to me in a spirit of collegiality and respect. Bob's insights forced me to rethink some of my work and—in the process—render it better. The massive reports by the two anonymous readers for Princeton University Press led me to rewrite and reorganize the manuscript substantially. I owe great thanks to the quantity and quality of their comments, which were truly amazing and way beyond the usual substance and tone common to this academic exercise. My friend Jeff Weintraub was, as always, a fountain of knowledge, insight, and encouragement. I will always be grateful for his having read the entire manuscript and his commenting on it to such benefit for my final product. Jeremiah Riemer's regular e-mails alerting me to relevant issues in the European press, his assistance in translating some passages from the original German text into the current English, and his solid friendship remain priceless. My doctoral students Alice Weinreb and Stacy Swennes helped me immensely with aspects of the research as well as the manuscript preparation.

Lastly, I owe much thanks to Richard Wolin, whose work I have admired for years but whom I did not know personally until that wonderful day in late March 2004 when we found ourselves both at Princeton and Richard introduced me to the editor of his just-published *The Seduction of Unreason*. It was thus that I met Brigitta Van Rheinberg, who assumed the perhaps thankless task of becoming the editor of this book as well. All I can say is that there ain't none better than Brigitta. Working with her on this project was more than a pleasure. It really was a privilege and a wonderful experience that I will always cherish. Through Brigitta I met Ruth O'Brien, who—together with Brigitta—has organized the "Public Square" forum jointly sponsored by Princeton University Press and the Graduate Center of the City University of New York. Ruth asked me to present my work in this forum in April 2005, which I gladly did and which became a precursor for this book. I am greatly indebted to Ruth's kind words about my study in this book's foreword. It is an honor to have my work be the first published in what promises to be a series of superb books authored by leading scholars of fascinating and controversial subjects.

My darling wife Kiki's patience, love, and support proved once again to be indispensable sources of comfort, confidence, and encouragement throughout the ordeal that the writing of any book always becomes. I owe her more than I can ever hope to express properly. Since I seem unable to keep my promises to Kiki that this will be my last book and major project for awhile, and that we will take lengthy vacations in exotic places, she decided to join me in my next endeavor as my co-author on a book about the changed discourse toward animals as representatives of the weak over the past four decades in advanced industrial democracies. I will forever associate this book's creation and production with our late Stormi's and recently adopted Cleo Rose's constant companionship. As our friend Krista Luker so well put it: Golden retrievers are definitely this world's bodhisattvas. I would like to dedicate this book to the memory of Karl and Ruth Deutsch and of my father, Ludwig Markovits, transatlantic souls and beings all.

# UNCOUTH NATION

# *INTRODUCTION*

Any trip to Europe confirms what the surveys have been finding: The aversion to America is becoming greater, louder, more determined.[1] It is unifying West Europeans more than any other political emotion—with the exception of a common hostility toward Israel. In today's West Europe these two closely related antipathies and resentments are now considered proper etiquette. They are present in polite company and acceptable in the discourse of the political classes. They constitute common fare among West Europe's cultural and media elites, but also throughout society itself from London to Athens and from Stockholm to Rome, even if European politicians visiting Washington or European professors at international conferences about anti-Americanism and anti-Semitism are adamant about denying or sugarcoating this reality.

There can be no doubt that many disastrous and irresponsible policies by the Bush administrations, as well as their haughty demeanor and arrogant tone, have contributed massively to this unprecedented vocal animosity on the part of Europeans toward Americans and America. George W. Bush and his administrations' policies have made America into the most hated country of all time. Indeed, they bear responsibility for having created a situation in which anti-Americanism has mutated into a sort of global antinomy, a mutually shared language of opposition to and resistance against the real and perceived ills of modernity that are now inextricably identified solely with America. I have been traveling back and forth with considerable frequency between the United States and Europe since 1960, and I cannot recall a time like the present, when such a vehement aversion to everything American has been articulated in Europe. "There has probably never been a time when America was held in such low esteem on this side of the Atlantic" wrote the distinguished British Political Scientist Anthony King in *The Daily Telegraph* on July 3, 2006, summarizing a survey that revealed a new nadir in the British view of America. No West European country is exempt from this phenomenon—not a single social class, no age group or profession, nor either gender. But this aversion and antipathy reaches much deeper and wider than the frequently evoked "anti-Bushism." Indeed, I perceive this virulent, Europe-wide, and global "anti-Bushism" as the glaring tip of a massive anti-American iceberg.

Anti-Americanism has been promoted to the status of West Europe's lingua franca. Even at the height of the Vietnam War, in the late 1960s and early 1970s, and during the dispute over NATO's "Dual Track" decision (to station Pershing and cruise missiles primarily in Germany but in other West European countries as well while negotiating with the Soviet Union over arms reduction), things were different. Each event met with a European public that was divided concerning its position toward America: In addition to those who reacted with opposition and protest, there were strong forces in almost all European countries who expressed appreciation and understanding. In France, arguably Europe's leader over the past fifteen years in most matters related to antipathy toward America, the prospect of stationing American medium-range missiles, especially if they were on German soil, even met with the massive approval of the Left in the late 1970s and early 1980s. This distinguished the French Left, arguably among the most ardently anti-American protagonists anywhere in contemporary Europe, from all of its European counterparts. That America's image was far from hunky dory in the Europe of the mid-1980s but still far exceeded its nadir reached since 9/11 and the Iraq War is attested to by the following passage from a Pew Survey:

> The numbers paint a depressing picture. Just a quarter of the French approve of U.S. policies, and the situation is only slightly better in Japan and Germany. Majorities in many countries say America's strong military presence actually increases the chances for war. And most people believe America's global influence is expanding. The latest survey on America's tarnished global image? No, those numbers

come from a poll conducted by *Newsweek* ... in 1983. The United States has been down this road before, struggling with a battered image and drawing little in the way of support even from close allies. But for a variety of reasons, this time it is different: the anti-Americanism runs broader and deeper than ever before. And it's getting worse.[2]

To be sure, as this study will be careful to delineate, opposition to U.S. policies in no way connotes anti-Americanism. But even in the allegedly halcyon days of pre-1990 West European–American relations, a palpable antipathy to things American on the part of European elites accompanied opposition to policies.

However, the climate between then and now has changed fundamentally. The fact that European elites—particularly conservative ones—have consistently been anti-American since 1776 is one of this book's central themes. But as of October 2001, six to eight weeks after 9/11 and just before the impending American war against the Taliban regime in Afghanistan, a massive Europe-wide resentment of America commenced that reached well beyond American policies, American politics, and the American government and proliferated in virtually all segments of Western Europe's publics. From grandmothers who vote for the archconservative Bavarian CSU to thirty-year-old socialist PASOK activists in Greece, from Finnish Social Democrats to French Gaullists, from globalization opponents to business managers—all are joining in the ever louder chorus of the anti-Americans. The "European street" has been more hostile to America than ever before. For the first time, anti-Americanism has entered the European mainstream.[3] If anti-Americanism has been part of the *condition humaine* in Europe for at least two centuries, it has been since 9/11 that the rise of a hitherto unprecedented, wholly voluntary, and uncoordinated conformity in Western European public opinion regarding America and American politics occurred. I would go so far as to characterize the public voice and mood in these countries as *gleichgeschaltet*, comprising a rare but powerful discursive and emotive congruence and conformity among all actors in state and society. What rendered this *Gleichschaltung* so different from those that accompany most dictatorships was its completely voluntary, thus democratic, nature. Especially leading up to and during the Iraq War, there appeared an almost perfect concordance among a vast majority of European public opinion, the European "street" by way of the largest demonstrations in European history, the media, most political parties, and many—if certainly not all—European governments. Western Europe spoke loudly and passionately with a unified voice that one rarely, if ever, encountered in such openly contested pluralist democracies.

The Bush administrations' policies have catapulted global and West European anti-Americanism into overdrive. But to understand this "overdrive," we need to analyze the conditions under which this kind of shift into high gear could occur. This book is intended to make such a contribution. Its aim is to show that the West Europeans' unconditional rejection of and legitimate outrage over abusive and irresponsible American policies—not to mention massive human rights violations à la Abu Ghraib, Guantanamo, secret CIA cells, and others of such ilk—rest on a substantial sediment of hatred toward, disdain for, and resentment of America that has a long tradition in Europe and has flourished apart from these or any policies.

Here, in short, is the book's overall argument: Ambivalence, antipathy, and resentment toward and about the United States have comprised an important component of European culture since the American Revolution at the latest, thus way before America became the world's "Mr. Big"—the proverbial eight-hundred-pound gorilla—and a credible rival to Europe's main powers, particularly Britain and France. In recent years, following the end of the Cold War and particularly after 9/11, ambivalence in some quarters has given way to outright antipathy and unambiguous hostility. Animosity toward the United States migrated from the periphery and disrespected fringes of European politics and became a respectable part of the European mainstream. These negative sentiments and views have been driven not only—or even primarily—by what the United States *does*, but rather by an animus against what Europeans have believed that America *is*. Anti-Americanism has been a core element, indeed at times a dominant one, among European elites for centuries. The presidency of George W. Bush, the American response to the terrorist attacks on September 11, 2001, and Bush's unilateral decision to commence the war against Iraq all led to a dramatic increase in hostility to the United States in Europe's "respectable" opinion. Moreover, for the first time since World War II, long-standing elite resentments against the United States fused with popular sentiments to create a kind of political and cultural perfect storm: Short-term crises brought long-standing antipathies to the surface. While the politics, style, and discourse of the Bush administrations—and of George W. Bush as a person—have undoubtedly exacerbated anti-American sentiment among Europeans and fostered a heretofore unmatched degree of unity between elite and mass opinion in Europe, they are not anti-Americanism's cause. Indeed, a change to a center-left administration in Washington, led by a Democratic president, would not bring about its abatement, let alone disappearance.

Chapter 1 features my definition and conceptualization of anti-Americanism. In particular, I argue that anti-Americanism constitutes a particular prejudice that renders it not only acceptable but indeed commendable in the context of an otherwise welcome development in a discourse that favors the weak.

Chapter 2 presents some historical features of European anti-Americanism in order to demonstrate that all of its present components have been alive and well in Europe's intellectual discourse since the late eighteenth century. In particular, this chapter highlights how integral and ubiquitous the anti-American tropes about Americans' alleged venality, mediocrity, uncouthness, lack of culture, and above all inauthenticity have been to European elite opinion for well over two hundred years.

Chapter 3 features a bevy of examples from many walks of life that highlight the pervasive and quotidian nature of anti-American discourse among European publics. I have collected all my examples from areas outside of what one would conventionally associate with politics *precisely* to demonstrate that the European animus against things American has little to do with the politics and policies of the Bush administration—or any other administration, for that matter—and is alive and well in realms that prima facie have few connections to politics. I consider many examples from diverse topics, such as language, sports, work, higher education, the media, health, law and the judicial system, and miscellaneous items (the presence of Halloween, for instance) in seven West European countries to demonstrate that the antipathy toward America and things American reaches much beyond politics and the discourse of one or two countries alone. By analyzing a bevy of newspaper and magazine articles from the 1990s, I hope to demonstrate that the presence and passion of anti-American discourse among Europeans much preceded the administrations of George W. Bush. The West European media report almost nothing that they associate with America in a neutral, matter-of-fact manner. Most things engender a palpable tone of irritation, derision, annoyance, dismissal. Terms such as "Americanization" and its equivalents—"American conditions," for example—have in the meantime assumed an exclusively pejorative connotation in present European discourse. They have become a *Schimpfwort*, a derogatory term for anything that one wants to discredit and stigmatize even if the issue at hand might have little to do with the real existing America or its conditions.

To show that these prima facie innocuous put-downs of American things (so what if one dislikes the alleged "Americanization" of cricket, of political correctness, of spelling, of antismoking laws, of family life, of business practices) do cumulatively constitute a palpably negative whole, I then proceed to summarize in chapter 4 the findings of some key surveys of the recent past that leave no doubt that a majority of Europeans have come to dislike America, if not with massive passion, then surely with a tangible opinion that matters politically.

Anti-Semitism is the subject of chapter 5. Rather than viewing this chapter as an in-depth analysis of anti-Semitism in contemporary Western Europe, I devote attention to this phenomenon solely because anti-Semitism has consistently been such an integral part of anti-Americanism and because the virulence in the hostility to Israel cannot be understood without the presence of anti-Americanism and hostility to the United States. Thus, I see my presentation of anti-Semitism and anti-Israelism as a subset of my larger discussion of anti-Americanism. Anti-Semitism's connection to anti-Ameri-

canism appears to be empirically forceful and compelling if conceptually far from necessary or stringent. The same pertains to the relation between anti-Semitism and opposition to Israeli policies, even
Israel's existence as a state. While opposition to Israeli policies and
to Israel's existence are in and of themselves far from being anti-
Semitic in any conceptually stringent manner, both do in reality—
and despite protests to the contrary—often include anti-Semitic
tropes and moments. These, in turn accompany anti-Americanism.
In this syndrome, Israel, due to its association with the United
States, is eo ipso perceived by its European critics as powerful, with
both being mere extensions of one another. Being an American ally
and also powerful in its own right renders Israel an obvious target
on the part of most European critics who oppose both power in
general and American power in particular. But there must be something else at work here as well, because America has many other
powerful allies that never receive anywhere near the hostile scrutiny
that Israel confronts on a daily basis. No European academic has
attempted to boycott British—or for that matter Spanish or
French—universities because Britain, Spain, and France are American allies that happen to be very powerful and can easily be construed—certainly from the logic of the sanctity of national liberation
that has been so central to the Left since the late 1960s—to occupy
foreign land in Ulster, the Basque Country, or Corsica, respectively.
So it is not only because Israel is an American ally and powerful that
it has so massively irked European elites and publics for decades.
Clearly, the fact that Israel is primarily a Jewish state, combined with
Europe's deeply problematic and unresolved history with Jews, plays
a central role in this singularly difficult relationship. Since this issue
invariably accompanies European anti-Americanism and Europe's
irritations with America, it had to be considered in this book.

In chapter 6, I conclude my study by arguing that Europe's anti-
Americanism has become an essential ingredient in—perhaps even
a key mobilizing agent for—the inevitable formation of a common
European identity, which I have always longed for and continue to
support vigorously, though I would have preferred to witness a different agency in its creation. Anti-Americanism, I argue, has already

commenced to forge a concrete, emotionally experienced—as opposed to intellectually constructed—European identity in which Swedes and Greeks, Finns and Italians are helped to experience their still-frail emotive commonality not as "anti-Americans" but as Europeans, which at this stage constitutes one sole thing: that they are "non-Americans." Anti-Americanism will serve as a useful mobilizing agent to create awareness in Europe for that continent's new role as a growing power bloc in explicit contrast to and keen competition with the United States, not only among Europeans but also around the globe. Anti-Americanism has already begun to help create a unified European voice in global politics and will continue to be of fine service to Europe's growing power in a new global constellation of forces in which an increasingly assertive Europe will join an equally assertive China to challenge the United States on every issue that it possibly can. Thus, I argue, for the first time in anti-Americanism's two-century existence among Europe's elites—hitherto particularly pronounced among its cultural and conservative representatives—anti-Americanism has now assumed a "functional" role of mobilization and in politics. It now matters because it might in fact affect things. Or to use the language of the social sciences: Anti-Americanism in Europe has begun to mutate from the world of having been almost exclusively a "dependent variable" to becoming an "independent" one as well.

Two important qualifications need mention as this introduction's closing thoughts. First, anti-Americanism in Europe has always been accompanied by an equally discernable pro-Americanism, which, though less apparent these days, has far from disappeared. From America's "discovery" by Europeans, it has consistently embodied for them simultaneous opposites: heaven and hell; a desired panacea and a despised abomination; utopia and dystopia; dream and nightmare. Surely, any analysis of Europe's relations with America, or a comprehensive assessment of how Europeans viewed America over the past 250 years, would necessarily have to include pro-Americanism alongside anti-Americanism. But that is not my project here. I am not weighting European anti-Americanism vs. European pro-Americanism in this book. Of course there were eras in European history during which it could easily be argued that pro-American sentiments outweighed anti-American ones. But even during these times—such as after World War II and during the height of the Cold War—anti-Americanism never disappeared from European discourse and sentiment. This book is not about the history of European-American relations, nor is it an account of how Europeans perceived America over time. Instead, it focuses solely on the very real phenomenon of the persistence and current accentuation of an antipathy that—I believe, as have others—is worthy of an exposé all its own. While any analysis of the relation between Gentiles and Jews would, by necessity, have to include philo-Semitism alongside anti-Semitism, I believe that the study of the latter all its own is valid. The same pertains to racism. Surely, any solid treatise of relations between or among different ethnic groups or races necessitates a presentation of all aspects of these relations, both positive and negative. However, a study solely of the negative and pejorative—i.e., racism—remains valid in and of itself. The same pertains to a study of anti-Americanism.

Second, this book deals exclusively with the countries of "Old Europe," featuring Germany and Britain in particular, with France accorded solid attention as well, and complemented with examples from Spain, Italy, Austria, and Portugal (as well as Greece in chapter 5). Obviously, the Scandinavian and Benelux countries would have been worthy of consideration, but a cursory acquaintance with their views of America allows me to believe that the results presented here would not have been noticeably different. This would not have been the case with Ireland's inclusion since a strong pro-American sentiment continues to prevail on the levels of both elite and mass opinion in that country. However, the book's most serious shortcoming in my view is its complete exclusion of Eastern Europe because all indications point to the strong fact that my findings there—in terms of both the present and the past—would have been diametrically opposite to the ones I encountered in the western half of the continent. In addition to purely pedestrian reasons for this omission, which pertain to my ignorance of any East European language beyond Hungarian and Romanian, and lack of temporal and monetary resources, one methodologically sound argument might at least partially justify this restricted presentation of Europe: Eastern Europeans' overwhelmingly positive views of America stem largely from their having perceived the United States as their sole ally against the much-despised Soviet Union. Thus, for this study, the comparability of contemporary anti-Americanism in France, Germany, and Britain is much more conceptually stringent and theoretically compelling than it would be with Poland, Hungary, and Romania thrown into the mix since all the countries considered in this study have furnished, in a political, economic, cultural, and—except Austria—military alliance with the United States, what was once known as "the West."[4]

*CHAPTER 1*

------------------------------------------------------------

# Anti-Americanism as a European Lingua Franca

## Anti-Americanism:
### What America *Is* vs. What America *Does*

Anti-Americanism is a particularly murky concept because it invariably merges antipathy toward what America *does* with what America *is*—or rather is projected to be in the eyes of its beholders.[1] The difference between "does" and "is" corresponds well with Jon Elster's distinction between "anger" and "hatred." Elster writes: "In anger, my hostility is directed toward another's action and can be extinguished by getting even—an action that reestablishes the equilibrium. In hatred, my hostility is directed toward another person or a category of individuals [Americans and/or Jews/Israelis in the case of this study, A.M.] who are seen as intrinsically and irremediably bad. For the world to be made whole, they have to disappear."[2] But even in hatred one needs to draw a difference between "I hate what you do" and "I hate you." Joseph Joffe aptly differentiated between these two concepts in a lecture on anti-Americanism at Stanford University: "To attack particular policies—say, the refusal to sign on to Kyoto, the Complete Test Ban or the Landmine Ban—is *not* anti-American. These issues are amenable to rational discourse. . . . To argue that the U.S. defied international law by going to war against Iraq may be true or false. It is certainly not anti-American."[3]

What, then, is the "real thing," the real anti-Americanism? In his analysis, Joffe groups anti-Americanism with other forms of "anti-isms" that—for him—must satisfy the following five conditions:

1. Stereotypization (that is, statements of the type: "This is what they are all like.")
2. Denigration (the ascription of a collective moral or cultural inferiority to the target group)
3. Omnipotence (e.g., "They control the media, the economy, the world.")
4. Conspiracy (e.g., "This is what they want to do to us surreptitiously and stealthily—sully our racial purity, destroy our traditional, better, and morally superior ways.")
5. Obsession (a constant preoccupation with the perceived and feared evil and powerful ways of the hated group)

Moreover, like all anti-isms, anti-Americanism constitutes "a ballet of shifting grounds and unfalsifiable denigrations whose main function, one must conclude, is to establish moral and cultural superiority vis-à-vis the Yahoos of America. In other words, it is not the facts that create the anti-ism, but anti-ism that creates and selects its own facts."[4]

Thus, anti-Americanism has characteristics like any other prejudice in that its holder "prejudges" the object and its activities apart from what transpires in reality.[5] Here I avail myself of Paul Sniderman's pioneering work on prejudice. In a number of major studies, Sniderman and his colleagues demonstrate that prejudice has the following minimal characteristics:

- judging an individual not by her or his personal qualities but in reaction to her or his group membership, which is invariably seen in a pejorative light;
- seeing prejudice not as something "archaic" and retrograde but indeed as a social ordering that exists among all groups and social strata in allegedly modern and tolerant societies;
- the almost innate preference for those that are like us, even in the flimsiest way, as opposed to those that are not, a clear in-group preference over any out-group; and

• the formation of stereotypes, which, far from simplemindedness, irrationality, and retrograde thinking, has an important ordering function and thus seems to be ubiquitous.[6]

Just as in the case of any prejudice, anti-Americanism also says much more about those who hold it than about the object of its ire and contempt. But where it differs markedly from "classical" prejudices—such as anti-Semitism, homophobia, misogyny, and racism—is on the dimension of power. Jews, gays and lesbians, women, and ethnic minorities rarely if ever have any actual power in and over the majority populations or dominant gender of most countries. However, the real existing United States does have considerable power, which has increasingly assumed a global dimension since the end of the ninteenth century and which has, according to many scholarly analysts and now as a commonplace, become unparalleled in human history with the passing of the Cold War in the late 1980s and early 1990s. Because of this unique paradox, the separation between what America *is*—i.e., its way of life, its symbols, products, people—and what America *does*—its foreign policy writ large—will forever be jumbled and impossible to disentangle. Indeed, I see as one of this book's main tasks—particularly through the "nonpolitical" examples assembled in chapter 3—to approximate just such a disentanglement as best one can.

While other public prejudices, particularly against the weak, have—in a fine testimony to progress and tolerance over the past forty years—become largely illegitimate in the public discourse of most advanced industrial democracies (the massive change in the accepted language about—and thus the legitimate behavior toward—women, gays, the physically challenged, minorities of all kinds, and animals, to name but a few, over the past three decades in the discourse of advanced industrial societies has been nothing short of fundamental), nothing of the sort pertains to the perceived and the actually strong. Thus, anti-Americanism not only remains acceptable in many circles but has even become commendable, indeed a badge of honor, and perhaps one of the most distinct icons of what it means to be a progressive these days precisely because it is directed against something that by no stretch of the imagination

can be construed as weak. Therefore, by being anti-American, paradoxically, one adheres to a prejudice that, ipso facto, seems to confer
on its bearer the stamp not of intolerance but of legitimate resister
and opponent against a truly powerful force in the world. Power
and its perception play—as I shall argue in this book—a parallel and
highly related role as to how Jews and Israel fare in the world of
accepted public opinion: While classic anti-Semitism still remains
by and large illegitimate in the discourse of advanced industrial democracies because it constructs Jews as weak and victims, the position against Israel can be legitimately fraught with an unlimited
number of invectives because Israel is perceived as a powerful agent
victimizing Palestinians, who—not by chance—are often perceived
as assuming the role of the Jews to Israel's status as the new Nazis.
Anti-Americanism, like any other prejudice, is an acquired set of
beliefs, an attitude, an ideology, not an ascribed trait. Thus, it is
completely independent of the national origins of its particular
holder. Indeed, many Americans can be—and are—anti-American,
just as Jews can be—and are—anti-Semitic, blacks can—and do—
hold racist views, and women misogynist ones.[7]

The reason I am mentioning this is that often the very existence
of anti-Americanism is denied by dint of Americans also adhering
to such positions. It is not a matter of the holder's citizenship or
birthplace that ought to be the appropriate criterion but rather her/
his set of acquired beliefs about a particular collective. Indeed, as
Linda Gordon and Andrew Ross argue, anti-Americanism became—often for understandable and justifiable reasons, though
mostly flawed in substance and form—an integral part of the American Left's discourse and world view.[8] But here, too, context means
everything. Delighting in Michael Moore's *Bowling for Columbine* or
*Fahrenheit 9/11* in an artsy movie theater in Ann Arbor, Madison,
Cambridge, or Berkeley is a completely different experience and has
a vastly different meaning from having Michael Moore mutate into
a veritable folk hero in Germany and much of Western Europe. To
the West European public, Moore has become a convenient shill for
voicing one's resentment toward America loudly and uninhibitedly
since—after all—if Moore as a quintessential American, baseball cap

and all, says all these derogatory things about Americans, so can Europeans without being accused of harboring anti-American sentiments.[9] Europeans delight in Moore regardless of whether he expresses justified criticisms of deplorable aspects of American politics and society or whether he sinks to the level of the crudest anti-Americanism imaginable, as he did, for example, during a lecture in Munich where he proclaimed to an audience roaring with jubilant laughter that Americans are stupid: "That's why we're smiling all the time. You can see us coming down the street. You know, 'Hey! Hi! How's it going?' We've got that big [expletive] grin on our face all the time because our brains aren't loaded down." To the English paper *The Mirror*, Moore proclaimed triumphantly that Americans "are possibly the dumbest people on the planet . . . in thrall to conniving, thieving smug [pieces of the human anatomy]."[10] Statements like these, just a few of the many Moore has uttered, have nothing to do with justified criticism of policies but are merely expressions of injurious and demeaning prejudices. In the two mentioned here, Moore addresses two standard elements of traditional European anti-Americanism: first, the amicableness of Americans that always strikes Europeans as phony, superficial, and inauthentic; and second, Americans' purported stupidity and simple-mindedness.[11]

Moore's language fuels such enthusiastic approval in Europe because—on the one hand—it now seems legitimate, even laudable and progressive, to express prejudices and derogatory views concerning Americans publicly in a way that one may no longer do precisely because advances in the discourse and demeanor of tolerance over the past forty years have made the expressions of similar derogatory sentiments regarding other nationalities unacceptable;[12] and because—on the other hand—these negative tropes are magnified and fortified by several degrees by Moore's being so quintessentially American. With the exception of the British yellow press and the stands of European soccer stadiums, public expressions of humiliation like these are no longer acceptable in today's Europe. In this context, a German friend quite correctly told me the following: "It would be unthinkable for books like *Stupid White Men* to hold leading positions for months at the top of Germany's best-seller list if these stupid white men were anybody but Americans, say if they were Italians, Frenchmen, or Brits, let alone Germans. No German author would ever dream of publishing an equivalent book on Germans, and if he or she did, the book would surely not catapult to the top of the charts as it has in Moore's case." Racist lyrics by rappers do not become less racist by virtue of their being articulated by African American artists, but their very quality changes completely when the same lyrics are uttered by whites. Few people have a more deprecating sense of humor than Jews. Yet it makes a whale of a difference whether the jokester is Jewish or not. The content defines, but the context lends meaning.

The German proverb "Der Ton macht die Musik" (the tone makes the music) informs this study since it captures the important insight that form matters at least as much as substance, indeed that form is often the same as substance. Accordingly, this study is as much about the "how" as it is about the "what." In particular, it holds that a steady—and growing—resentment of the United States (indeed, of most things American) has permeated European discourse and opinion since the fall of the Soviet Union in 1991 and thus the end of the bipolar Cold War world that dominated Europe since 1945. However, it also argues that the manifest nature of this antipathy hails from a very long and fertile history, and that it is only superficially related to the dislike of George W. Bush and his administrations' policies. The latter have merely served as convenient caricatures for a much deeper structural disconnect between Europe as an emerging political entity and a new global player, on the one hand, and the United States, its main, perhaps only, genuine rival, on the other. Anti-Americanism in Europe long preceded George W. Bush and will persist long after his departure.

## Anti-Americanism: Some Definitions

Lest there be any misunderstandings or conceptual uncertainties as to what exactly I mean by anti-Americanism, here is the definition offered by Paul Hollander:

Anti-Americanism is *a predisposition to hostility* toward the United States and American society, a relentless critical impulse toward American social, economic, and political institutions, traditions, and values; it entails an aversion to American culture in particular and its influence abroad, often also contempt for the American national character (or what is presumed to be such a character) and dislike of American people, manners, behavior, dress, and so on; rejection of American foreign policy and a firm belief in the malignity of American influence and presence anywhere in the world.[13]

Alvin Rubinstein and Donald Smith second Hollander's definition of anti-Americanism with their own in which they see anti-Americanism "as any hostile action or expression that becomes part and parcel of an undifferentiated attack on the foreign policy, society, culture and values of the United States."[14] And Todd Gitlin offered the following trenchant view on this topic: "Anti-Americanism is an emotion masquerading as an analysis, a morality, an ideal, even an idea about what to do. When hatred of foreign policies ignites into hatred of an entire people and their civilization, then thinking is dead and demonology lives. When complexity of thought devolves into caricature, intellect is close to reconciling itself to mass murder."[15] Agreeing with all three of these definitions, I see anti-Americanism as a generalized and comprehensive normative dislike of America and things American that often lacks distinct reasons or concrete causes. Anti-Americanism has all the tropes of a classic prejudice. Beyond that, anti-Americanism also constitutes a well-identified and well-established "ism"—thus bespeaking its entrenched institutionalization and common usage as a modern ideology. Indeed, with many of the major "isms" of the twentieth century, such as "communism," "socialism," "Leninism," "fascism," and "Nazism," either moribund or certainly past their prime as ideas and, above all, as movements with international appeal, a definite global charisma, and the panache of antinomy and a direct challenge to the existing order, "anti-Americanism" might indeed have assumed at least partly such a function in the world. By being "anti-American," one ipso facto seems to stick it to "the Man," even if West Europeans, in notable contrast to peoples of the developing world, objectively constitute the very same "man." However, it is the subjective that matters. And there, by being anti-American, West Europeans see themselves as part of a global opposition movement—perhaps even its vanguard—against the American order, the American establishment. The following incident offers a fine illustration of how arguably the most privileged people, the utmost winners of this world, still experience a sense of antinomy, of opposition, even of revolt when the object of antipathy centers on things American. On January 5, 2005, Gerhard Casper, the former dean of the University of Chicago Law School and former president of Stanford University, attended a production of Friedrich Schiller's famous play *Don Carlos* in Munich's Kammerspiele theater, which—together with the Residenztheater—furnishes one of that city's most stalwart institutions of high brow culture. In a wonderfully poignant dialogue between King Philip II, the autocratic, austere, and cruel ruler of Catholic Spain at the height of its power in the sixteenth century, and Rodrigo, marquis of Posa, the latter implores the king to ease his brutal rule and give the people of the rebelling protestant provinces of Flanders and Brabant their much-deserved freedom. Rodrigo's passionate plea ends by his throwing himself at the king's feet and exclaiming "Geben Sie Gedankenfreiheit" (O give us freedom of thought).[16] In the Munich production attended by Casper, this plea was immediately followed by Posa reciting the "Universal Declaration of Human Rights" of 1948, at which point the packed house broke into thunderous applause that in every facet of its expression was clearly meant to address a current political grievance way beyond the play itself. Casper writes in his e-mail to me: "I took this particular change [adding the 'Universal Declaration of Human Rights'] and audience reaction to be aimed at [President George W.] Bush. A sophisticated Bavarian acquaintance of mine confirmed that interpretation. I guess Bush is Philip and Iraq is Flanders. I saw this, of course, against the background of the canonical nature of *Don Carlos* in German life. A Hamburg audience during the Third Reich broke into applause after 'Geben Sie Gedankenfreiheit.' I think similar incidents occurred in the GDR [German Democratic Republic]."[17]

I would go one better than Casper and his "sophisticated Bavarian acquaintance," precisely based on Casper's fine contextualization of this iconic play with its iconic sentence, and claim that to many in the audience in the Kammerspiele theater who applauded so passionately at this telling scene that evening, sixteenth-century Flanders was not so much contemporary Iraq as it was contemporary Germany. German bourgeois audiences do not muster this kind of spontaneous and deeply felt passion for Iraq, but they most certainly do for Germany in the context of their seeing it as America's victim suffering under the yoke of America's political rule and cultural influence. And in this context, it would not have been the first time that a major sentiment in Germany experienced America's war against Iraq in parallel terms to its war against Germany a half century before. During "Operation Desert Shield" in 1991, Germans had employed terminology in their description of the American role in Iraq that was idential to their depiction of America's war against Nazi Germany.

And lest my point gets lost here, let us remember that this feeling of antinomy and opposition did not emanate from Bolivian peasants or Mexican laborers whom America and its policies have wronged repeatedly and continue to do so. This sentiment arose from the most privileged people in this world who, if anything, have only benefited from America's role in their country's recent history. To this Munich audience in 2005, Bush and America were the emotional equivalents of what Hitler and the Nazis were to the Hamburg audience in the Third Reich, and the Communist dictators were to theater-goers in the former German Democratic Republic.[18]

Whereas the word "Anti-Americanism" itself might not have been explicitly used until the beginning of the twentieth century, the sentiments that it denotes have been commonly understood and employed in Europe since the late eighteenth century, if not before.[19] Anti-Americanism exists: it is visible, palpable, audible, readable. It is one of the most powerful anti-isms that constitute legitimate discourse virtually all over the world, most certainly in contemporary Western Europe.

### Anti-Americanism: America as Europe's Antonymous Other

Even under the aegis of Bill Clinton, whom European intellectuals embraced wholeheartedly as a kindred spirit, as a kind of honorary European à la Woody Allen[20]—particularly during the Lewinsky scandal and the ensuing impeachment proceedings—Europeans started the conscious construction of Europe being America's other. "Europe: The Un-America" proclaimed Michael Elliott in an article published in *Newsweek International* in which he dismissed any semblance of a common transatlantic civilization.[21]

Many European intellectuals basically appropriated Samuel Huntington's (in)famous and controversial notion of the "clash of civilizations" and used it to characterize what they perceived as the increasing divergence between Europe and the United States rather than—along the lines of Huntington's original argument—a clash between the predominantly Christian West and the Islamic world.[22] The Swiss legal theorist Gret Haller has written extensively to a very receptive and wide audience about America being fundamentally—and irreconcilably—different from (and, of course, inferior to) Europe from the very founding of the American Republic.[23] To Haller, the manner in which the relationships among state, society, law, and religion were constructed and construed in America are so markedly contrary to its European counterpart that any bridge or reconciliation between these two profoundly different views of life is neither possible nor desirable. Hence, Europe should draw a clear line that separates it decisively from America. In a discussion with panelists and audience members at a conference on European anti-Americanism organized by the Sir Peter Ustinov Institute at the Diplomatic Academy in Vienna, Austria on April 29, 2005, at which I shared the podium with Gret Haller, she explicitly and repeatedly emphasized that Britain had always belonged to Europe, and that the clear demarcation was never to run along the channel separating Britain from the European continent, but across the ever-widening Atlantic that rightly divided a Britain-encompassing Europe from an America that from the get-go featured many more differences from than similarities with Europe. The last few years merely served to render these differences clearer and to highlight their irreconcilable nature.

The widely voiced indictment accused America of being retrograde on three levels: moral (America being the purveyor of the death penalty and of religious fundamentalism, as opposed to Europe's having abolished the death penalty and adhering to an enlightened secularism); social (America being the bastion of unbridled "predatory capitalism," to use the words of former German Chancellor Helmut Schmidt, and of punishment as opposed to Europe being the home of the considerate welfare state and of rehabilitation); and cultural (America the commodified, Europe the refined; America the prudish and prurient, Europe the savvy and wise.)[24]

Indeed, in an interesting debate in Germany about so-called defective democracies, the United States seems to lead the way bar none. Some critics regard the "liberal," "ultraliberal," or "merely liberal" nature of certain democracies—viz. America—as the most poignant manifestations of their defectiveness. Without a substantial "social" component, a democracy's defects are so severe that one might as well consider labeling such a system nondemocratic, at best as defectively democratic.[25] Leading the charge in this debate is Thomas Meyer, who "is not just a well-known public figure, but also the most important behind-the-scenes intellectual of the Social Democratic Party (SPD), who co-authors every party platform, runs the party-affiliated Political Academy and heads the SPD Commission on Basic Values. His influence reaches up to the very top of the party establishment and cannot be measured alone in terms of book sale figures or public appearances."[26] Meyer's featuring the United States as the paragon of "defective democracies" only rivals his comparable contempt for Britain, which he regards as deeply flawed and thus a "burden" and even a "threat" to Europe and the EU. His view on this topic emanates from his important work on Europe's identity, the essence of which Meyer perceives to be a clear repudiation of the United States and a thorough rejection of most things American.[27]

To be sure, no serious observer of the United States would dispute the considerable defectiveness of its political system, particularly as practiced since the advent of the so-called Reagan Revolution, thus well preceding the presidency of George W. Bush. But what matters in this context is not so much the often appropriate indictment of the defects of American democracy, but the total silence about the defects of German and (West) European democracy, which—if anything—is extolled as a true, or nondefective, model-like democracy to be emulated by all. As one of this argument's major progressive critics has correctly countered, surely most segregated and alienated immigrants in the suburbs of Paris or the dreary streets of Berlin would be less likely to extol German and French democracies as free of any defects. Indeed, if one extends the "social" dimension to include the successful integration of immigrants, surely America's democracy would emerge much less defective than the alleged models of Western Europe.[28]

A major part of the European disdain for America's defective democracy also pertains to the continued existence of the death penalty in the United States. While the death penalty ought to be rejected on many grounds and constitutes for me one of the most objectionable manifestations of contemporary American politics, its existence does not eo ipso render a country less—or even un—democratic. Was France prior to 1981 less of a democracy than it is today on account of having had the death penalty before? What about Great Britain until 1965, when the death penalty was abolished for all crimes, excluding military offenses, such as treason, for which the death penalty was not abolished until 1990? And what about the fascinating issue of Article 102 of the Federal Republic of Germany's "Basic Law," which abolished the death penalty in 1949, not so much for humanitarian reasons but to protect the lives of convicted Nazi war criminals by preventing their execution at the hands of British and American authorities? As Charles Lane writes in a perceptive article, "far from intending to repudiate the barbarism of Hitler, the author of Article 102 [a right-wing German politician] wanted to make a statement about the supposed excesses of Allied victors' justice."[29] Germans at the time—indeed, until the 1960s—

most certainly wanted their common murderers to be executed by the state. They just did not want this to happen to Nazi criminals and mass murderers for whom both the Social Democrats as well as the Christian Democrats bombarded American and British authorities for clemency. To be sure, in the course of the Federal Republic's successful postwar history, the death penalty lost its popular appeal and is now opposed by a solid majority of Germans. But was the Germany of the 1960s a more defective democracy than the one today? Or do Europeans ever mention India, the world's largest democracy, and Japan, both of which still have the death penalty, as defectively democratic because of its presence?

The same pertains to Americans' bearing of arms. Again, this might not be to one's liking and there are fine reasons to see this as a problem and oppose it vigorously. But does the large presence of guns in America and their relative paucity in Europe render the former more democratic than the latter? Does the fact that some American states, such as New York and Massachusetts, have much tougher gun laws than France make them more complete democratic polities?

But much of the disdain that European intellectuals accord America does not even bother with such nuanced differentiations. Instead, it is thematically and historically comprehensive. America no longer represents something "different" from Europe, but rather it mutates into its much-disdained "other." As such, local peculiarities that contemporary Europeans might find odd, maybe not even to their liking, but which they tolerate, become items of irritation and ridicule upon perceiving them in America and certainly serve in their eyes as prima facie evidence for America's inferiority and evil. America's "otherness" is not accepted as such by Europeans or even considered under the rubric of that motto "Other countries—other customs." On the contrary: The American "other" serves the purpose of turning America on the whole into a laughingstock, of mocking, ridiculing, and sanctimoniously instructing America, but never viewing it as an equal on the same plane with Europe. There are many examples of this comprehensive blaming, complete ridiculing, and wholesale rejecting of America in the contemporary European intellectual scene, but perhaps few are more encompassing than the Austrian journalist Eric Frey's *Schwarzbuch USA* (Black Book on the USA), whose more than 460 pages feature every real and purported evil committed by the United States with a relish and gusto second to none.[30] The undertone of Frey's book—as well as of most anti-American voices—is not only accusatory but also of the what-on-earth-else-can-one-expect-from-these-people-and-their-society-and-politics mode.

Just like anti-Semitism, so, too is anti-Americanism antonymous. Everything and its opposite pertains: too religious, too secular; too idealistic, too materialistic; too elitist, too populist; too prudish, too pornographic; too individualistic, too conformist; too anarchic, too controlling; too obsessed with history, not having any history; too concerned with culture, not having any culture; too dominated by women, too controlling of women. America, in the view of some Europeans, is so obsessed with freedom and individualism that this obsession impedes genuine individuality and creates what one conservative German critic of the United States tellingly labeled "freedom Bolshevism" (Freiheits-Bolschewismus).[31] In short, the motto is clear: Damned if you do, damned if you don't.

It was well before George W. Bush was close to running for president that French Foreign Minister Hubert Védrine inveighed against the United States as a "hyperpower"—*hyperpuissance*—that needed to be brought down by an "un-American" Europe obviously led by France. To Hubert Védrine, the clarion call of Europe's rise against the United States centered on the following American ills that all good Europeans had to fight tooth and nail: "ultraliberal market economy, rejection of the state, nonrepublican individualism, unthinking strengthening of the universal and 'indispensable' role of the U.S.A., common law, anglophonie, Protestant rather than Catholic concepts."[32]

The *Kulturkampf* had commenced long before George W. Bush's arrival in the White House. Indeed, this very term has frequently been used as a rallying cry by European intellectuals and cultural elites in their battle against the United States. Overt hostilities in language and attitude that have remained taboo against any other

culture or country among European intellectuals and elites have attained acceptability when it concerns America. Overt anti-Americanism has become a badge of honor in certain European circles.
Thus, a well-known German director, Peter Zadek, stated: "*Kulturkampf*? Count me in. I deeply detest America."[33] Or take the British novelist Margaret Drabble: "My anti-Americanism has become
almost uncontrollable. It has possessed me like a disease. It rises in
my throat like acid reflux."[34]

## Anti-Americanism: "Surplus" Dimensions in Europe

In this book I am interested in what—following Russell Berman's
study—I call "surplus anti-Americanism," an extra amount of resentment, hate, negativity, and mockery that has nothing to do with
criticism of any policy or action, and which can even be an obstacle
to such criticism.[35] As I will illustrate above all by the examples in
chapter 3, what I have in mind by "surplus" is a generalizing, stereo-
typing, and pejorative characterization that contributes little or
nothing to understanding the phenomenon at hand but does much
more to reinforce the persistence of already existing prejudices.
Anti-Americanism in Europe often accommodates this kind of ex-
cess, a surplus that negates the very essence and existence of America
rather than criticizing its political actions. This seems to distinguish
Europe's anti-Americanism from that of other regions. As my University of Michigan colleague Meredith Woo-Cummings has shown
in a working paper on changes in public opinion in the Republic of
Korea, antipathy there toward the United States does not draw on
any of the depth, resentment, negative features, and traditions of
the European variant; instead, it clearly emerges from a rejection
of American policy, from what America does rather than from the
character or essence of America (its being).[36]

As if to confirm the difference between Korean and European
anti-Americanism, Salman Rushdie sees parallel patterns in the difference between the anti-Americanism of the Muslim and European
worlds. The former, according to Rushdie, chiefly enlists political

reasons for its antipathy to America, but the latter is anti-American in its essence and entire behavior:

> These days there seem to be as many of these accusers outside the Muslim world as inside it. Anybody who has visited Britain and Europe, or followed the public conversation there during the past five months, will have been struck, even shocked, by the depth of anti-American feeling among large segments of the population. Western anti-Americanism is an altogether more petulant phenomenon than its Islamic counterpart and far more personalized. Muslim countries don't like America's power, its "arrogance," its success; but in the non-American West, the main objection seems to be to American people. Night after night, I have found myself listening to Londoners' diatribes against the sheer weirdness of the American citizenry. The attacks on America are routinely discounted. . . . American patriotism, obesity, emotionality, self-centeredness: these are the crucial issues."[37]

Explicitly extrapolating Rushdie's view of anti-Americanism becoming a ubiquitous trope in the discourse of British elites of the left and right, Alvaro Delgado-Gal sees similar patterns for the virulence of anti-American sentiment in Spain. Identical features that once characterized the deep anti-Americanism of the Spanish Right under Franco are now alive and well in the discourse of the Spanish Left.[38]

Anti-Americanism in many developing countries has an entirely different political character and legitimacy than it has among Europeans.[39] In the developing world, compared to what appears to be the case among Europeans, condemnation of what America *does* claims much greater attention than condemnation of what America's *is*—and for good reason. In parts of Latin America, Southeast Asia, Africa, and the Middle East, there are millions of people whose grievances against the United States could easily be classified as vehemently anti-American, but they are born out of real-life experiences where the United States has often behaved brutally, murderously, and to the clear detriment of these regions and its inhabitants. To put the point crudely: I find that anti-Americanism among Vietnamese, Guatemalans, and Nicaraguans—to name just a few examples—has a completely different historical and political status from its equivalent among Germans, the French, or the British. America has often wronged peoples of color, and its policies have frequently harmed countries in the developing world. None of this applies to Europeans—quite the contrary.

For Europeans, unlike the rest of the world, America was associated with an overcharged image and complex entity. This was so because America was, of course, a European creation, though one that, in contrast to earlier constructions founded by Europeans, had deliberately distanced itself from its origins and become the very first country to conduct a successful war of independence against its European colonial rulers. As we shall see in the next chapter, Europeans were already vehemently anti-American at a time when they still had power and the Americans had hardly any (at least compared to Europe). To many European intellectuals, America was nothing but a threatening parvenu from its very inception to this day. In the eyes of these critics, America's essence consisted of venality, vulgarity, mediocrity, and—most important of all—a palpable and ubiquitous inauthenticity that, in the eyes of Europeans, permeates every aspect of American life. Add to this a sense of danger and attraction, and the irritating and intimidating mix of America the Beguiling emerged. The power discrepancy vis-à-vis America so frequently lamented by Europeans is empirically just not tenable as a significant source of their anti-Americanism. Anti-Americanism was already a European constant in periods during which Europe clearly had the more powerful position vis-à-vis America (from the late fifteenth to the late nineteenth century), when power between the two continents was evenly balanced (from the beginning of the twentieth century until the fascist and Nazi dictatorships in Europe were crushed), as well as in the period during which the United States dominated at least the western half of Europe (until the collapse of the Soviet Union). It is interesting and telling that, at the very time when Europe's power and autonomy vis-à-vis America is clearly increasing rather than decreasing, European anti-Americanism is becoming an unprecedented Europe-wide lingua franca and thus a legitimating discourse for Europe as a new power.

### Anti-Americanism: Europe-wide Rather Than
   Country-Specific Features

One of this book's main points is that anti-Americanism features
no country-specific tropes and thus indeed is totally pan-European.
Reading anthologies on the subject, which usually treat different
European countries in separate chapters, one is struck by how the
common features of anti-Americanism in Europe massively out-
weigh the country-by-country differences.[40] For me, anti-Americanism in Germany does not differ at all in its texture, its topics, its
features, and also its social carriers from that in Britain, France, Italy,
Spain, or any other West European country. To be sure, anti-American sentiments have indeed varied in their manifest expressions both
diachronically and synchronically, but in their core, anti-Americanism's characteristics pertain Europe-wide. One of these key Europe-
wide ingredients relates to anti-Americanism's persistent presence
on each country's radical right and left. Anti-Americanism has been
a topic of absolute importance for both the Right and the Left and
has formed, certainly since the 1920s, one of the few constant common grounds between these two political poles.[41] This kind of convergence is not, of course, something that people with these two
political orientations share on a daily basis, though conceptual (if
not necessarily organizational) points of agreement between left-
wing and right-wing radicals on the matter of anti-Americanism are
nothing new in Europe. The French saying, "*les extremes se touchent*"—the extremes converge or touch each other—actually does
not seem to be the case with the far Left and the far Right on most
of their preferred views, with two important (and tellingly related)
exceptions: hatred for America and for Israel. The reasons and motivations might be different (though those have become increasingly
blurred as well), but the manifestations are eerily similar. Perhaps
the only remaining difference between the anti-Americanism of the
Right and its counterpart on the Left is that adherents of the former
proudly stand by their resentment while those espousing the latter
always deny this by using the self-exculpatory "but": "We are not

anti-American, but anti-Bush. We are not against the American people, but the American government. We have nothing against America, *but*. . . ."[42] Over and above the presence of a right-wing and a left-wing component in every European country, one can also distinguish (roughly speaking) between a cultural and a political-economic aspect of European anti-Americanism. Together these dimensions—right/left; culture/political economy—yield a four-dimensional field with the following content:

>**Left/political economy.** America, as the leading capitalist state, is inherently imperialist. It is the progenitor of all evil modern inventions of the capitalist accumulation process, from Taylorism and Fordism in its industrial phase, to various postindustrial flexibility schemes today. It stands at the summit of everything that is reactionary worldwide. America is a predatory power keen on controlling the entire world. The United States launched the Cold War in Europe to repress all indigenous progressive movements that could potentially have transformed countries such as Italy, Greece, Germany, and others in Western and Southern Europe into socialist entities. Most West European governments have been nothing but American lackeys. Tellingly, this dimension has mutated in the course of the post–Cold War, post-9/11, post–Iraq War era in which the local governments are now seen as much more autonomous of the United States and—sometimes—even as welcome allies of the people in their joint attempt to resist America's bullying. While the German left viewed German social democracy as America's lackey in the 1970s and 1980s, Gerhard Schröder—especially during his years as chancellor—mutated into a veritable hero of the German (and European) Left by dint of his opposition to America and its policies well beyond the Iraq War. "Show 'em, Gerhard" and "Don't succumb, Gerhard" were just two of the often-heard and seen slogans adorning political rallies in Germany throughout 2003. Globalization is Americanization, and according to this equation Western Europe is a victim of American capitalism in exactly the same way as the developing countries.

>**Right/political economy.** Here we find two variations. The first, the Tory-Gaullist-conservative version, exhibits (roughly speaking)

the following characteristics: America, because of its vulgar nature, cannot assume the role, so urgently needed, of leading the free, white, Western world. Owing to its permissiveness, and lacking traditional elites, the political system of the United States is disorganized, confused, and completely unsuited to rule its own country, much less the world. The United States is structurally and historically incapable of exercising serious political leadership. America is weak, shallow, inexperienced, naive, and ultimately not an adversary that the enemies of the free world can take seriously. The second variant is the nationalist-völkisch (ethnic-racial) one: America is on the verge of destroying the authenticity of other peoples, their institutions, and their autonomy. It is a political duty for every country to act decisively in opposition to this oppression and national annexation. Since this variant of right-wing anti-Americanism also includes a strategy of national liberation, it is much closer on that dimension to the Left's anti-Americanism than to the conservative variant mentioned just before.

**Left/culture**. American culture is the expression of an alienated, brutal, capitalist society that, acting exclusively on behalf of profits for large corporations, has produced a soulless, formless, and inauthentic mass culture that can never mutate into anything resembling authenticity, let alone art. The American culture industry produces cheap, thoroughly worthless things in order to make a quick profit on the mass market in which misguided, manipulated, and exploited individuals are robbed of their true and authentic identity by the alienating force of a capitalist society. McDonald's, *Dallas*, Coca-Cola, and so on are worthless commodities that are useless except to flush money into the cash registers of the ruling class. This is how its members buy politicians who impose their interests not just in the United States but everywhere in the world, with military brutality, and also by means of a constant dumbing down of culture and public discourse.

**Right/culture**. American culture does not deserve the name. The United States has never been capable of producing anything of lasting value. Even worse: America uses its financial power to buy and/or (as is typical for the nouveaux riches) superficially imitate real, that is, European, culture. American culture is by definition a nonculture since Americans do not have a proper history and disdain tradition.

American "culture" is shallow at best, but really a Jewish-influenced, mongrelized mishmash featuring inferior elements like blacks and women. The danger of American culture resides in its appeal to the European masses; its universal attractiveness is what constitutes its depravity. Above all, American culture is a subversive force that destroys the authenticity of the people and the binding power of völkisch (ethnically or racially nationalist) identity.

In the field of politics, therefore, the European Left fears American power much more than does the Right. It is the other way round in the realm of culture; there, the Right is much more worried than is the Left. Both camps are fused in their rejection of American culture as inauthentic, with the Left viewing this above all as a consequence of America's commercialism and capitalism, and the Right seeing it as the outcome of America's supposed lack of history and tradition, in other words, as a result of Americans' not having the profundity, intellectualism, and that indispensable mixture of education and character formation Germans call "Bildung."[43] If to the European Right America's main evil lies in its excessive egalitarianism and racial permissiveness, then to the Left it is America's inequality and racism that are its hallmarks. Both see it as an overly materialistic society dominated for the Left by "finance capital," to which the Right has frequently added the qualifier "Jewish."

Perhaps, however, the European aversion to America has less to do with right or left or any other reason more profound than the perfectly respectable human need to hate the big guy. After all, nobody in Germany—apart from some Munich residents, opportunists, or parvenus—can stand the Bayern München soccer team, and not simply because this team had always been frowned on and continues to be referred to as the "Jew team,"[44] but also for the simple reason that for decades on end it has dominated German soccer and has won every imaginable trophy and championship. America (apart from many New Yorkers) rejoices when the mighty Yankees fail. Ditto for the Los Angeles Lakers in basketball. In Spain there was a nationwide cry for joy in the 2003-04 season when the Galacticos of Real Madrid did not prove successful in a single European or national competition. To hate Manchester United is a national sport in England.[45] And, as far as Harvard is concerned, I have never heard colleagues talk about an "evil empire" when discussing any other university.

Whether justified or not, everywhere the big guy is viewed by others as arrogant and haughty, as sanctimonious, unfair, and merciless, since he simply must have achieved his greatness in some crooked way and at other people's expense. This applies exactly to the position of the United States today vis-à-vis Europe and the world. Just as Germany and Germans until recently have always been viewed by the inhabitants of neighboring countries as threatening, arrogant, and sanctimonious no matter what they actually did specifically, simply owing to Germany's disproportionate size, so it is with what America represents for its immediate geographic and political neighbors like Canada and Mexico, except in America's case its neighborhood has come to include the entire world in the course of the twentieth century, including Europe.[46] Being the main player in what was not coincidentally called "the American century" brought with it the burden of the eight-hundred-pound gorilla, or Mr. Big. Still, the following fact bespeaks the depth of European anti-Americanism: Long before the United States—figuratively speaking—became the equivalent of the New York Yankees, the Los Angeles Lakers, Manchester United, or Real Madrid, when it was still struggling for its existence in a fourth-tier minor league, it was already being viewed and feared by Europeans as an uncouth and threatening giant.

## Anti-Americanism: Comparisons to Anti-Europeanism

Just as an imagined America has served all kinds of purposes for Europeans, so too have the different notions of Europe that Americans created in the course of their history served to sketch out a sense of "being different" for Americans. The phenomenon of America as Europe's counterimage and vice-versa has best been characterized by Bernd Ostendorf, certainly one of Germany's most profound America experts, as a "compulsive *folie à deux* for over three centuries with a remarkably stable set of choreographies, but with a rather uneven, historically specific set of performances."[47]

I detect, however, an important difference in the respective agencies of this *folie à deux* on the two continents: Whereas, in the United States, the carriers of prejudice and antipathy toward Europe have been located predominantly (if at all) among the lower social strata, American elites (especially cultural elites) have consistently extolled Europe, and they continue to do so.

This love for and emulation of European tastes, mores, fashions, and habits remained a staple of American elite culture even during the country's most nativist and isolationist periods. Practically all sophisticated culture in America is European. One need only look at the humanities departments of any leading American university to observe this continuing cultural hegemony, which, even in the persistent attempt to negate its own Eurocentrism, resorts to ideas and methods that are completely European. American elites continue to be completely fixated on Europe, in spite of the repeated fear voiced in Europe that America might be drifting toward Asia. That drift exists—although only partially—in the economy, but by no means in the realm of culture. A European vacation after final exams remains more or less obligatory for every graduate of an elite university in the United States. Every aspect of the consumer profile of American elites—from classical music to cuisine, from cars to vacation spots, from interior decoration to preferences in clothing—shows a clear predisposition for Europe and things European.

In massive contrast to the negative and pejorative—at best ambivalent—notions that the word "American" conjures up in Europe, "European" invariably invokes positive tropes among Americans (elites and mass alike), such as "quality," "class," "taste," and "elegance," be it in food, comfort, tradition, romance, or eroticism (as in European massage, European decor, European looks . . . and the list can go on and on). Every Madison Avenue ad agency knows full well that the best way to sell quality and rare curiosities to American elites is to conjure up European associations.

The rancor against Europe in American mass public opinion is of a completely different magnitude from anti-Americanism in Europe. In American politics and society, Europe is—if anything—a sporadic and insignificant element of the public discourse. For most Americans, Europe as such is a lovely vacation spot, something fine, quite tasteful, old, safely remote, and—basically—a matter of indifference. Surely this very indifference provides additional grounds for Europeans' anti-Americanism, since it intensifies the European notion of Americans' narrow-mindedness. But, above all, this American disinterest offends European pride. It is, as everybody knows, worse when one is not hated but simply ignored.[48]

Even linguistically there is no American counterpart to the European concept of "anti-Americanism." The word "anti-Europeanism" certainly exists as a concept, but except for the Europhile readers of the *New York Review of Books*, this is an almost unknown, and above all unused, concept for most Americans.[49] Until the very current debate conducted on both sides of the Atlantic about anti-Americanism, the term "anti-Europeanism" did not really exist. That these two terms—and by implication their social reality as well—do not have at all the same weight in their respective historical and societal contexts is demonstrated by the following bit of Internet research: If one enters "anti-Europeanism" into Proquest, a search engine for scholarly journals and papers of record in Great Britain and the United States, 669 entries appear. For "anti-Americanism" the tally comes to 14,170. Google yields 2,420 entries for "anti-Europeanism" but 116,000 for "anti-Americanism," which in the world of search engines is the equivalent of "no longer countable." Gerard Baker performed a similar experiment with Yahoo. Entering "anti-Europeanism in America," he got 358 items. But "anti-Americanism in Europe" gave him 21,400, whereby the round number, as Baker properly notes, is simply Yahoo's way of reporting "we haven't got a clue how many are out there but here's the first batch."[50]

This is confirmed by Herbert J. Spiro's research. In a historically oriented essay about anti-Americanism in Western Europe, Spiro writes that expressions like "anti-Europism" or "anti-Europeanism" do not occur in either American linguistic usage or ways of thinking.[51] This does not mean that even the slightest anti-Europeanism in the United States should be tolerated or justified. But to equate it with the phenomenon of European anti-Americanism would simply be wrong, both analytically and politically.[52] The former is the temporary, marginal affair of conservative Bush fans who make themselves look laughable before the American public with things like "freedom fries," while the latter is a resentment occurring on the entire European continent whose potential for politics and society is becoming clearer with each passing day. Gerard Baker wrote the following perceptive passage about this issue:

> I will wager that, rough as the diplomatic road may get with the Europeans, no American will throw a brick through the gaslit windows of bijou brasserie chains in the Midwest, or carve rude messages about German labor-market rigidity into the back of a Porsche 944. . . . For every Euro-hater in the conservative establishment there are at least half a dozen Americans ready to laud Europe. The cultural elite still likes to decry US TV and it longs for the virtues of British television, blissfully unaware that almost every piece of trash on American TV screens—from *American Idol* to *I'm a Celebrity, Get Me Out of Here*—has a British provenance. Many will chatter fondly about French cinema—though I doubt any of them has actually seen a French film since *Belle de Jour*. You can still reduce Americans to whispering awe by telling them that you attended Oxford or the Sorbonne, even though the average State University of Wherever knocks the best European academic institutions into a cocked hat. And they might scoff at the nonsense of medieval pageantry, but they will roll over like a royal corgi at the prospect of an honorary gong. And it is not just the National Public Radio–listening, Chablis-swilling, cosmopolitan elite of Washington and New York I am talking about, either. Out in the great heartland, you will find attitudes to Europe that are far from hostile.[53]

The phenomenon is well captured by the words of Paul Lee, chief operating officer of BBC America: "There is no door you can't open [in America] with a British accent."[54]

In a wide-ranging interview with Germany's paper of record, the *Frankfurter Allgemeine Zeitung*, the French intellectual Bernard-Henri Levy spoke about his experiences in the United States which formed the basis for his best-selling book *American Vertigo: Traveling America in the Footsteps of Tocqueville*. When the German journalist asked Levy how he—being an avowed atheist, a French intellectual of Jewish origin, the paragon of cosmopolitanism—was received in rural and "middle" America, where surely folks of Levy's ilk are less than welcomed, Levy answered unequivocally: "I was received much more cordially than any American would have been in France had he been pursuing a similar project to mine. I never experienced any personal animosities, let alone anything that might vaguely be construed as francophobia."[55]

Over the course of their history, Americans were often vehemently anti-French, anti-German, anti-Russian, anti-British, and anti-Communist, but they were never anti-European. A significant aspect of acculturation in America always involved rejection of things from "the old country." The attempt to create a new world required distance from the "Old World." In this sense one may speak of Americans differentiating themselves from Europe. But this does not even begin to reach the degree of aversion that is contained in Europeans' anti-Americanism, since the latter—in contrast to the former—was (until the unilateralism of the Bush administration) chiefly borne by European elites and not by the majority of Europe's citizens.

The situations in Europe and the United States are reverse images of each other. "Ordinary" Europeans have never harbored the same aversion to America as their elites have done. As routine surveys in West European countries since the beginning of the 1950s have brought to light, a solid majority of Europeans were constantly expressing positive attitudes toward America; only 30 percent on average had a negative opinion.

In contrast to other antipathies and prejudices against different collective entities, negative attitudes toward America increase with higher social status and class affiliation. Some European observers believe that one of the main reasons for the vehemence and durability of antipathy that European elites display toward America derives from their equating America with a despised proletarian culture that also involves something tempting and irresistible. "Anti-Americanism," writes Mary Kenny on the phenomenon in Great Britain, "is almost exclusively confined to the upper, or upper-middle, classes. It comes from Oxbridge (and public school) intellectuals, your Hampstead and Islington chattering classes, your Guardianistas with the holiday home in France, and also your old colonials resident in the shires. Rarely do you find anti-Americanism among the British masses, among the lower-middle classes, and least of all, among the proletariat."[56] With a few deviations, these class- and status-specific characteristics of British anti-Americanism also applied to the Continent until the advent of George W. Bush, whose policies and persona have successfully forged a hitherto unprecedented convergence in the antipathies toward America on the part of European elite and mass publics. But before we analyze this convergence and anti-Americanism's wide-ranging presence in contemporary Western Europe's quotidian culture, a brief presentation of anti-Americanism's European history is in order. It is to this topic that we turn in chapter 2.

------------------------------------------------------------

## CHAPTER 2

# European Anti-Americanism:
# A Brief Historical Overview

The lack of understanding by the Germans, but not only
the Germans, for Anglo-Saxon traditions and American
reality is an old story.
  —*Hannah Arendt*

During my research on this topic, I embarked on an excursion into
history to find out whether the kind of anti-Americanism currently
sweeping Europe is indeed unique. Even if anti-Americanism today,
quantitatively viewed, has come to occupy a new hegemonic hold
on the daily discourse of Europe's elites and citizens—and even if it
currently enjoys a legitimacy never before articulated so clearly
among all population groups and in nearly every political camp (so
that there is now an extraordinary convergence of opinion between
elites and the general population on this subject)—the themes and
structures of anti-Americanism are anything but new. On the contrary, European elites have consistently and passionately expressed
the same negative sentiments about America for centuries. In both
substance and tone, what stands out is this continuity, rather than
change. There never was a "golden age" in which European elites
genuinely liked America. To be still more precise, an era never existed in which European intellectuals and literati—European
elites—viewed the United States without a solid base of resentment,
or better, *ressentiment*.[1] Accompanying this resentment, one will usu-

ally find envy, jealousy, hatred, denigration, as well as a sense of impotence and repressed revenge. Add to this the ingredient of schadenfreude, and this resentment becomes part of a potent mixture of simultaneous feelings of inferiority and superiority.

As odd as this may seem, this goes back all the way to 1492 and the so-called discovery of the so-called New World—what was to become America and the Americas—by Christopher Columbus. To Europeans at the end of the fifteenth and start of the sixteenth century, Columbus himself spread the tale of America's attractive, even golden, primitivism, to which he simultaneously ascribed decadent and frightening features.[2] As Ira Strauss argues in a perceptive paper, a simpler, preideological fear of and resentment toward America emerged among Europe's elites—both the aristocracy and the clergy—who understood all too well that the changes in the world that Columbus's journeys wrought could potentially undermine their established positions and ordered views.[3]

Well before America had any power, and well before it was an independent country, tropes emerged in the ways in which it was perceived that were to become mainstays of European anti-Americanism to this day: venality, vulgarity, mediocrity, inauthenticity, but also a clear sense of danger in its indefinable but manifestly evident attractiveness. Even before the United States became "Mr. Big"— the eight-hundred-pound gorilla—which it would grow into in the course of the twentieth century, even before it posed any real danger to France and Britain—"Messrs. Big" of the era—Europeans felt a certain loss of agency vis-à-vis America, a sort of incapacitation as if something was going to befall them inexorably from this new entity, which Europe had no power or will to resist. The German term *Selbstentmündigung*, best translated as a self-induced abdication of agency, aptly captures this phenomenon. Thus, the argument that America's disproportionate power when compared to Europe's alleged powerlessness lies at the heart of European resentment toward the United States and things American simply does not hold up. Clearly, even when the United States had virtually no power (and it was certainly powerless compared to the big European players such as Britain and France), Europeans bore hostility toward this new entity. From the very beginning of European interaction with the Americas, European elites have continued to view America as a threatening parvenu.[4]

Many Europeans, of course, were fascinated by the "New World." America's admirers saw it as a kind of paradise, an ideal and idyllic refuge from the narrowness, traditionalism, and injustice of the "Old World." From the very beginning, America always was both to Europeans: utopia and dystopia, dream and nightmare. I will not concentrate on the favorable dimensions in this chapter because—like in the book as a whole—my topic is *not* a comprehensive analysis of the European view of America, but rather the phenomenon of anti-Americanism in Europe. In this chapter, then, I explore a variety of European sources writing about the United States. In all of these texts, be they literary, scientific, or political, these European writers criticize different aspects of America or Americanness. What unites them all is not so much their content as it is their voice, their tone. Whether inveighing against the climate or the animals, the cityscapes or the rural wastelands, the table manners or the dancing styles, the architecture or the work habits, the clothing or the language, these European thinkers share an almost paranoid fear and discomfort, a sense of threat, a palpable resentment, of whatever it is in America that attracted their attention.

From the get-go, America, both in the abstract and as a physical reality, represented something uncanny and dangerous for Europe and the Europeans. This perceived threat, apprehended at least partly as an existential danger, seemed to be aimed at both European power and European culture. America's vastness, its undeveloped spaces for settlement, delighted Europeans. At the same time, many feared America as a castrating "other," as something alien that hardly inspired confidence, as an entity whose remoteness and otherness was definitional to its potentially irresistible attractiveness. Antipathy and aversion to America thus became a solid component of the elite discourse in Europe long before the United States emerged as a global power. Many Europeans viewed the land in America as barren, as it was not able to produce the European crops (and hence the European cultures) to which the settlers were accustomed. Despite its reputed sterility, they paradoxically still craved it. Indeed, their need to see this land as "available," in order to justify their claiming it as their own, resulted in their defining it as uninhabited, an "empty landscape." This meant, on the one hand, simply denying the existence of native peoples; on the other hand, it worked preemptively to justify programs of deliberate and indirect genocide.

## "Degeneration"

The French naturalist Georges Louis Leclerc, better known as Comte de Buffon, played an extremely important role in developing theories of the fertility of the American landscape and its impact on human bodies, both "Indian" and European. Buffon was especially interested in sexual organs and human and animal sexual behavior. By studying patterns of reproduction, Buffon argued that the biology of the Indian body marked him or her as infertile and indolent, in turn maintaining that these traits were the inevitable result of living on American soil. Taking sparse body hair as proof of an immature and weakly developed sex life, Buffon came to the conclusion that men's inability to achieve an erection and women's deficient menstruation were the decisive characteristics of the indigenous population: "In the savage, the organs of generation are small and feeble. He has no hair, no beard, no ardor for the female."[5]

Popular European visual representations of Native Americans present a striking contrast to parallel images of African peoples. Unlike these traditionally oversexed and childlike Africans, with a focus on large breasts and buttocks, Indians were almost asexual. They were still, silent, seemingly resigned to their fate of extermination, presumably unable to maintain their population because of an innate sterility. Buffon argued that the New World was just that: new. This adjective brought with it positive connotations of potential, excitement, energy, but it also implied lack of maturity, development, and sophistication, a view that Europeans have shared about America to this very day. Rather than arguing, however, that America would simply, given sufficient time, develop along the same lines as Europe, Buffon claimed that this status of immaturity was a definitional, permanent aspect of America, again a view that has not abated among Europeans—European elites in particular—over the past 250 years. A strong believer in the idea that environment forms individual bodies and psyches, Buffon claimed not only that the Native Americans, in their lack of sexual drive and overall energy, were produced by the American land, but also that Europeans (as well as their livestock and crops), once transplanted into this space, would also mysteriously be sapped of their vitality, be deprived of their virility, and physically shrivel and shrink: In sum, they would "degenerate," just as America itself was a sort of degenerate (in the cultural, not moral, sense) Europe.[6]

Comte de Buffon's "degeneration thesis" gained immense popularity and a wide audience among Europe's elites throughout the eighteenth and nineteenth centuries and was also supported by other European interpreters of America, such as the Dutch naturalist Cornelius de Pauw, who decried the existence of America as "the worst misfortune" that could have happened to all humanity. As with Buffon, not only the state of humanity but that of the plant and animal kingdoms reflected this degeneracy. De Pauw, for example, noted that the New World's dogs never barked.[7] For de Pauw, the defeat of the native inhabitants at the hands of European settlers was proof of the former's degeneracy, which he attributed in turn to the hostility of the American landscape and climate. Frequent and heavy rainfall, high humidity, and swamplike soil conditions not only weakened the natives but also had the effect of retarding the development of the new settlers and their animals, as they lost all their will and capacity to procreate. Feebleness, degeneration, and corruption were accordingly the inevitable consequences not merely of physical contact with, but equally of mental, spiritual, cultural, and ethical proximity to, America and everything American.[8] The view of America as "backward," derived from these early biological theories of retarded development, remains to this day a central component of European elite opinion.[9]

## "Indianization"

Since the "discovery" of the American continent by Columbus, it was the major differences between Europe and America, rather than the similarities, that shaped European images of this new territory. During the first centuries of Europe's occupation of America, Europeans understood this difference to be both dangerous and potentially infectious. William Cronon's classic ecological history of the early British colonies shows in detail how these early immigrants desperately attempted to replace what was alien, what was American about America, with the familiar European structures they had just left behind. By examining these settlers' decisions about agricultural, architectural, and cultural policy, Cronon demonstrates persuasively that one of their primary goals was in fact "to reproduce the mosaic of the Old World in the American environment."[10] Indigenous fauna and flora were to be replaced by European imports; cows, pigs, and horses to supplant beavers, bears, and buffalo; and wheat and rye to substitute for maize and acorns. Despite the fact that these decisions were detrimental to the health of these settlers (European architecture was ill-suited to the American climate, and native foods were far more productive than imported grain crops), they perversely insisted upon this doomed experiment of re-creating Europe in America. This fear of "Americanness" thus was paradoxically linked with the earliest phases of European expansion into the New World.

The greatest danger Europeans saw in America was the New World's reputed capacity to infect the Old World by attacking the Europeanness of the Europeans living there. Like Eve's apple, America seduced innocent Europeans by ruining everyone who tasted the forbidden fruit. From the moment of their arrival in the New World, Europeans were afraid of indigenous peoples and products. This fear existed in the physical sense—that new foods might be indigestible, or native ways of dress bad for health—but also in a spiritual or intellectual respect, insofar as American objects and ways of life threatened the very core of European identity by potentially transforming the partaker into an American. As Trudy Eden put it,

morally and physically they feared that "consumption of the Amer-
indian diet . . . would eradicate their Englishness."[11]

Europeans developed a fear of a supposed "Indianization" that
might befall them under the influence of the New World. Nothing
seemed more dangerous to them than the apprehension that the
boundaries separating them from the "natives" might become invisible or fluid. Clothing, hair length, and beards became important
markers distinguishing Europeans from the "others." Thus, natives
in European clothing, sporting riding boots or even short hair, triggered anxiety that was amplified even further by seeing Europeans
with long hair, dressed in loincloth and sandals. Tanned and long-
haired Europeans aroused aversion, as did light-skinned Indians.[12]
Both Indian-looking whites and white-looking Indians not only implied that racial and cultural categories were inherently arbitrary
and instable; they also represented a specific fear of the impact of
America on European bodies, the possibility that the one could become the other.[13]


## Elite Anti-Americanism

European antipathy toward America can also be traced to July 5,
1776, the beginning of the republic. Thus, Herbert J. Spiro: "Anti-
Americanism has been endemic among the ruling classes in continental Europe since 1776 at the latest. Ordinary continental Europeans, by contrast, acted pro-American, often enthusiastically and
sometimes even existentially."[14] Originally, anti-Americanism was
an ideological value supported by educational elites and the aristocracy, while less well-to-do and underprivileged Europeans demonstrated sympathy for America by emigrating there. By dint of being
attractive to Europe's masses—surely not the aristocracy's
friends—America attained yet another threatening dimension to
Europeans (European elites in particular) that it never lost, at least
not until the end of the Cold War and the advent of the Bush administration: that of being an unbridled seducer of essentially immature and heteronymous objects like the masses and children. To
this day, one encounters the widely held view in Europe that Ameri-

cans are like children, implying they are immature, impressionable, without sound judgment, anchorless, lacking tradition or history. Moreover, to this day as well, there exists the fear that Europe's masses—childlike in their own way—also succumb to America's superficial veneer that woos innocents to something worthless at best, at worst well-nigh deadly. Thus to this day, Europe's elite discourse often depicts America not as proletarian, which at least to leftist Europeans has the connotation of authenticity, but rather as commodified, commercial, vulgar—values that exude inauthenticity, plasticity, and heteronomy. European elites' image of America as "Las Vegas," "Disneyland," basically as "white trash"—or what the British call "chav"— has a distinguished pedigree: gaudy jewelry, expensive-but-tacky clothes, garish makeup, platinum blond hair, tattoos, vulgar demeanor, in short inauthentic and kitschy glitter best captured by the term "uncouth." This disparaging image of America cultivated by European elites was also linked to how the young United States embodied modern capitalism hostile to an aristocratic order. Thus, for example, during the Civil War, leading members of the political classes in France and Britain openly rooted for the Confederacy, which they rightly assumed to be much more akin to their own aristocratic ways. Indeed, they feared the brash, capitalist, industrial North, whose victory would inevitably make the United States a formidable political rival for global domination.[15]

From the get-go, there was something eerily seductive about the place, something not simply explainable by the new life that it offered to millions of Europe's population. It was similar, yet different; weak, yet powerful; repellent, yet attractive. In notable contrast to any other country, from the very beginning the enemy for European elites was not "America the Conqueror—not the 'Imperial Republic'—but America the Beguiling."[16] Nobody has expressed this powerful sentiment better than Johnny Hallyday, that self-styled French Elvis Presley, in the ambivalent lyrics to his song "Quelque chose de Tennessee": "That force which pushes us toward infinity; there is so little love but so much desire/envy."[17]

America as a European obsession has a long, complex relationship, one constantly vacillating between flashes of adoration and profound antipathy.[18] The allure of America, generally succumbed to by the European masses rather than elites, remained a permanent mystery and thorn in the side for European critics of the United States. From the outset, the upper classes saw something primitive about America, but simultaneously something horribly and excessively modern. Thus, the very Romantics who should have adored America for its reputed primitiveness in fact loathed the nation for supposedly destroying nature and being ruled by competition and the dollar. For its critics, America thus represented polar opposites but at the same time was also squarely in the middle, signifying the banal and mediocre, associated with notions like "stupefying" and "dreary." In the late eighteenth century, it was the unimaginative small towns of New England; in the nineteenth century, it was the deplorable social conditions in the industrial metropolises like Chicago and New York; in the twentieth century, it was life in America's suburbs, and finally the dullness of the shopping malls and exurbs. With a way of thinking going back to the eighteenth century at least, America was not only alien and different to European observers, but also inferior. This contradictory trope of modernity as barbarism is a constant of negative European perceptions of America.

In the following sections I cite examples of anti-American prejudices from Germany, Austria, Britain, France, Norway, Russia, and Spain in order to show the pan-European character of this resentment and disdain. These examples are nowhere near to being exhaustive. Instead, they are samples intended to convey the breadth of anti-Americanism that has informed European discourse at least since the early nineteenth century, if not earlier. From its very beginning, anti-Americanism constituted a Europe-wide—and not a country-specific—phenomenon in terms of its form and content, as well as its analytical foundation, concepts, and political and social functions.


## German Immigrants

Let us begin with Germany. Between 1830 and 1890, many Germans left their homeland for political, religious, or economic reasons. Most of them emigrated to the United States of America. In 1914 four million Americans of German descent lived in the United States. Two large waves of immigration, between 1846 and 1857 and again between 1864 and 1873, made Germans the largest group of immigrants in the United States throughout most of the nineteenth century. Between 1860 and 1890, Americans of German origin represented the largest single ethnic group in the United States.[19]

Germans, perhaps because of the sheer scale of their immigration as well as the complex idea of German nationalism, were particularly focused on maintaining their Germanness in the New World. They did this by cultivating the German language and culture. Even in the early phases of immigration, German immigrants imagined they were threatened by Americanization, or that Americanness was in opposition to Germanness. To counter this danger and preserve their own identity, they pursued the creation of German enclaves, at the core of which were German-speaking schools.

It was therefore no surprise that the American government classified the German immigrants and their communities as particularly resistant to assimilation. Benjamin Franklin, who declared German-speaking public schools in his home colony of Pennsylvania illegal in 1751 (during the British colonial period, in other words), was so deeply concerned about German immigrants' reluctance to assimilate that he worried they would "Germanize us instead of our Anglifying them."[20] As early as the midnineteenth century, Germans in the United States and in Germany founded numerous associations and organizations whose sole purpose was to facilitate the cultivation of their mother tongue, and to protect the home culture from the constant assault of Americanization.

Because so many Germans came into contact with America and Americans, Germany provided the most productive and widely read authors in Europe dealing with the New World. Hundreds of books about the most varied topics and incidents were published for Germans in the United States, but also for interested readers in Germany and other European nations. There were nonfiction books about America's flora and fauna, its politics, opportunities available to Germans across the Atlantic, and the dangers and risks awaiting immigrants. In addition, there were multiple sorts of novels, popular treatises, theater pieces, and songs, and virtually all imaginable forms of printed materials.

In spite of the enormous number and thematic variety of these publications, there was something of a thread running through them: the desire to use America as a vehicle for Germans to understand their own identity. To be sure, this did not differentiate Germans from any other group of Europeans. Nonetheless America, due to the unusually large number of German immigrants, and Germany's own particularly tortuous relationship to nationhood and questions of unity, became particularly embroiled in the conflict-laden process of German state and nation building throughout the nineteenth century and thus was implicated in the construction of German identity.

One of the most influential German books from this period, dealing explicitly with the interaction of American and European identities, was the 1838 bestseller *Die Europamüden* (The Europe-Weary) by Ernst Willkomm.[21] In this today almost forgotten novel, the author presents America as a primary alternative to a Europe that is growing old and falling into decline. Willkomm describes America as a primitive, young, and for this very reason strong country, full of energy, freedom, and irresistible appeal. On closer examination, however, it becomes clear that the author is not praising this autochthonous power of America in a manner that is sui generis; instead, he is using it as an ideal site to provide a new homeland for a race outfitted with German blood, German perseverance, and German power. From Willkomm's perspective, America's greatness is most closely linked to its capacity for helping an authentic Germanness become manifest.[22] In other words, the glory of America was not in its own national identity, its Americanness, but rather in its ability to strengthen and augment Germanness.

Such essentially positive if German-centered visions of America faced ever stronger disapproval in Germany during the late 1840s and early 1850s. Fear of revolution and growing concern at the huge numbers of emigrants abandoning their homeland for the other side of the Atlantic led governments throughout Germany to promote books with a negative tone about the New World. Travel guides and printed material for those seeking to emigrate started to emphasize America's limitations and problems. They warned emigrants that things did not look as rosy in the flesh, on American soil, as they might appear from a distance back home in Germany. Such criticisms of America and the American way of life focused specifically on countering popular myths about abundance, ease of life, and freedom, insisting that "America is anything but a paradise . . . one has to work a lot harder than in Germany to get anywhere."[23]

In 1855, as a reply to Willkomm's romantic vision of the New World, and against the background of increasing postrevolutionary German emigration, Ferdinand Kürnberger, an imprisoned activist from the revolution of 1848, published his notorious novel *Der Amerikamüde* (The America-Weary). As cultural critic Rüdiger Steinlein notes, Kürnberger's main concern is to present America to the German reader as a thoroughly negative fantasy land.[24] America appears as a destructive, terrifying space, aimed directly at undermining and destroying the unique culture and way of life of Germany. Emigrants to the United States would not find a youthful, fresh, unadulterated place, but instead a society driven by greed and profit and unacquainted with folkways or fatherland, a place where the metropolis of New York served as an admonishing example of the excesses of the United States as a whole. For the author of this novel about suffering, death, and spiritual loss, the dilemma of Germans who immigrated to America did not have to do so much with assimilation or dissimilation, but rather with social ethics and identity. The loss of German and the acquisition of American values struck Kürnberger as proof of the corruption of the self, and of the final destruction of a positive and communal premodern, precapitalist identity by the very incarnation of evil: "Yankeeness" (Das Yankeetum).[25]

In the course of the following decades, as Germans increasingly came to view themselves as potential victims of America's insatiable drive for capitalist growth, prey to all the negative consequences of modernization, they began to identify with North American Indians and their fate. For millions of Germans, the original inhabitants of the United States became a symbol of suffering under the "Yankeeness" of the whites. Literature and scholarship fabricated a myth, still present to this day, of the peace-loving Indian living in harmony with nature, both of which (Indians and nature) fell victim to white Yankee brutes. This myth not only misrepresents Native Americans, it also hinges upon the (untrue) notion of racial extinction. Following this idea, German authors lamented the extermination of what was once so "noble a race" and—in a rewriting of Buffon's thesis— accused white Americans of being at fault for the "degeneration" and ultimate demise of the Indians.

Here, of course, they were not entirely wrong. There can be no doubt that European immigrants to the New World are to blame for the degradation, persecution, and finally the large-scale death of American Indians. German and European criticism of white America is wholly justified here. What seems odd, however, is the special emotional affinity of Germans with Indians, since there were also millions of German emigrants to the United States who—presumably as Americans—participated in this genocide. But somehow Americans of German origin remained immune to this accusation, and to their fellow Germans' hatred of white America. The land of the Yankees thus became opposed to both Indians and Germans, an existential threat to the one, and, by extension, to the other.

### Karl May: "Noble Savages"

Another aspect of German-American Indian relations, though one not specific to Germany, is an effusive praise of the American natives as "noble savages" whom the Germans viewed as kindred souls in defending their culture against the assault of America's materialist and venal civilization. This is most evident in the many Westerns of Karl May, whose adventure novels were standard reading for every middle-class boy in the first half of the twentieth century, and still to a lesser degree today. The main character in the books is a German (the narrator), a blond gentle giant named Old Shatterhand, who, together with his "blood brother" Winnetou, chieftain of the Apaches, fights the good fight against a wide assortment of bad guys (venal Englishmen, drunken Scotsmen, cowardly Frenchmen, cunning Jews, brutal Comanches and Sioux). The villains' names tell all: "Roulin, Leflor, Lertrier or Newton, Burton, Butler . . . the scum of that melting pot that is originally the hope of the Zionist Zangwill, to whom New York harbor appears as the entrance to a 'New Jerusalem' and for whom the gradual mingling of immigrant groups, regardless of skin color or religion, guarantees America's greatness."[26] Karl May stylizes the Apaches—in crucial alliance with German immigrants like Old Shatterhand, Old Surehand, and (of course) Old Firehand ("head forest ranger by profession, forced to leave Germany for political reasons that caught many an honest man in their whirl"[27])—as a kind of bulwark of nobility against modern capitalism and Yankee individualism, which are subverting and undermining traditional German/Indian values. The German studies scholar Peter Uwe Hohendahl confirms this assessment of Karl May's work but places it in a broader German literary context.

> Authors like Kürnberger with "America-Weary" (1855) and Baudissin with "Peter Pitt" (1862) preceded him. . . . May's critique of capitalism seldom goes beyond tracing individual evil characters, yet the intention is unmistakable. The Yankee is the representative of capitalism; his striving for profit dominates him so completely that other human emotions are suppressed. Wherever he meets less profit-oriented people, he immediately exploits them. Then it is Old Shatterhand's job to redress this kind of injustice. . . . May shares the anti-capitalist sentiment of the literary intelligentsia.[28]

According to Karl May, the Indian was "initially a proud, daring, valiant, upright, truth loving huntsman, loyal to his fellow tribesmen, he became, through no fault of his own, a slinking, lying, mistrustful, murderous, redskin. The white man is to blame for that transformation."[29] In May's novels, there are two distinct elements to whiteness. There is the racial category, based on skin color and genetic origins, to which all Europeans and Euro-Americans belong. In addition, however, he has a moral yardstick for race definitions, a categorization that creates an opposition between two primal groups of "whites": Germans and Americans. Both belong to the

white race, but the mercilessness of the Americans toward the Indians, the former's cowardice, underhandedness, and other physical
and moral defects, prompt Old Shatterhand to question his alle-
giance to his own racial identity, and to cry out in horror: "I felt
ashamed to be a paleface."[30]

## Karl May: Germans in the Prairie

In May's books, Germans never speak ill of Indians, in glaring contrast to the Americans, who constantly make disparaging remarks
about the "redskins." In these narratives, vehement moral criticism
is centered on the continued mistreatment of Indians by white
Americans, who take pleasure in exploiting, torturing, and killing
Indians; indeed, it is this moral criticism, rather than the lives and
experiences of the Indians themselves, that is the author's primary
concern. Richard Cracroft, one of the few American commentators
on May's writings, aptly summarizes the narrative structure of May's
work: "while surveying, Karl May becomes acquainted with the re-
volting cruelty of the American, and must frequently exert his Teutonic wisdom and strength to teach a few Teutonic manners."[31] The
evil of the Americans thus only makes sense in contrast to the good-
ness of the Germans. For, unlike the American, the German is perceived by all as "a brother of redmen," and indeed explicitly identified
by the "red man" as his "dearest friend and brother." Not only are
May's Germans morally superior to white Americans, they are also,
unexpectedly, better cowboys and trappers. Indeed, American-born
men often have to acknowledge reluctantly that native Germans are
"cut out to be Westerners," indeed miles ahead of "real" Americans
in their ability to understand and master the American landscape.[32]

Certainly the number of Germans riding around in May's Wild
West is really quite considerable. Every cowboy who has integrity,
toughness, or empathy, who performs the deeds of the "Westerner"
with skill and compassion, turns out to be a person of German origin, who still has "those German feelins racin' around in [his]
blood." As one such talented cowboy explains to Old Shatterhand,

"You might think I was born and bred to this life, but to tell the truth—now don't fall over in amazement—I'm a German immigrant just like you."[33]

Indeed, observers acquainted with May have noted that the novelist exported so many Germans into the American West "that the United States often resembles a German colony."[34] Accidental meetings in the prairie, during hunting or some other relevant activity, resemble get-togethers of some secret organization at which the obligatory opening question, "Who are you?" often triggers the stereotypical reply, "I'm German." "Being German" for Karl May was more than just a question of birthplace; it was also a matter of moral integrity and, above all, of the sharing in a "German culture" never explicitly named yet all the more meticulously depicted—one that most certainly was superior to American culture, something that May along with millions of other Europeans considered an oxymoron. True faith and good education distinguish Germans from white Americans, who come across in May's novels as blasphemous and utterly uneducated. Indeed, it is Old Shatterhand's "Europeanness"—meaning his Germanness in a cultural sense, and not his whiteness in any kind of purely racial category—that constitutes his intellectual and spiritual-religious superiority, distinguishing him not only from the Indians, but also Anglo-Americans: "Of course, the furthest thing from my mind, as an 'enlightened European,' was lending any sort of secret miracle-working credence to the mutual benefit of a few drops of blood. I knew how to distinguish between the substance and the external symbol."[35]

## Karl May: Americans—Indians—Germans

The magical triangle of these three competing ethnic communities (Americans—Indians—Germans) is, of course, no accidental construction; rather, it expresses a negative, almost obsessive passion of the German people: America. To understand the gap between a generally positive or romantic view of the New World's scenic expanse and the constant demonizing of America's culture, politics, and population—of "Americanism"—it is important to recall that America at the time was perceived as a very real political threat simply because of its appeal to the German populace. In Karl May's day, "Germany sent waves of immigrants to the United States, where they were subject to great assimilatory pressures that rendered them lost resources to the newly united German nation-state."[36] This loss was not something to be taken lightly; indeed, one of the major arguments for the development of a German colonial presence in Africa was the hope that it would reduce the flow of immigration to the United States. It was, it seemed, better to have Germans in an African colony, where they were not only directly linked to the German nation-state but in lesser danger of assimilating, than in the dangerously alluring America. Behind the negative and disparaging assessment of American culture stood a latent fear of the attraction that it exercised on millions of would-be emigrants.

In the imperialistic discourse of Germany at that time, the slogan *Volk ohne Raum* (a people without land) came into popular use. This phrase expressed a sort of self-identity otherwise unknown among the imperial powers, one that provided a specifically German variety of motivation for the general, Europe-wide antipathy toward America. Behind the pathos of Karl May and other contemporary Germans concerning the boundlessness of the American land lurked a secret wish to possess a country so big. These desires were of course to remain unfulfilled (indeed, America seemed to be colonizing Germans, more than Germans America), adding particular bitterness to the fact that so many of their fellow Germans chose to go to America. For many Germans, this emigration was more than a simple loss. It was treason.

It is customary in Europe to reproach Americans with accusations of the genocide against the Indians. In Germany this accusation has a special status. The reasons are obvious: by constantly referring to America's Holocaust, Germans obtain a kind of sense of righteousness that is especially soothing because they see in America, controlled by its "East Coast intellectuals" (a common code word for Jews), the country that continuously and unrelentingly reminds them of their Nazi past. By turning the tables and accusing the

Americans of genocide, they kill two birds with one stone. On the one hand, by placing them on the same level as the Nazis, Americans are deprived of the moral right to criticize, which raises the hope that these cheeky and annoying critics will finally leave Germans in peace.[37] In addition, it allows Germans to reidentify themselves, to adopt an identity opposite to the traditional one of "Nazi." Katrin Sieg's book *Ethnic Drag* provides a detailed explanation of this very point: of how the German obsession with Indians and Indian role-playing games, which continue to this day, can be traced back to guilt regarding the Holocaust. She argues that dressing up like Indian victims of genocide offers a chance to transform the status of "German" from that of "evil Nazi" to that of an innocent victim of American cruelty.[38]

One of the key aspects of Karl May's writings, and of the continued fascination with American Indians through the twenty-first century, is the way in which this positive identification with the Indians and a moral criticism of America provided an important forum for imparting a much more complex view of and sentiment for America among Germany's (and Europe's) mass publics than the rather uniform anti-Americanism of the elites.[39] The divide between elite and popular opinion regarding America and the Wild West is demonstrated by the bizarre and fascinating annual summer festivals in the Bavarian town Eging am See (Pullman City) and the central German town Hasselfelde (Pullman City II), and the famous Karl May Festival in Bad Segeberg. There are more than a dozen similar "Wild West theme parks" in Europe, from Spain to Scandinavia. But nowhere are they as widespread and on such a high level qualitatively as in Germany, explicitly a direct legacy of Karl May. These festivals are for "the people," not the elite. Not even during one of my frequent visits to soccer stadiums have I detected such a clear class division between myself (as a university professor) and the bulk of the audience. In these theme parks there are hardly any intellectuals to be found, nobody from "high society," just "ordinary" people living out their fantasies.

While elites in Germany and Europe rarely allow themselves to develop any positive wishful thinking about America, much less make this a public affair, it has always been different among the normal population. While the German masses by no means embrace America unambiguously, there is certainly a more complex duality of emotional responses to the construct of "America." Torn between the traditional lure of the frontier, of the tropes of freedom, large scale, opportunity, Las Vegas, and Disneyland, on the one hand, and a national pressure to dislike the country constantly portrayed as a profound threat to their own nation, on the other, the German masses, much like their counterparts elsewhere in Europe, frequently tempered their disgust for the United States with a strange sort of romantic nostalgia or enthusiastic imitation. For the elites, of course, the story was quite different.


## European Intellectuals

From the late eighteenth century until today, a strong negative assessment of things American has far outweighed any positive views of the United States on the part of German intellectuals and elites. The dichotomy of Germany's "Kultur" versus America's "Zivilisation" arose to contrast the latter's materialism, vulgarity, and shallowness with the former's idealism, nobility, and depth. Beginning with Hegel, virtually all German observers condemned the political immaturity of the United States, mainly defined by the lack of a European-style state. As long as the United States failed to establish a European-style polity and state structure—and the prognosis looked bad given the size of the country as well as its civil turbulence (which was an outgrowth of its multiethnic and immigrant population)—the United States, Hegel concluded, would remain forever peripheral to world history.

Only an orderly political power similar to that of the European states, one with a clearly defined tradition, an aristocracy schooled in the art of governance, a bureaucracy obedient to authority, and at most two religious communities accepting the status quo—only this constellation guaranteed a functioning state order. Without these factors, only the economy, meaning capitalism, remains something barely capable of establishing an order, propped up by a vague constitutional legitimacy that, as anyone could see, could only lead to political chaos and cultural mediocrity.

In this regard it is interesting that, for Hegel and other European thinkers of this normative provenance (and especially for the great British political thinker Edmund Burke), the compulsively chaotic system of American politics and statehood had a flip side represented by a barely concealed dictatorship of the uncontrolled American people.[40] This theme has survived to the present day: too much individual freedom coexisting with collectivist conformity. Following this trend of loathing America precisely because it preached a freedom nowhere to be found, Heinrich Heine hated America, that "monstrous prison of freedom, where the invisible chains would oppress me even more heavily than the visible ones at home, and where the most repulsive of all tyrants, the populace, hold vulgar sway." In America, according to Heine, "there are no princes or nobles there; all men are equal—equal dolts!"[41]

Jacob Burkhardt equated the allegedly a- and anti-historical nature of American society with total vacuity. He described the "*a-historical Bildungsmensch*" (educated person) who was vegetating in America's blandness, monotony, mediocrity, and uniformity. His only escape consisted in his inevitable—and pathetic—imitation of Europe's mores and values.[42] Nikolaus Lenau bemoaned America's "horribly dull" nature, where one could not find a "brave dog" nor a "fiery horse, and no passionate human being." Above all, the land was so sullen and dreary that it clearly could not sustain any nightingales or singing birds of any kind.[43] This barrenness of nature transposed itself onto American society, culture, education system, and people, all of whom Lenau viewed as lacking imagination, burdened by small-mindedness, and enslaved by a practicality and mercantile outlook that was dreadfully insipid and vacuous.

Simon Schama has argued that the flimsy frame construction of American houses served as prima facie evidence for Germans of America's rootlessness, an attribute that was, to the Romantics, an unforgivable sin.[44] This association of America with rootlessness became, of course, a major staple of German views of America, well beyond the reach of radical Right and Nazi blood-and-soil ideology. Thus, for example, in many a current discussion pertaining to the often-claimed advantages of the "Rhenish" as opposed to the American model of economic and social management, one often hears that, in contrast to the ills of America's "flexible" labor markets, which exact a high degree of geographic mobility from workers, Germans are much more tied to home and hearth, which they allegedly value much more than their American counterparts do.

Friedrich Nietzsche hated America as the epitome of the modern, which he foresaw as the inevitable conqueror of Europe. Long in advance of Hollywood movies, jazz, rock, and rap music, the spread of American culture was likened to a form of disease. Its progress in Europe seemed ineluctable. "The faith of the Americans is becoming the faith of the European as well," Nietzsche warned.[45] And Nietzsche's student Arthur Moeller Van den Bruck, probably most famous for having popularized the phrase "The Third Reich," proposed the concept of *Amerikanertum* (Americanness) which was to be "not geographically but spiritually understood."[46] Sigmund Freud viewed the United States as embodying the most pronounced manifestation of everything that he found despicable in modern civilization. It was a place that was solely governed by the almighty dollar, that had "no time for libido," that was simply an "anti-Paradise." "What is the use of Americans, if they bring no money?" he once asked Ernest Jones. He confided to Jones that "Yes, America is gigantic, but a gigantic mistake."[47]

Martin Heidegger frequently mentioned "Americanism" as a soulless, greedy, inauthentic force that undermined Europe.[48] And through the fine scholarship of Georg Kamphausen, we have impressive evidence of how major German social theorists and sociologists like Werner Sombart, Ernst Troeltsch, Ferdinand Tönnies, Robert Michels, Karl Mannheim, and Max Weber harbored deep resentment and disdain for American academic life, American intellectual accomplishments, and America as a whole.[49] All of these authors bemoan in one way or another America's lack of historical awareness, its overdeveloped bourgeois mentality, coupled with its underdeveloped aristocratic ways. This uniquely American combination of an overly strong bourgeoisie accompanied by a lack of refined tastes and talents ultimately leads to superficiality, venality, and a lack of quality, subtlety, and—of course—authenticity. Kamphausen argues that these observers' unwillingness to view America free from their preestablished clichés led not only to faulty representations of American political processes and social structures, but also to a defensiveness and opposition concerning America, something that had major epistemological and methodological consequences for German sociology: "European arrogance vis-à-vis the New World is mostly purchased at the cost of a heroic pessimism appealing to the essentialist gravity of an allegedly higher morality that only the state appears capable of guaranteeing."[50] Some of the main pillars of German sociology, Kamphausen concludes, thus arose out of the arrogant answers of German sociologists who "discovered" America for domestic purposes because they could not—or would not—analyze it sui generis. That German academia has remained remiss in the proper study of America to this day becomes evident in a fine study by Reinhard R. Doerries, who shows how the development of American history as an academic discipline at German universities continues to remain woefully neglected by the authorities as well as among the educated classes.[51]

The era after World War I witnessed an increase in tension between European elites and the masses regarding the value and appeal of the United States. While previously popular affection toward the United States among Europeans had most tangibly been reflected in mass waves of immigration, now for the first time new forms of mass communication allowed those unable or unwilling to physically leave Europe for America to experience some of America in Europe. This they did unabashedly, by dancing the Charleston, flocking to movie theaters, idolizing film stars, grooving on jazz—in short, by making key aspects of American culture part of European life. This new dimension did not supplant, but rather paradoxically enhanced, popular suspicion of, even hostility toward, the politics and government of the United States, fanned by the growth of communism on the left and fascism on the right, both of which shared a deep dislike of America—a dislike joined by very similar manifestations but moti-

vated by ostensibly different reasons. If anything, elite resentment
of America grew in the Europe of the interwar period. Suddenly
America—for elites and masses alike—no longer had to do with some
distant abstraction or projection, but rather with concrete things directly affecting the daily lives of millions of European citizens. It is
thus little surprise that, as would be the case with rock and roll after
World War II, after World War I jazz was vilified as decadent "nigger
music" purportedly promoted by profit-hungry Jews who, by undermining the authentic and indigenous qualities celebrated by the
elite, ultimately seemed intent on undermining the very fabric of
European life. Along with jazz, all aspects of mass culture, including
fashion, popular art, and lifestyle choices, were decried as American,
and thus inferior, shallow, and tasteless. What made European elites
hate these items even more was the fact that, despite all their alleged
and oft-repeated shortcomings, they remained immensely seductive,
indeed irresistible, to Europe's masses.

## "American Imperialism"

Although the basic pattern of anti-Americanism was established in
Germany and the rest of Europe long before the 1920s, I would like
to discuss briefly a few new aspects that moved into the forefront of
this discourse during the interwar period, as they have to this day
lost little of their topicality. Perhaps the most important of these
new themes is American imperialism. There were, of course, isolated voices in Europe that had branded the United States an imperial power immediately after its war with Spain in 1898. Nonetheless, it was above all the physical presence of American troops in
Europe and the significance of America for European postwar policy
(Wilson's influence on the Paris peace negotiations, etc.) and economic development (the American government's involvement in the
Dawes Plan, which vastly increased the importance of American
corporations' commitments on the continent) that led to the widespread perception of America as an imperialist state.

From this perspective, Europe rapidly came to see itself as a victim of America; indeed, Europeans began to feel a sort of solidarity

with the countries of South America, nations more directly oppressed by the harsh imposition of American power.[52] The fact that
at the same time huge areas of Africa and Asia still suffered under
European colonial rule seemed irrelevant to these anti-American
anti-imperialists. On the contrary, thanks to their own empathetic
status as victims of American imperialism, Europeans were given
carte blanche on matters of imperialist covetousness and could
sweep any European-caused injustice under the carpet.

To this day the image of Europe as an imperial victim of America,
both economically and culturally, has remained one of the most
powerful ways to mobilize both continental and British anti-Americanism. The threat of American imperialism functions here as an
integrating factor bringing together the European Right and Left.
In hardly any other area of the European political self-image over
the course of the last ninety years has there been such similarity
between the extreme Right and its counterpart on the Left as in
their respective versions of anti-Americanism. The special German
twist to this right-left blend was the circumstance that a sort of na-
tion-based socialism was perceived as a promising counterbalance
against the global yoke of Anglo-American capitalism. This legacy
lives on in some political circles in Germany, as witnessed by the
notorious "locust" campaign of the SPD in April 2005: Here American hedge funds were depicted as locusts descending on the German
economy, sucking its assets dry and leaving behind nothing but
empty carcasses. IG Metall, Germany's metal and engineering
workers' union and a close ideological ally of the SPD, followed this
campaign one month later with its own, which featured mosquitoes
that not only sucked the blood of German workers but were explicitly American and exhibited stereotypically Jewish features (see
more on these two incidents in chapters 3 and 5).

## American Presidents

The second aspect of European anti-Americanism after 1918 was a
pronounced aversion to certain American politicians; this, too,
proved to be a quite durable prejudice. With the major exception of

John F. Kennedy (and, to a lesser extent, Bill Clinton), all other twentieth-century American presidents were frowned upon by European elites—either disliked (Wilson, Roosevelt, Johnson, Nixon, Reagan, Bush *fils*, Bush *père*) and/or not taken seriously as political persons and ridiculed (Harding, Coolidge, Hoover, Truman, Eisenhower, Ford, Carter, Reagan, Bush *fils*, Bush *père*).[53] In the interwar period, animosity was focused on Woodrow Wilson. The European Right treated him as the prototype of the wimpy internationalist, pursuing self-serving American interests under the hypocritical guise of national self-determination as a general principle.

The losers of the war among the German and Austrian Right were strikingly similar, both in the tone and substance of their spite, to French and British right-wing forces on the victorious side. To both nationalist conservative and völkisch currents on the German right, Wilson was viewed as the incarnation of sanctimoniousness who contributed to the enslavement of the German people by not standing up to the revanchist French and perfidious Britons. Conversely, their counterparts in French right-wing circles criticized his yielding to Germans and Austrians. Down the line, the European Right regarded Wilson as a marionette of liberal "East Coast" forces. Among the moderate Left, "the breakdown of Wilson's peace policy was interpreted as pure, innocent failure to oppose overpowering political laws. Social democrats saw him as a humanist who stood no chance of prevailing against capitalist circumstances, who had fallen victim to the capitalists. Liberals occasionally reprimanded him for weakness of character and inexperience in European affairs; at best it was noted that he had 'nourished false hopes.' "[54] Communists viewed Wilson as the compliant henchman of American capital. (Their hatred was, however, minor in comparison with how the Nazis had criticized Franklin Delano Roosevelt in the 1930s and 1940s.)

## "Verjudung" (Judaization)

This leads to a third new factor in European anti-Americanism—the "Judaization" (*Verjudung*) of America and the increasingly strong overlap between anti-Americanism and anti-Semitism. This phenomenon, too, is not completely new. German, but also other continental European, anti-Semites and haters of Britain have been united since the eighteenth century by a preoccupation with the "small shopkeeper mentality" of "perfidious Albion," a theme that lent itself easily to anglicized America. The kind of modernity that was becoming ever more successfully represented by the United States and Great Britain (and that thus appeared ever more threatening) was attributed to a Western liberal and Judaized "merchant commercialism" (*Händlertum*) that was opposed by a cultured German "heroism" (*Heldentum*).[55] Anglo-American capitalism and its allegedly close links with Judaism and Jews has been a standard trope of continental antimodernism since the early nineteenth century, if not before. Be it the more "organic" and "corporatist" ideas of Catholic conservatives like the author and editor Karl Freiherr von Vogelsang, or the more radical prefascist ideologies of men such as Georg Freiherr von Schönerer, leader of the racialist Pan-German movement, for many thinkers Jews, America, Albion, and capitalism have remained an inseparable conglomerate for the continental opposition to modern capitalism. In the 1920s this aspect of German and European anti-Americanism enjoyed an unprecedented popularity and public legitimacy, the legacy of which has lasted til today.

Whether one looks at the passionate anti-American bestsellers of Adolf Halfeld (*Amerika und der Amerikanismus. Betrachtungen eines Deutschen und Europäers* [America and Americanism: Observations of a German and European, 1927] and *USA greift in die Welt* [The USA Reaches into the World, 1941]); Giselher Wirsing's *Der maßlose Kontinent. Roosevelts Kampf um die Weltherrschaft* [The Immoderate Continent: Roosevelt's Struggle for World Domination, 1942]); or relevant articles in both the popular and serious press (even publications by the Social Democrats and Communists are occasionally susceptible), everywhere Jews figured as the powerful string-pullers behind everything that was important about and in America. The "New Deal" became a "Jew Deal," and conspicuously Jewish-sounding names of prominent Americans are explicitly noted in such publications.

Even the WASP patrician Franklin D. Roosevelt gained the reputation of being related to the "Jewish clan," since he, like his uncle Theodore, came from the East Coast state of New York. Unfortunately, even to this day millions of Europeans have been convinced that the "Judaized" metropolis of New York City calls all the shots in America and—by extension—the world. Although for many German-speaking observers in the nineteenth century the eastern coastal region of the United States was already an area "whose characterization coincided with stereotypes against the 'Jew,' "[56] only after World War I did this geographic expression become a synonym for purported Jewish domination over America or for a Jewish-dominated American supremacy over Europe and the world. Since that period, America has been seen (and not just in Germany or even Europe) as a "Judaized" country. Indeed, according to Doron Rabinovici, it was perceived as "the Jew" among the world's nation-states.[57]

## "Weak Soldiers" and "Shotgun Dames"

If the accusation about the softening impact of America on individual bodies goes back to Buffon's degeneration thesis of the eighteenth century, it was primarily in the course of World War I that the image of the weak American soldier emerged. Neither in the First nor in the Second World War did Germans view American soldiers as their military match. American troops had neither discipline nor endurance, neither team spirit nor courage. Any potential display of competence was regarded with suspicion; after all, they lacked an officer corps as brilliant as the Germans'. American soldiers were seen as childlike and unable to withstand a real challenge. Since money and material issues were the primary concern of the United States, such a nation could hardly produce decent soldiers. Germans made fun of the "Negro army" that the Americans had sent into battle in World War I in order to spare the white race. According to this German (and European) logic, the Americans' victory in World War II was attributable solely to their superiority in the production of war goods. German soldiers frequently still cite the belief that it was only the combination of "the Yank with his equipment" and "Ivan with his reckless human masses" that was capable of defeating the brave and upright German soldier. "Like the Indians in the 19th century," one German soldier said after D-Day, "we were vanquished only by more powerful weaponry."[58]

That the contempt for America in the military field has not entirely disappeared, even in today's peace-loving Germany, is attested to by some of the indignant e-mails I received as a response to my article about the sixtieth anniversary of the Allied landing in Normandy.[59] The e-mail writers unanimously claimed that the GIs would never have won the war if they had been required to fight with the same level of equipment as the Germans. By no means did such views come entirely from conservative or right-wing circles, which have long regarded the American military as soft and incompetent. People from the Green and Social Democratic milieus—where German pacifism is chiefly at home today—also displayed this contempt for the courage and ability of American GIs, thereby indirectly demonstrating how deeply Germans feel the resentment of things American.

These e-mails were in fact confirmed at an individual level by what the SPD intellectual Tilman Fichter frankly and openly proclaimed to British journalists: According to Fichter, one of the West German Left's leading ideologues and—naturally—a devoted man of peace, the American armed forces have always been worthless, even today: "Even a group of British boy scouts is a better military troop than today's American army."[60] Fichter continued to say that, if worse comes to worst and Germans participate in the Iraq War, German soldiers should only do so by serving under a British, rather than American, high command.[61] Fichter's claim is made with an implicitly racial bias since his criticism of the capabilities of the American military hinges upon the idea that American soldiers today are nonwhites and therefore suffering from a lack of both discipline and ability, thus making them, of course, eminently unsuitable to lead Germans in battle. Fichter's reasoning for this sorry state of the American soldier certainly seems new, if his prejudice and racism most definitely are not: With the purported decline of the East Coast in American politics and the parallel rise of the South and Midwest, today's American army is largely recruited from among the inhabitants of black ghettos and from Hispanics, who (according to Fichter's implicit message) produce substandard performance. Anti-Americanism in Germany has by now assumed such a magnitude that even a Social Democratic intellectual openly reaches for an essentially racist line of argument to drive home his point about the inferiority of the American soldier.[62]

Even as late as 2006, millions of Germans still struggle to come to terms with the facts of their defeat at the hands of the Americans twice in one century, especially with their vanquishers purportedly being a people they have been encouraged to despise and regard as inferior. In the peace-loving outlook that has become a highly stylized popular ideology in today's Germany, a kind of revanchist wishful thinking against Americans manages to flourish subcutaneously. On this level, the same masses that embrace American popular culture nonetheless maintain a profound negative bias toward those aspects of America that seem different, threatening, or simply foreign.

Another traditional angle of this popular distrust of Americanness is that of gender. As far as America's supposed gynocracy is concerned, there are simply too many facets to mention them all. What they all have in common, however, is a pejorative character: whether it be the Wild West's "shotgun dames" (in German, *Flintenweiber*), who project domination and power, or the matriarchal family structures of the Indians that rob the men of their (already weakly and beardless) manhood; whether it be the American male, who loses his manhood to a woman because, in a thoroughly materialistic and utilitarian world, his only role is making money, or the fact of America's lack of culture being a result of female dominance; whether it be the lasciviousness with which women intimidate and seduce men or their prudery and chastity as dictated by Puritanism and religious fanaticism—in European eyes, what prevails in America is a perverted balance of the sexes, one that might prove horribly contagious to countries and cultures coming into contact with the New

World. As we shall see in chapter 3, European notions about the relations between the sexes in America today are no closer to reality than they were in the 1890s or the 1920s.

For many of the most virulent America-haters, race and gender in America were explicitly linked, forming an amalgam of horror and perversion. It needs no elaboration that the National Socialists (like most European fascists) despised America. America stood for all the social and political dimensions they perceived as contrary to the essence of their own ideology. The Nazis saw in America an uncultured, mediocre mass society shaped by half-breeds and ruled by a Jewish-dominated plutocracy that envisioned its mission as the attainment of total world domination (politically, economically, and culturally). For the Nazis, Americanism equaled Judaism, and both had to be destroyed:

> [Americanism's] expansion follows the growing power of Jewry in exact parallel. And, like everything encouraged by Jewry, American-ism's lack of culture and lack of manners, its youthful depravity cam-ouflaged as liberality in the "century of the child," is also conscious make-believe. . . . The Jews have succeeded—using jazz and film, magazines and smut, by glorifying gangsters and free love, trivializing perverse inclinations—in preoccupying the American people so thor-oughly in other fields that [the American people] does not take any part in shaping its destiny and no longer even conducts what it calls politics with its head, but rather below the belt. . . . Almost all the peoples of the earth have confronted or are confronting the task of overcoming Americanism, a ubiquitously pleasant reversion into a barbaric lack of culture, by the power of self-contemplation. . . . It is pointless to fight Americanism using unpolitical methods, as if it were merely some sign of ethical-cultural degeneration. But it has already been overcome when one digs up its roots and finds them labeled with the unmistakable insignia "Made in Israel."[63]

But what rendered America truly despicable and dangerous in the eyes of the Nazis was the fact that this total mediocrity, this inau-thentic entity, somehow still exuded an irresistible attraction on the German (and European) masses. To be sure, the Nazis saw it as their task to crush this attraction, but in the meantime they realized its potency and were reluctantly obliged to indulge it, lest its interdiction cause dissatisfaction, even revolt. Thus, the National Socialists felt it necessary to play jazz, swing, and ragtime on the radio during the war to prevent their own soldiers from switching to the U.S. army channels.[64]

On the whole, the German Left exhibited nowhere near the anti-Americanism that was common to the Right. Karl Marx and Friedrich Engels were great admirers of the Union and backed it wholeheartedly in its battle against the Confederacy. But as Thomas Haury shows, one also finds plenty of passages from Marx in an unequivocally anti-American pitch, which indicate a certain ambivalence vis-à-vis America on Marx's part. Nevertheless, "compared with the anti-American lamentation of his contemporaries Nikolaus Lenau . . . and Heinrich Heine . . . Marx argued in a significantly more reflective fashion."[65] Above all, Marx emphasized and admired the progressiveness of bourgeois America against feudal Europe. Wilhelm Liebknecht and Karl Kautsky were in fact decidedly friendly toward America. In general, the continental European Left, especially the social democratic and republican forces up to the end of World War I, was markedly more pro-American than the European Right. In contrast to the British Labour Party, which was severely anti-American as early as its foundation in 1900, German and Austrian social democracy, at least until the 1930s, saw America with a certain degree of sympathy, if never able entirely to disregard the common cultural disdain acquired from the hegemonic discourse in which these parties existed as countersocieties.

With the establishment of the Soviet Union, however, the attitudes of the European Left toward America began to change for good. Adherents to communism and others to the left of social democracy now showered their affections on a country that—with the exception of the war years 1941 to 1945—became one of the most important bearers of anti-Americanism. A telling example of this shift is the German satirist and writer Bertolt Brecht: "Originally, he shared the pro-modernist enthusiasm for America in Germany that reached its climax in Germany around 1924-26."[66] By the end of the 1920s, however, Brecht had changed into a critic, and by the start of the 1930s he greeted America with contempt. As Dan Diner put it, "America and capitalism became interchangeable metaphors—and the Soviet Union appeared as an optimistic counterworld."[67] Brecht verbalized his personal shift thus: "The mistakes of the Russians are the mistakes of friends; the mistakes of the Americans are the mistakes of enemies."[68] The normative transformation Brecht underwent is the rule among European intellectuals who did not have an anti-American attitude a priori. I do not know of a single instance in which a formerly anti-American intellectual developed into a friend or admirer of America.

## Anti-Americanism in Great Britain

It was not just German and Austrian elites who expressed habitual contempt for America. Let us take a look at Great Britain, a country that in Germany and elsewhere on the European continent has always been perceived as a close ally of the United States. Indeed, recently it has been explicitly represented as Washington's lackey and servile lapdog, as in Tony Blair's being nothing but George W. Bush's poodle. Just as continental Europeans routinely regard Great Britain as an appendage of the United States, America is often—mistakenly—viewed by continentals as an extension of Britain transplanted across the Atlantic. Owing to the linguistic and cultural affinities between these two political entities, continental Europeans believe that Britons view America quite differently than they do. On the contrary, only one theme encountered in Germany is missing from the British view of the United States: the "small shopkeeper's mentality" (*Krämerseele*) and other clichés articulated in that hazy atmosphere where German culture, the German spirit, and the German soul are set against a "Judaized" and profit-oriented pragmatism. In Germany—as in France (albeit for other reasons)—anti-Americanism is mixed with a strong antipathy to the English and Great Britain. In what the Germans call *die Angelsachsen* and the French dub *les anglosaxons*, this attitude has a generic label whose negative connotations are to this day common knowledge in German- and French-speaking regions. Apart from the fact that British anti-Americanism naturally harbors no anti-British resentment in the same way as the German and French versions, British, French, and German (or continental European) anti-Americanisms are virtually congruent conceptually and normatively.

British writers were in fact some of the most vociferous critics of America in the nineteenth and twentieth centuries. Perhaps precisely because of the perceived linkages and similarities between Great Britain and its former colony, British literature frequently displays a disparaging and critical voice when it comes to the United States. In this literature, it is not so much the content of the critique, but rather the voice of the author, that defines its anti-Americanism. As early as 1832, the Englishwoman Frances Trollope, matriarch of the talented Trollope family of writers, published her book *Domestic Manners of the Americans*, which became a bestseller on both sides of the Atlantic.[69] The book contained all the negative stereotypes already circulating in the Old World at that time, many of which still have resonance today. Americans, according to Trollope, were hypocrites. They talked arrogantly about freedom but kept slaves. The worst example of this collective hypocrisy, she wrote, was Thomas Jefferson. Trollope reproached him for holding slaves himself as a plantation owner in Virginia, and one who was rumored to have fathered a child with a young slave.[70] The British woman also made fun of the patriotism openly displayed by Americans, which one encountered everywhere in both town and country. She was especially appalled at the lack of manners and the vulgar utilitarianism she imagined as formative to every kind of behavior in the New World. According to her, Americans ate, they did not dine, as she noticed with disgust that every meal was gulped down with incredible rapidity, and conversation hardly took place while eating. The intake of food did not constitute a pleasure for Americans, instead serving only the function of supplying calories for work. In addition, Trollope was terribly concerned about Americans' obsession with efficiency, which supplanted any space of tranquility or self-reflection, and which obeyed only the logic of production and profit.

She found it horrible that American women preferred working in a factory to being a housekeeper, to her mind a consequence of the unappetizing equality of the sexes that accompanied democracies. As with many Europeans, the position of the American woman—too active in public life, too dominant in private—did not suit Trollope. And of course she complained about the American weather, which struck her as too extreme, incommodious both for work and for leisure.

*Domestic Manners of the Americans* was an enormous success in Great Britain because the book used every stereotype of cultural inferiority and crude materialism imputed to the New World as a way of making the Old World feel better about its own identity in relation to the United States. Trollope supported the British reading public's belief that this ex-colony, which was already preparing to challenge the motherland's position as leading industrial nation and world power in the not too distant future, was nothing more than an arrogant parvenu. It was ultimately not simply the specific criticisms that she levied against America that made her book such a representative and influential text for the voice of modern anti-Americanism; rather, it was her unwavering tone of moral indignation and righteous horror, this sense of the simultaneous absurdity and very real danger of America, that set a tone, and assured the book's international popularity. Here is Simon Schama on this topic:

> *Domestic Manners of the Americans* made Frances Trollope, at the age of 52, a sudden literary reputation, and £1,000 from the proceeds of the first runaway edition. Her book was popular in Britain precisely because it documented all the stereotypes of cultural inferiority and boorish materialism which the Old World was avid to have confirmed about the New, and thus assuage its increasing uneasiness about upstart America. Stendhal read Mrs. Trollope, chuckled, made heavy annotations, and concluded complacently that there was indeed something of the "smell of the shop" about the country. Baudelaire thought it the Belgium of the west.[71]

This brings us to Charles Dickens, who had already toured the United States in 1842 as a superstar, not only because his books

*Nicholas Nickleby* and *Oliver Twist* sold extremely well over the counter, but also because the dramatizations of these books were hugely successful on the American stage. Dickens's *American Notes* and *Martin Chuzzlewit* vastly eclipsed Frances Trollope's critique of America as far as the curtness of his language and the extent of his contempt, derision, and mockery.[72] Dickens provides an exclusively negative portrayal of America in both books. With the exception of Boston and Harvard, which he and countless European intellectuals before and since enjoyed precisely because they are so "un-American," Dickens is outraged at every aspect of America: there are too many immigrants, it is heterogeneous, populist, dirty, brutal; its politics are corrupt, fixated on individual persons, and violent; the press is sensational and unreliable.

In these two books dedicated explicitly to the United States, Dickens mocks the American accent and the degeneracy of the English language he hears and reads. He finds laughable the Americans' notion that their country arouses envy throughout the world. Instead of discerning what the Americans praise as their trademark meritocratic system, Dickens sees nothing but plutocracy and an all-dominating avarice. The inhabitants of the New World strike him as conceited, ill-mannered, repulsive, sanctimonious, immoral, boastful, uncultivated, tasteless, moralizing, insulting, insulted, abusive of liberty, materialistic, religious and blasphemous at one and the same time, and (how could it be otherwise?) living under miserable climactic conditions in a hateful, inhospitable landscape. Dickens describes the Mississippi as a "slimy monster hideous to behold," a visual abomination and a breeding ground for illness. Not only does he find American cities hideous, but so too the uncultivated land, which was so wild and ugly "the eye was pained to see [it]." In total, America comes off quite badly, particularly when compared with the beautiful and liberating British natural landscape.[73]

Like many Europeans before and after him, Dickens accuses the Americans of not achieving anything with their potential, of ultimately being capable only of destructiveness. He is speaking to the oft-heard belief referenced in that previously quoted statement from Eric Frey's *Schwarzbuch USA*: "The United States *could be* such a wonderful country." For Dickens as for Frey, however, the follow-up thought is never that the United States would be a great country if they only did this or that, if they reformed themselves this way or that way, but instead only if they gave up existing. This European criticism is therefore never constructive, but rather essentialist. Thus Dickens's derision of America in *Martin Chuzzlewit* and *American Notes* ultimately has nothing to do with a critique of America. He flatly and uncompromisingly rejects the United States. It is a land inherently lacking the possibility of reformation or redemption.

In his own *American Notes*, Rudyard Kipling talks about the Americans' absence of manners, which he ascribes (along with their crude language, with its painfully laughable accent) to their lack of culture. American journalists needed to be treated, according to Kipling, like "little, very ill-mannered children." American patriotism and the display of religiosity struck him as exaggerated and silly; he ascribed both to the country's youth and its population's cultural defects. Kipling was appalled at the amount of violence in the country and by what struck him as an incomprehensible lack of political order. Everywhere he encountered chaos—for example, San Francisco was a "crazy city" inhabited by "insane people."[74] On the one hand, Kipling did not shy away from writing about the African American population in racist tones; on the other hand, he was amused by the aristocratic affectations and pretensions of southern plantation owners who did not think twice about practicing lynch justice. As the height of his contempt, Kipling compares the barbarism of this supposedly civilized America with that of India, about which he had published so many writings brimming with racist clichés, the very clichés that made him one of Victorian Britain's most successful authors and most typical representatives.

## Anti-Americanism from France

In a sense, the history of anti-Americanism in France is perhaps the most interesting in Europe. In contrast to all the other major European countries—Great Britain, Germany, Spain, Italy, even the

Austro-Hungarian monarchy[75]—France and the United States have never fought a war against each other.[76] What is more, the United States was allied with France, officially or otherwise, more often than with any other European country. France stood as godfather to the American republic at its birth in the War of Independence against Great Britain, and the ideas of American independence from 1776 greatly influenced the French Revolution of 1789. Possibly for this reason French sentiment toward the United States constantly vacillates between a close bond and a constant rivalry, a tension that ultimately has worked to bias the French population profoundly against America. Although the quantitative dimension of a construct as complex as anti-Americanism is hard to measure even with the most refined survey methods, I feel confident in claiming that anti-Americanism in France has had the strongest public presence among the European countries across the last two centuries.

Of course, this also has to do with France's colonial past, which placed it in permanent competition with Great Britain. In this competition, France frequently came off second best, especially on the American continent, where, following the defeat on the Plains of Abraham in September 1759, the victorious British largely limited French influence to Quebec (La Belle Provence). One element of French anti-Americanism thus results from an undifferentiated aversion to everything Anglo-Saxon and English in general. With the French it is not so much the kind of skepticism about modernity (money, capitalism, trade, markets) that dominates German resentment of America. What tends to matter for the French are rivalries of power politics, jealousy, and a sense of inferiority rooted in the Seven Years War. From this point on, France always has either come out the loser in a direct confrontation with Great Britain or, even worse, has been able to restrain its German neighbor only with the assistance of the Anglo-Saxon powers.

There are also specific cultural fetishes and phobias unique to France. No European country pursues so rigid a linguistic policy as France, a nation that has always viewed its language as both an anti-American and an anti-English bulwark. Of course in Germany, too, there have been occasional efforts to keep the German language clear of foreign (meaning, as a rule, English and French) influences.[77] And, of course, there are still organizations in Germany, like the Verein Deutsche Sprache e.V. (German Language Association), that have made a mission out of protecting the German language from contamination by American English. But nowhere in Europe is there such a concordance—one emotionally tangible to the populace and capable of being politically mobilized—between state and society as when it comes to the defense of French against the ubiquitous English language. And while this defensiveness might be geared in general toward the influence of "English," it is both explicitly and implicitly clear that it is specifically "American English" that poses the biggest threat.

Let us now take a look at the ideas French intellectuals and scholars have entertained about America and the Americans. Comte de Buffon, mentioned earlier, launched the "degeneration thesis" that became so critical for the way that America was received by Europe. Voltaire viewed America as a "belated" continent, primitive and underdeveloped, if possessing an admirable strength and purity. In general, those French voices that did admire aspects of America, for example Chateaubriand, tended to single out the nation's indigenous population or wildness for praise, not its civilization or development. For more critical "philosophes," America was simply inferior.

In the revolutionary years, when the French themselves saw the young United States as their most important ally against the British Empire, they found Americans ungrateful and arrogant. For the great conservative thinker Joseph de Maistre, the United States not only incorporated everything bad but was also a danger to Europe. And, as already cited, people as influential as Baudelaire and Stendhal were at best unimpressed, at worst revolted, by the United States. Not just politics but American bodies and mores disgusted French observers. There were many French authors who did not find Homo Americanus of either sex particularly appetizing: too big, fleshy, and fat. The size of American meals frightened French observers as much as their inferior quality. While Jules Huret regarded chewing "funny gum" as progress compared to the consumption of chewing tobacco, which had to be grotesquely spit out, he attributed this strange American habit to the hyperactivity of the people and the land: the jaws and teeth of the Americans, like every other part of the American anatomy, enjoyed no rest. Instead, they had to be in good shape for the tough, oversized portions of beefsteak that were served for breakfast.[78]

American football struck Huret as barbarian, despite the fact that he experienced the sport in the fine society of a Harvard-Yale game. He was shocked by the brutality of the students in the stands, who egged on their teams with cries like "Kill him" and "Break his neck!" Another French writer, Urbain Gohier, found the behavior of the public at American sporting events quite nasty: the collective bellowing, the symptoms of mass hysteria he described as "burning fever," the riotous assembly of the fans into tribal-like formations that gave these events a primitive air. For French observers like Georges Duhamel, the novelist and playwright from the first half of the twentieth century, American sports, especially football, both symbolized and embodied the destructive force of America on human culture at its most basic level: "a game that leads to such a frenzy of brutal struggle cannot be good for civilization." For many shocked French male observers, even worse than the brutish athletes were the cheerleaders, whom Gohier satirized as "amazons." On the one hand, they were the most unfeminine creatures a French man could possibly imagine. On the other hand, they reminded him "of the prostitutes in the Mediterranean ports," performing "a suggestive and furious *danse du ventre*." Duhamel found it appalling, if admittedly erotic, that an American woman, smoking a cigarette and showing her legs in nylon stockings, might drive along country roads at fifty miles an hour. He keenly concluded that women in America must be holding the reins of power, having snatched them from their weakly protesting husbands and fathers.[79]

Hundreds of other French men and women have seen to it that this image of America has been disseminated throughout France. For example, there was Frederic Gaillardet, the nineteenth century French journalist, for whom American women dominated not only their husbands, but also the entire country. The American male was a slave who had long since lost his status as king of the castle. He was grateful simply to be maltreated by his spouse rather than physically abused. Gaillardet called the American woman a "republican duchess" who had "moved up from the footstool to the throne."[80] In accord with the character of the country, she was not a sovereign, but rather a despotic ruler. Even French politicians were not immune to these prejudices within French popular culture. Two-time French Prime Minister Georges Clemenceau could not stand Woodrow Wilson, treating him with contempt although Wilson was a highly cultivated man, renowned political scientist, and the former president of Princeton University.[81]

As in Germany, anti-Americanism intensified in France after World War I. Despite the fact that the two nations had fought on opposite sides, the tone and content of their attack on America were identical. Both countries were united by hatred of Wilson and American politicians, hatred of American business, whose overseas commitments did not suit their respective economies, hatred of Jews, and hatred of the perceived destroyers of native or authentic culture. Even at this time there were all kinds of conspiracy theories circulating about the international political ambitions of America. Americans were accused of entering the war just as the European powers were exhausted in order to ensure a shift in global power in their favor after the armistice.

Soon after 1918, whatever feelings of gratitude there might have been toward the Americans, who had helped the French to end the war victorious, were gone. (This pattern reoccurred after May 1945.) Intellectuals on the left and right inscribed anti-Americanism on their banners, which they waved in public to great success. A few relevant book titles testify to the basic normative alignment of this political trend: in 1927—the same year Adolf Halfeld published his bestseller *Amerika und Amerikanismus* (America and Americanism) in Germany—Jean-Louis Chastanet, a left-wing member of the French assembly, published his anti-American and anti-Semitic work *L'Oncle Shylock* (Uncle Shylock), in which "Uncle Sam" is controlled by the Jew Shylock. In 1929 Octave Homberg brought out his book *L'Impérialisme américain* (American Imperialism), and the anti-Semitic Kadmi-Cohen followed a year later with the widely read title *L'Abomination américaine* (The American Monstrosity). In 1931 the right-wing intellectuals Robert Aron and Arnaud Dandieu wrote *Le Cancer américain* (The American Cancer). And 1931 was also the year in which future Minister of the Interior Charles Pomaret's *L'Amérique à la conquête de l'Europe* (America at the Conquest of Europe) appeared.

Whether author and economist André Siegfried, three-time Prime Minister André Tardieu, novelist and playwright Georges Duhamel, nihilist author Louis-Ferdinand Celine, or Charles Maurras, founder of the fascist journal and popular movement *Action Française*, whether the philosopher Jean-Paul Sartre or the feminist thinker Simone de Beauvoir, from radical Right to radical Left, France's intellectual elite was almost unanimously anti-American. This alignment remained constant for a long time in both milieus, with some brief exceptions in the early 1980s, France's short post-Solzhenitzyn era when its intellectuals unequivocally confronted the Soviet Union's Stalinism head on, thus creating a short-lived atmosphere of pro-Americanism. Apart from this interlude, most French contemporary intellectuals, just like their eminent predecessors mentioned above, have been panic-stricken about the alleged standardization of the world and of French life by America. In the eyes of these thinkers, what was at stake was nothing less than a defense of human culture. One example ought to illustrate this point. To underline the cultural wealth of Europe as compared with America's supposed cultural wasteland, Simone de Beauvoir compared the French ball game pétanque with bowling. Boules or pétanque is played in the shadows of majestic trees on a village square, where the unevenness of the ground is part of the game. Bowling is played in lifeless, sterile halls, where perfect spheres race at rapid speed across millimeter-perfect lanes toward completely identical plastic figures, in order to be sent back to the players by machines.[82]

Very brief mention of the anti-Americanism in the works of a Norwegian, Russian, and Spanish writer, respectively, serves to show that all the themes accentuated by British, French, and German writers and thinkers were also present in other European cultures. The Norwegian Nobel laureate and later enthusiastic follower of

National Socialism Knut Hamsun merged his pronounced anti-Americanism with a solid dosage of Anglophobia and that other oft-articulated requisite, anti-Semitism. Hamsun viewed America as a land of tasteless and avaricious materialism bereft of cultural or artistic achievements. A cheap imitation of Europe, America was the embodiment of inauthenticity. Everything about America seemed unclean: in politics, in the mixing of races and social classes, in the economy, and in culture. The American ideology of freedom, according to Hamsun, was deceiving millions of emigrants by offering them something that did not exist. In general, dimensions were getting dramatically out of hand: everything seemed too big, too fast, too uncontrolled, too materialistic, and too vulgar. American politics struck him as infantile but at the same time corrupt, brutal, and merciless. Even the affected admiration of American elites for the British struck him as servile, a sign of cultural insecurity and hypocrisy.[83]

That Maxim Gorki, a bona fide man of the Left, expressed nearly identical views about America as the fascist Hamsun once again shows the strong affinity between the European Right and Left on this issue. In his two books, *The City of the Yellow Devil* and *In America*, Gorki mercilessly picked New York City and the nation on the whole to pieces.[84] Freedom in America, according to Gorki, was nothing more than a deceitful instrument of the yellow devil—gold. Gorki perceived America, despite the never-ending rhetoric of freedom, as completely unfree, since its society was thoroughly conformist, mediocre, and inauthentic. The gigantic wealth of John D. Rockefeller and J. P. Morgan had consigned the founders and champions of American freedom, especially George Washington and Abraham Lincoln, to complete oblivion. Skyscrapers and Sunday newspapers weighing ten pounds were all well and good, but they were not productive: people bereft of ideas and culture disported in the former, and the latter contributed nothing to society except advertisements and shallow reporting. To Gorki, Americans seemed high-handed, laughable when it came to their patriotism, and much too energetic and industrious (an attribute not meant as a compliment!). Their energy made them destructive, and their industry lacked any imagination. Like robots, they slaved away in this wretched country and this terrible city of New York without ever experiencing true beauty and leisure. In his writings, America was a Moloch, an evil machine that could only be corrected by a socialist revolution.[85]

Lastly, the conservative Spanish intellectual José Ortega y Gasset speaks for many of his European counterparts when he characterizes the essence of the United States as consisting of practicality and technique. To be sure, for Ortega y Gasset, both of these are clearly European inventions of the eighteenth and nineteenth centuries that have been transposed to the United States, where—in their in-authentic reincarnation—they give the country its sole claim to fame. Subsequently, Ortega y Gasset articulates an oft-repeated mantra of European disdain for America: that the United States can-not claim any greatness because it has no history, has little experi-ence, and has not yet truly suffered. Ortega y Gasset concludes that "it is illusory to think that this people [the Americans] could posses the virtues of command."[86]

The vignettes in this chapter are not intended to offer a compre-hensive overview of anti-Americanism's presence in Europe's intel-lectual discourse of the past two centuries. Rather, they merely serve to highlight the fact that the common themes constituting anti-Americanism existed in many European cultures, and that they have remained constant and consistent in their emphases to this day. It is to the present situation that we now turn in the next two chapters.

---------------------------------------------------------------

# The Perceived "Americanization" of All Aspects of European Lives: A Discourse of Irritation and Condescension

This chapter is devoted to the analysis of diverse themes that have just one thing in common: They have almost nothing to do with "grand" politics. By way of this exclusion I hope to analyze the kind of European resentment against America that might be called "surplus" anti-Americanism, or the anti-American "bonus." The subject is anti-Americanism for its own sake, where resorting to general assumptions about the United States contributes nothing, either descriptively or analytically, to understanding the topic at hand, but instead chiefly serves the purpose of confirming and mobilizing preexisting prejudices. Above all, the negative references to America serve mainly to defame and denigrate, not to explain, compare, and analyze. Thus, my research here focuses on subjects like language, sports, work, higher education, the media, health, law and the judicial system, crime, urban development, and a miscellaneous assortment of general vignettes and various topics that are part of everyday life but basically unconnected to governments, states, parties, and other explicitly political actors and institutions.[1] Using this approach, I hope to illuminate the *identity* dimension (what America *is*) of European anti-Americanism and minimize (if not completely filter out, which I believe is not possible) its *conduct* dimension (what America *does*). I am thus following the methodological claim asserted by Melvin L. DeFleur and Margaret H. DeFleur, who in their study *Learning to Hate Americans* aim to establish what they call a "dual pattern" that differentiates clearly between "attitude objects" pertaining to the United States government and its policies, on the one hand, and the American people, on the other.[2] My empirical material derives from seven West and Central European countries: Germany, Austria, France, Great Britain, Italy, Spain, and Portugal. Even though the examples in this chapter hail disproportionately from Germany and Britain, with France being a distant third and the other countries restricted to a few cases, I believe that these instances capture the tone of a discourse about America in Western Europe that has become pervasive and not at all country-specific.

I would like to mention two vignettes that feature my interests in this chapter: The first is best characterized by what Eric T. Hansen—an American journalist who has lived for twenty years in Germany but who, by his own account, has not come to feel like a German even though he writes and dreams exclusively in German—calls "felt Americanization."[3] A pretty twenty-year-old girl from Passau confessed to Hansen that she felt "deeply American." "There was bitterness in her voice, as if she had been robbed of her natural culture in the cradle," Hansen wrote. Hansen has heard people talk incessantly about their inevitable "Americanization" and, of course, the "Americanization of Germany." In this context, for example, he mentions a book by Michael Rutschky called *Wie wir Amerikaner wurden. Eine deutsche Entwicklungsgeschichte* [How We Became Americans. A German coming-of-age story] in which it is asserted that Germany lost its soul because of Americanization. Hansen goes on to write that there are currently "about 12,000 Turkish fast food shops and 23,000 Italian restaurants in Germany in addition to 1,650 hamburger restaurants. Yet nobody talks about Germany's Italianization" or even the "Italianization" or "Turkization" of Germany's culinary habits. As I made a point of showing in the preceding chapter, European feelings of anxiety, irritation, and contempt toward America are nothing new; they can look back on a solid 250-year tradition. This "felt Americanization," a mixture of anxiety about invisible dangers and irresistible temptation that is supposedly on an unstoppable course toward undermining and corrupting the integrity of the German essence surreptitiously, can be distinguished only by degree from the National Socialist delusion about the "Judaization" that the Nazis attributed to similarly demonic forces attacking a helpless German people. In both phenomena, what stands out is the notion of a complete self-incapacitation of the Germans, who are supposedly subjected to terrible things done against their will by two exogenous, overpowering, and irresistible forces. But it is not only the Germans who feel themselves surreptitiously Americanized and losing their essential identity. Other West Europeans, too, like the following voice from Spain, bemoan a loss of agency, a seeming self-incapacitation vis-à-vis America's cunning and compelling ways, which are clearly experienced as dangerous and undesirable but against which one appears to be helpless. "I am frightened for the simple reason that we cannot deny that every day cultures and societies look more like the American style, and its way of thinking is being imposed indiscriminately on everybody. For this reason, I stop to think about the consequences of the imminent phenomenon of Americanization and all that remains is: I am frightened."[4]

Second vignette: On July 9, 2004, the *Frankfurter Rundschau* published an article by Helmut Müller-Sievers, a professor of German literature and classical philology and chair of the department of comparative literature at Northwestern University. The article was entitled "The American Campaign under the Sign of the Churches" and was the first in a series written for this paper on the forthcoming presidential election in November of that year. As might be expected, the author reproduced the usual clichés about American ignorance and inauthenticity, which in this case he attributed to a lack of understanding and misinterpretation of true Lutheranism and of Luther's teachings on the part of American "evangelicals." One of the sources of this American ignorance was the "vastness of American space . . . , which in Texas, in Nebraska, [and] in Montana is so empty, so disjointed and hostile, that it practically cries out for a God as a reason."[5] Even more interesting and telling than the article, though, was the following apposition that the intellectually highbrow Web site Perlentaucher ("Pearl Diver"—a daily digest of major articles from the cultural pages of German-speaking Europe's serious periodicals) added by way of introduction to the text it posted on the Internet that day: "God, it is an awful country."

Two thoughts went through my head as I read this: First, that Perlentaucher would never have added a remark like this about any other country on Earth: not North Korea, nor Saudi Arabia, Germany, nor even Israel, although the daily breaking of taboos about the Jewish state in Germany and Europe does seem to indicate that it may not be too long before this also becomes inevitable, given how so many Europeans and Germans are already heading in this direction. (I will say more on this in chapter 5.) An apposition like this either would not have occurred to the editors in the case of any other country or, if it had passed through their minds, they would have guarded against relating it to those readers interested in what the left-liberal *Frankfurter Rundschau* has to say. Secondly, however, it was clear to me that this sentence reproduces exactly what Germans and Europeans must be thinking about America today, even if they take seriously only half of the daily dose publicly presented to them concerning America. On the basis of my regular perusal of the West European press on the subject of "America" over the last fifteen years, I shall be so bold as to conclude that the commentary appended by Perlentaucher placed that Web journal right in the mainstream of the German and European press.[6] This very tone and intellectual attitude toward America are hegemonic in the German and European media. Today, the "ugly American" is a prominent and ubiquitous figure in all of Western Europe's public discourse.

## The Myriad Threat of Americanization, American Conditions, the American Way, Just Simply America

In current German usage, the concepts "Americanization" (*Amerikanisierung*) and "American conditions" (*amerikanische Verhältnisse*; *amerikanische Bedingungen*) almost invariably stand for something negative, bad, and above all threatening, something that absolutely has to be avoided or—if the European patient has already contracted this ailment—somehow needs to be alleviated or diminished. One also often encounters the past participle *veramerikanisiert*, which—by adding the prefix *ver* to *amerikanisiert*—lends "Americanization" a noticeably pejorative dimension. In contemporary European discourse, "Americanization" has become a wholly acceptable and fashionable *Schimpfwort* (swear word), used frequently by the Right, Left, and Center in economics, politics, culture, the social world—pretty much any conceivable realm. Indeed, Lutz Erbring, one of Germany's leading media researchers, argues that the term *Amerikanisierung* has mutated into a "virulent Schimpfwort" in Germany's public discourse.[7] Erbring's research demonstrates that the German media liberally and regularly resort to negative stereotypes about America and Americans that they would not use in the case of reporting on any other country, certainly never on anything pertaining to Germany. As Erbring points out correctly, the term *Schneisen*, as in the title of the newspaper article "Schneisen durch Bagdad gebombt" ("Aisles/Lanes created by bombing of Baghdad" in which the translation of "Schneisen" as "aisles" and "lanes" in no way captures the connotation that Germans associate with that word, namely the carpet bombing by the Allies during World War II) is obviously meant to create an analogy between German and Iraqi victims. When discussing the *Don Carlos* incident in Munich, I already mentioned how Germans—particularly the German media—have habitually invoked parallels between the bombing of Baghdad and that of German cities (Dresden in particular).

In my research into hundreds of German texts, to be sure, I did run across a few that associated "Americanization" with something like "progress," "freedom," "emancipation," or some other positive value. Some writers did use these concepts neutrally and merely descriptively, but the overwhelming majority employed them to describe something pejorative, undesirable, worthy of contempt, laughable, and/or dangerous. In Western Europe, in all political camps independent of social position, nationality, age, or sex, the code word "Americanization" elicits such a degree of rejection that it pays for politicians to deploy this feeling for purposes of mobilization and legitimation. In brief, "America" has become a ubiquitous negative symbol in the western part of the continent. America's normality has become abnormal to Europeans. A good example of this is how the Oklahoma City bomber Timothy McVeigh, an American mass murderer and fascist, was portrayed by one of the leading German and European publications as an ordinary American who even—it can't get any more American than this!—wanted to stage and market his own execution.[8] The United States is regarded as dangerous, commercial, nationalistic, undemocratic, intolerant, antiwelfare, crude, religious, puritanical, vulgar—as the exact opposite of how Europeans think about themselves, of how they like to imagine and portray themselves.

German Chancellor Gerhard Schröder, brilliant politician that he was, understood this only too well in 2002, which is why his successful reelection campaign that year explicitly evoked and contrasted "our German way" of running a society against implicit "American conditions" and juxtaposed "German" with diametrically opposed "American" values.[9] There is no doubt that it was these implicitly hinted anti-American sentiments fully understood by all and thus rarely in need of explicit elaboration that contributed to Schröder's popularity among the German public in the 2002 campaign and also helped him and the Social Democrats annul a more than twenty-point lead that the conservative opposition had gained on the Social Democrats only six weeks before the September 18, 2005, parliamentary elections. German patriotism—especially of the Social Democratic variety—was mainly built on accentuating the differences between Germany and America, which in turn necessitated the negative invocation of American tropes in matters having little to do with America but in need of legitimating matters dear to the Social Democrats in Germany.

This pattern—portraying unwanted changes as American or a consequence of Americanization—has been a prerogative of not only the German Left. Indeed, threats of alleged "Americanization" are voiced among conservatives just as readily to discredit their Social Democratic opponents. Thus, for example, Germany's Junge Union (the youth branch of the conservative Christian Democratic Union) hardly lags behind the Social Democrats when it comes to using the stigmatizing word "Americanization." In a declaration

entitled "Democratization instead of Americanization," Hildegard
Müller, the chair of the Junge Union, charged that a proposal by
Franz Müntefering, secretary general of the Social Democrats, to
implement electoral primaries on the American model was nothing
more than "ill-considered showmanship." The head of the Christian
Democrats' youth wing claimed: "Our politics is in need of democratization rather than Americanization, of competence in problem-
solving rather than air bubbles."[10] In Müller's view, which is shared
by millions of Germans and Europeans, democratization and Americanization have become incompatible opposites. And clearly
"Americanization" stands for "air bubbles"—fluff, show, inauthenticity—never for genuine problem solving. And not only among
young Christian Democrats, but also among such seasoned elder
statesmen as the Christian Democratic politician Heiner Geißler,
"American conditions" have been presented as something undesirable and threatening for Germany. In an interview with German
television's second channel ZDF (the news program *heute-journal*),
Geißler said that a welfare reform proposal for a law merging unem-
ployment with public assistance violated a basic principle of solidarity. "In this context," reported the Web newspaper *Netzeitung*, "he
warned against 'American conditions' in Germany."[11]

Moreover, using America and Americanization as a convenient
bogeyman to garner points in an internal conflict that has nothing
to do with America certainly is not confined to Germany. Thus, for
example, in the heated French debate in the spring of 2005 about
the approval of the European Constitution by the public, both sides
used "America" prominently in their argument against each other.
President Jacques Chirac and the proponents of the constitution
warned that only a strong and united Europe could effectively oppose the United States. Voting in favor of the European Constitution thus became an act of countering America. The constitution's
opponents gained much mileage by depicting the European Union
and its policies as a quasi-America, as a structure that—with its
"Anglo-American neoliberalism"—was well on its way to usurp Europe and its values and surreptitiously create an America in Europe.
Both the Austrian far Right led by Jörg Haider and citizen action

groups typically more self-defined as members of the Left invoked negative themes in their political campaigns centered on America. Haider implored voters not to let Vienna become Chicago ("Wien darf nicht Chicago werden")—why Chicago, why not Palermo or Liverpool or any number of European cities that are far from problem free? In Vienna, too, the civic action group "No to the North- east Highway Pass" mobilized successfully against a city highway by asking the question, "Do we need 'American conditions' in the city on the Danube?"[12] Beyond invoking a number of the conven- tional negative tropes about America and Americans, this group won its case buttressed by the argument that pedestrians do not exist in the United States. And in Portugal, the debate about the preservation of Portuguese culture in the face of an ever-growing influence by the European Union in many aspects of Portuguese life also frequently invoked the dangers of "the bastardization of national cultures, all of which face the same external threat— namely the cultural products of the United States—which they are left to confront disarmed and alone."[13] Here, too, the European Union is invoked as a defender against as well as a purveyor of much-dreaded Americanization.

In Austria, *Amerikanisierung, amerikanische Verhältnisse*, and *ame- rikanische Bedingungen* exhibit a negative connotation identical to that which exists in Germany. In Great Britain, "Americanisation" and "American-style" stand almost exclusively for negative develop- ments. Indeed, particularly the former often has the adjective "creeping" as a telling modifier in front of it, as in "creeping Ameri- canisation of the car's feel on the road" (the article never explains how exactly a car's handling becomes "Americanized," but that is not the point; instead, "Americanization" is invoked to convey something undesirable),[14] " 'the cult of guns' fuelled by creeping Americanisation through violent films,"[15] "the danger of creeping Americanisation" in the ever-growing girth of British novels,[16] "the declining standard of literacy—or perhaps creeping Americanisa- tion,"[17] "the creeping Americanisation of Halloween,"[18] and the "creeping Americanisation" in—of all things—cricket, a sport that Americans do not even play or follow.[19] At the heart of a study published in 2000, scholars from the University of Manchester also ranked "creeping 'Americanisation' " as the main reason for growing stress in Great Britain's working world.[20] And "creeping Americanisation" need not at all be associated with violence, commercialization, or any other kind of obvious or perceived deterioration. Indeed, it is coded negatively even if it concerns something presumably positive, like the alleged "niceness" in the discourse of British sports. But no, this, too, is bad and inauthentic, ergo part of an obviously "creeping Americanisation" as in the following statement: "The creeping Americanisation of British sport, in terms of ubiquitous coverage and potential for high-earning, means that niceness is at a higher premium than ever before."[21] I could give hundreds of examples like these from all imaginable walks of British life, but the point is clear: What all these "Americanisations" have in common is that they depict something deteriorating, negative, undesirable that allegedly has befallen the particular item presented in the article. And the constant usage of the attribute "creeping" clearly is meant to convey something that is "creepy."

If we are to believe major press outlets in France, the Americanization of French society has been far-reaching, relentless, and totally to the detriment of whatever the case may be. We encounter the *Americanisation* of French and European accounting practices, the constitutional system, electoral campaigns, the growth of single family clusters outside metropolitan areas, the use of credit cards, urban and suburban planning, sports, films, music, language, habits. Even the world of Parisian haute couture seems to have been bastardized by "a violent Americanization of taste." And of course antonymy in this all-around evil of *Americanisation* prevails. Thus, Regis Debray, who has made it his life's mission to berate America for every possible ill befalling French society, and who, like most of his colleagues hailing from the Left Bank in Paris, has derided America's religious zealotry, has recently changed the angle of his attacks. In a piece arguing that one of current French society's main problems was the paucity of a meaningful religious and spiritual life, he concluded that the results led to France's becoming a European variant of "an Americanized society in which there exists top quality for the connoisseurs of quality, vulgarity for the masses and no mediation in between."[22] Debray seems to have moved to the right on a number of issues in French politics. But one vector remains unchanged in this apparent transition: disdain for America and the completely negative connotation associated with anything related to *Americanisation*." In addition to the term *Americanisation*, one also encounters the almost exclusively pejorative *à l'Americaine* and quite often the dismissive *les Americains* or *ces Americains*—"the Americans" and "these Americans."[23] In Spain, *americanizacion* has an identically pejorative connotation as it does in the other countries considered in this chapter, perhaps with the exception that on occasion the term *norteamericano* in both its adjectival and substantive forms is used maybe to differentiate (good) Spanish America from (bad) English North America. But just as in Germany, France, and Britain, in Spain, too, *americanizacion* entails something menacing, subversive, cheapened, lessened, commercialized, inauthentic, something that makes things worse.

## "Americanization" and Language

Let us begin with the German expression *aus dem Amerikanischen*, which graces virtually every book or article translated from texts penned by authors that are perceived as "American."[24] What exactly is going on here? "Is 'American' "—according to Josef Joffe, the American-educated editor of the German weekly *Die Zeit*—"pronounced differently from 'English'? That also applies to 'Austrian' and 'Swiss.' "[25] But it would never occur to anybody in America, Canada, or Britain to label "a Gottfried Keller translation 'Translated from the Swiss' or Wittgenstein's *Tractatus* as having been 'translated from the Austrian.' "[26] "Why do the Germans want to force a language on Americans that they don't even speak? Because they write 'harbor' instead of 'harbour'? Then one would have to attribute a language of their own to the Austrians for saying 'Sessel' when they mean 'Stuhl' [for chair] or turn 'Januar' [January] into 'Jänner.' Because American slang is spoken differently from British slang? That's true, but in both countries the standard languages are about as identical as 'Austrian' and German."[27] What is "American" supposed to communicate to German readers? An accent? But then writings by an author from Glasgow would have to be titled "from the Glaswegian" or those by a writer living in Manchester as "from the Mancunian." John Lennon's books would have to be graced with the formulation "from the Liverpudlian" and those by Woody Allen with "from New Yorkish" or, to be more precise, "from the Brooklynese." If it's not about accent, is the criterion perhaps geography? Then Germans would have to use "from the Canadian" or "from the New Zealander." "Perhaps," Joffe continues,

> the meticulous German wants the empty phrase "from the American" to designate the country of origin. But then this is not meticulous enough. Then one would have to say that Brendan Behan was translated "from the Irish," Varga Llosa "from the Peruvian," and Nadine Gordimer from the "South African," Patrick White "from the Australian," and Ionesco "from the Rumanian French" and Conrad "from Polish English." Stop, that's not fussy enough. Walker Percy now gets to be translated "from the Alabaman-American-English" and Isaac Bashevis Singer "from the Yiddish-Polish-Hebrew-American." And [East German author] Sarah Kirsch is still writing "GDRish," a language that is just as remote from—or close to— "FRGish" as "American" from "English."[28]

The invention of this nonexistent language also cannot have anything to do with an author's U.S. citizenship; otherwise, an interview that Ariel Sharon gave to a U.S. newspaper would not have appeared in *Die Welt* with a remark from the editors that it was "translated from the American." "As is well known, the man was born in Israel, spent a year in England, and therefore speaks the kind of 'not so good English' that is practiced by millions all around the world."[29] And then (by the same logic) the writings translated into German but originally composed by people who happen to live in the United States but are not American citizens could also not be labeled "from the American."

The label "from the American" has, of course, very little to do
with being precise about accent, vocabulary, writing style, orthogra-
phy, geography, or citizenship. It simply has to do with the ascription
of a cultural inferiority. I cannot recall a single one of my numerous
stays in German-speaking Europe in which I was not at some time
confronted with the lovely statement, "The Americans don't even
speak proper English." A colleague of mine who has now been a
professor at Trinity College in Hartford, Connecticut, for more
than two decades told me that she grew up in Kaiserslautern and
learned English from American GIs. Instead of being rewarded for
her knowledge of the language, her secondary school teacher, who
knew far less English than this little girl, gave her nothing but
bad grades because she "didn't speak proper English, just American
dialect." As stated in the preface, I had virtually the identical experience at the prestigious secondary school, the Theresianische Akademie, that I attended in Vienna in the 1960s, even though I was fortunate enough—unlike my colleague from Kaiserslautern and
Trinity—to get straight A's in English in spite of my inferior "American dialect," my "faulty" American spelling, and after being reminded virtually on a daily basis that "in a prestigious institution
such as ours, where we educate Austria's elites, we do not talk American, do not walk American, do not look American because we are
not in the Wild West but in a civilized place." Italian elites also
regularly refer to American English as a dialect that they view as
inferior to British English.

It has long been known that the Verein Deutsche Sprache e.V.
(German Language Association) published "linguistic policy guide-
lines" in order to shield the German language from the influence of
"Anglo-American linguistic and cultural assets" leading to a "loss of
identity on the part of the peoples and popular groups concerned."[30]
The association has made it its mission to eliminate the German-
English hybrid "Denglisch" inside Germany. It has gained in follow-
ers and is beginning to make some inroads beyond the right-radical
and conservative circles that one would assume to be its most proximate purview.

In France, too, the decades-long battle waged against English (meaning almost exclusively "American") influences on the French language creating the much-invoked and much-despised "Franglais" is well known and needs little elaboration. All English (American) terms are given their French equivalents, and government policy exacts that these French terms be used in all official communication. Of course, in France, too, some books and articles are *traduit de l'americain*, though this term is used less frequently and with less regularity than it is in Germany. Some Dreiser novels are *traduit de l'americain*, and much of Faulkner's, Capote's, and Dos Passos's work appears fairly consistently *traduit de l'american*, but then again Sinclair and James are *traduit de l'anglais*, as are recent Jim Harrison novels where one encounters a *traduit de l'anglais* (*Etats-Unis*). Prior to the 1880s, one almost always encounters only *traduit par x* featuring the name of the translator and not the language from which the piece was rendered into French. To be sure, just like in Germany, almost every work emanating from Canada or Australia appears as *traduit de l'anglais*, although recently there have been a few instances where *traduit du canadien* has been used. What is particularly telling is that nonliterary texts from the social sciences, for example, are also subjected to this differentiation where there truly exist no differences at all between American and English. Thus, "from the American" appears regularly when the work of American economists and political scientists is translated into French and German, while it is, of course, "from the English" in the case of articles penned by their Canadian, Australian, and British colleagues. Some in France as well as in Germany argue that by differentiating an American language that is clearly separate from English, one actually enhances the authenticity of American English and thus places it on par with its original British variant. I have found a number of arguments along these lines in various discussion groups, mainly composed of linguists, on the Internet. This might in fact be technically the case and the honest conviction of the individual linguists involved. But given the valence of the hegemonic discourse about America—and most certainly American culture—among Europe's book-reading and book-translating elite, the construction of an "American" language in no way enhances this variant of English but rather serves as yet another signifier of America's cultural inferiority.[31]

There is a more interesting reaction against Americanisms in Great Britain, with an entirely new tenor. As mentioned in chapter 1, Britons (as well as anglicized Americans)—and especially literary figures, intellectuals, and members of the upper class—regard American English as inferior to the British version in every respect. After World War II, to be sure, it was accepted willy-nilly that American English had become prevalent in rock music and other youth-oriented spheres of British life. But then there was a hail of protests when British spelling—with reference to "international standardization"—made way for the American way of writing: "Forgive us. But we may be about to suffer a sense-of-humor failure," the left-liberal London daily the *Independent* announced. "According to the Qualifications and Curriculum Authority, the body responsible for overseeing exams in England, schoolchildren will soon be told to adopt 'internationally standardised' versions of certain words. We are not fooled. We know that means American versions." "In future, 'foetus' and 'sulphate' should instead, we are told, be written as 'fetus' and 'sulfate.' Well, this really makes us mad."[32] Of course, the article, written in American slang while railing against American English, mentioned the usual villains such as Microsoft ("the inventors of the pernicious 'US English' spellcheck"), Disney, McDonald's, rap music, and the Internet, and it talked about American English as a "fifth column in our own midst." The article concluded with the question: "Are we really going to take lessons in language from the land whose president came up with 'It depends what the meaning of "is" is'[?]"—for which its resounding answer was the Americanism "Hell, no!"[33] Even in the *Financial Times* one writer complained that, of the three thousand new expressions whose official entry into the English language was celebrated by the *Oxford Dictionary of English* in 2003, a great majority came from America.[34] "The research confirms what we have all long suspected: the Americanisation of English continues at a hectic pace."[35] And it is doing this in every branch of life, from television programs to movies, from the natural sciences and technology to the social sciences and art. Britons were becoming afraid that their country was about to "sink forever in the ketchup of American culture."[36]

For British journalism, the unavoidable consequence of Americanization seems to be "dumbing down" and "cretinisation," with respect both to the selection and presentation of topics as well as to their form and language.[37] This prejudice is so far-reaching that Britons today distinguish between an earlier American culture of language and literature whose influence on British culture was supposedly "good" and a contemporary American influence that is bad. In some of their demands they even go as far as the French. They ask the British state to check the current bad influence of American language and culture: "It is a long way from BB King to Snoop Doggy Dogg, from Lenny Bruce to Howard Stern, from VC to PC. And even though it may be the American Way, it is becoming less and less one that the enlightened Brit wants to follow."[38] It is therefore not surprising that a growing number from the British literary and cultural elite should be expressing their despair about America and its supposed influence on British culture by calling for boycotts of America.[39]

The bottom line is this: A large segment of Europe's cultural elite and literati fully agree with Paul Watzlavick's notion that American English has no historical and cultural value at all and is merely a convenient form of quotidian communication that—at best—produces cute neologisms that are versatile and practical.[40]

## "American Conditions" and Sports

Let us turn to sports. The world of soccer offers a fine example for my point precisely because, whatever one wants to argue about this sport and its culture, it is clear that the United States was at best an also-ran in it throughout all of the twentieth century, with no power or importance. America simply did not matter—and still matters very little—in the world of soccer. It was never a threat to Europe; or, to put the point in the right style, America was never a "player."

Nevertheless, the discourse about this game on the European side has always had a cynical, aggressive, irritating, and above all condescending tone.

When the United States was chosen to host the World Cup for the summer of 1994, much of the European media was appalled. Instead of rejoicing that the last important terra incognita for soccer was about to be conquered by the "beautiful game," Europeans loudly voiced the usual objections to American crassness, vulgarity, commercialism, and ignorance. They argued that giving the tournament to the Americans was tantamount to degrading the game and its tradition. Awarding Americans the World Cup in soccer was interpreted as an abomination, tantamount to holding a world championship in skiing in a country in the Sahara, or playing a major golf tournament in Greenland—an anomaly bordering on impudence, cheekiness, and inauthenticity since, in the European view, the environment wasn't suited to this sport. The facilities were denigrated, the organization ridiculed, the whole endeavor treated with derision. When the stadiums were filled like in no other World Cup tournament before or since, when the level of violence and arrests was far and away the lowest at any event of this size, the European media chalked this up to the stupidity and ignorance of Americans. Of course Americans came to the games, because they like events and pageantry, but did they really enjoy and understand the sport? Could they even learn to? Could they possibly grasp the beauties and "profundity" of soccer? The answer, most often, was an unequivocal no. And the only reason there was no violence was that the stadiums were frequented by families with mothers and little girls who knew nothing about soccer, instead of by knowledgeable old troopers and true fans as in Europe. Even Europe's hooligans gained positive press by dint of their authenticity compared to the artificial plasticity of the American crowd and the entire tournament.

When more than 60,000 people crowded into Giants Stadium near New York City on a Wednesday afternoon to watch Saudi Arabia play Morocco (surely no powerhouses in the world of soccer), this, too, was attributed to the vast ignorance of Americans regarding soccer. Indeed, European soccer connoisseurs proudly pointed to the fact that similar games in soccer-savvy Italy attracted fewer than 20,000 people in the 1990 World Cup held in that country.

Those few European journalists who bothered to write anything about American sports such as baseball, which, as always in the summer, was in full swing at the time, had nothing but contempt, derision, and ridicule for the game: no attempt to engage its traditions, no endeavor to understand it on its own terms, merely another vehicle to confirm one's prejudices about America. A number of Europeans mocked the discipline of the American public and took it as proof that Americans not only knew little about soccer (which is often true), but that their own kinds of sports—or "languages" as I like to call sport cultures, since these are similar in every respect— were not worth much and did not merit any enthusiasm. The reader will certainly recall an illustration from the previous chapter: For European visitors in the early twentieth century, American athletic events were much too rough and crude, both on the field and among the fans. At the end of the same century, Europeans were irritated because they were now too dull and tame. Regardless of what happens in America, and how, it irritates and upsets Europeans. Damned if you do, damned if you don't.

Michel Platini, the former French soccer great of the 1980s and in charge of organizing the subsequent World Cup in France, summed up his feelings and judgments in the vernacular of current Europe: "The World Cup in the United States was outstanding, but it was like Coca Cola. Ours will be like sparkling champagne." Surely Platini could not have meant to characterize the riots, the violence, the ticket scandals, the racial insults that occurred during the tournament in France as "sparkling champagne." And it is equally unclear what he meant by characterizing the American tournament as "Coca Cola." No matter, the code was clear to all: regardless of its actual success and its achievements, the American event was to real European soccer fans by definition crude and inauthentic (like Coca Cola), whereas the French—equally by definition—was inevitably going to be refined and profound (like champagne).[41] And to confirm Michel Platini's characterization of soccer's Coca-colonization by the Americans, which he voiced in 1994, French soccer officials were openly discussing the adverse affects of the "Americanization" of soccer on the eve of the World Cup tournament in France in June 1998. "Americanization" in this view not only entailed an undermining of the structures and traditions of soccer, but it also meant jeopardizing the game's authenticity and credibility on the field, as a sport.[42]

It was remarkable how differently the European media reported on the World Cup 2002 in Japan and South Korea, both newcomers to the world of soccer, just like the United States. Rave reviews were accorded to the facilities and organization in both countries. This contrasted sharply with the negative tone describing the equivalent structures in the United States in 1994 even though the global soccer federation (FIFA), for example, and soccer officials had nothing but praise for the American effort. What was viewed as inauthentic kitsch in the American context (the opening ceremony, for example, and other pageantries accompanying the tournament) was lauded as artistic, innovative, and indigenous in the Japanese and South Korean equivalent.

Lastly, in 2002 the American team was first ridiculed as an incompetent group of players who barely deserved to be in the tournament. The huge upset over Portugal was attributed to sheer luck. When Team USA advanced to the second round and then defeated its arch-rival Mexico, the press corps who were vocally rooting for the Mexicans during the game remained stunned in silence at the press center.[43] It was simply impossible to accord the Americans their victory because—in addition to being interlopers as players—this victory meant nothing to the American public, preoccupied as it was with its own sports and not with soccer. "By contrast, look at Mexico. 'This is war' proclaimed the headline of the Mexico City newspaper 'Reform,' which called the two competitors 'bitter rivals'."[44] In Mexico, millions were weeping and set on revenge. Mexico's loss to the Americans was a national tragedy, whereas the American win would barely register among sports fans in America, let alone have any bearing on the public mood. To most Americans, this major soccer event was, at best, a sideshow. For many European commentators, this was simply unforgivable. In notable contrast to the positive sentiment that was expressed toward Turkey, Senegal, and South Korea, the other Cinderella teams of the tournament, nothing but bitterness and derision was voiced toward the American team. Even in soccer, Europeans were viewing Americans not as welcome outsiders or newcomers but as ignorant incompetents, arrogant interlopers, and menacing competitors. Above all, even though in soccer America has been a minnow, Europeans continue to regard it as the eight-hundred-pound gorilla: threatening, powerful, clumsy, yet also inferior.

Only when the mighty Germans narrowly (and luckily) beat the Americans in a quarterfinal did some European commentators become interested in the American team. But this interest (and even some sporadic, timid praise) quickly turned into genuine alarm. For heaven's sake, the message now ran, the Yanks might actually achieve something in soccer, too. A concerned English friend of mine so tellingly remarked: "This is terrible. Now you Yanks are getting good at this, too. You are in the process of stealing our game. Imagine eleven Michael Jordans running onto the pitch at Wembley. That would be our end." Damned if you do, damned if you don't— it could not be articulated more clearly: When the Americans play poorly, they are irritating merely by doing so and because they remain aloof from everybody. When they finally play well, they are disliked because they have become threatening by joining the game.

Of course the German national team's manager Jürgen Klinsmann has repeatedly been mocked for and accused of various "Americanizing" transgressions in his leadership of the team, mainly, I assume, for having lived in Los Angeles for the past fifteen years of his life and being married to an American woman. When Klinsmann hired some fitness trainers from America for the German national team, all hell broke loose. Many sports reporters ridiculed and derided his "Americanizing" German soccer and attacked him relentlessly over this issue. Many tensions related to Klinsmann have been conveniently chalked up to his "American" ways. Major German soccer figures (such as Dieter Hönness) worried aloud about the German Soccer Federation (Deutscher Fussballbund, DFB) becoming "Americanized" without ever explaining what exactly this was supposed to mean.[45] But clearly, it was something that irritated them. I will, of course, follow the World Cup in Germany on location in the summer of 2006. Among many angles that interest me in this event, I will most decidedly look at the reactions to the American team's presence at the tournament. My findings will arrive too late to be included in this book.

This underlying irritation was further confirmed during my many lectures on comparative sports in Germany, especially on two book tours in support of the German edition of my book *Offside*.[46] In literally every forum in which I presented my book and work—from university campuses to bookstores; from rented public halls to semi-private settings; from Saarbrücken in the West to Potsdam in the East—at some point the question arose as to whether I did not believe that the absence of soccer's prominence in America's sports culture was not merely further prima facie evidence for American arrogance and part of the same syndrome of self-importance that also allegedly makes the United States such a reluctant participant in international organizations.

For Europeans, the outstanding position of women in American soccer and the excellence of the American women's team worldwide are further indications of the American tendency to undermine, distort, and soil holy European traditions. There are two aspects of women's soccer that bother Europeans: First, soccer is still a purely man's affair for every inveterate European soccer fan, and it should remain thus. Second, it is typical of European fans' outlook to be upset that this kind of soccer, this "antisoccer," not only is played in America but is even popular there, arguably more popular than the men's game. The European soccer fan sees a dual perversion in the presence of American women's soccer. Thus, for example, an article in the German weekly news magazine *Der Spiegel* proclaims that this women's soccer has nothing to do with sports—a standard European reaction to women's soccer in America.[47] "Typically American" were the first two words in the introduction to the article, so that the reader would know right away what to expect.

Germany is not a special case here, as was demonstrated by the gibes with which the French media greeted Marinette Pichon when she was chosen by her colleagues and coaches in the league as most valuable player for the Women's United Soccer Association (WUSA) in 2002. Pichon openly declared that she would never have been given the space to pursue her hobby, soccer, with the same intensity and joy in France as she was able to do in the United States.

For Italians, women's soccer is just an American anomaly mirroring all the cultural and psychological problems of this comic country: dominant women, subaltern men, commercialization, show, no tradition—simply silly.[48] "Brandi Chastain kicks, hits, runs to the raging fans, kneels down, tears the jersey from her body, and remains in her bra. She is perfect, the ideal embodiment of the Yankee woman: liberated and a victor. . . . Of course, this entire fuss leads, as always in America, to a public psycho-ordeal."[49] In the British soccer nations of England, Scotland, Wales, and Northern Ireland, women's soccer is regarded as a complete joke that only Americans in their perversion of all good things might have conceived. It is only in the egalitarian Scandinavian countries that America is not ridiculed for its women's soccer quite as much as it is in the rest of Europe.[50]

The purported Americanization of British sports has caused irritation for quite some time on the island. In every discussion about rule changes proposed or contemplated by FIFA, the British suspect the subversive, exclusively commercial influence of the Americans. Any potential challenge to tradition must involve the inauthentic, commercialized, and irreverent Americans. This is especially interesting because every authority on the subject knows that the United States is a weak, unappreciated, and above all far from fear-inspiring member of FIFA, especially compared with the great soccer powers Germany, England, and the other traditional players in international football.

It seems as if the British find every aspect of the sporting world's potential Americanization fearful and worth fighting. Thus, for example, they complain that their stadiums have increasingly come to resemble those in America and are now equipped with good seats, restaurants, and even dance floors.[51] Comfortable seats and the abolition of the "terraces"—those (in)famous standing room sections—

after the catastrophe at Hillsborough in Sheffield, where a hundred people lost their lives, have to be attributed to the Americanization of British sports, just like high ticket prices. Americanization is also held responsible for the transformation of British fans. Previously, the true fan who knew and attended the game came from the neighborhood. Now it is only affluent show-offs who are at these events simply to be there and be seen, without understanding much about the game or trembling along with the team.[52]

The taming of the fans and of the players is regarded as a hated by-product of Americanization. Americanization, according to the irritated voices of British sports fans and journalists, leads to the players having better manners among each other and in public. They become more professional, they inform themselves about the details of their contracts, and they hire tax advisers—serious transgressions in the world of the authentic un-Americanized footballer (soccer player) and his supporters (fans), to use the appropriate British expressions.

But it is not just better manners and more civil behavior on the part of fans and players that is attributed to Americanization and assessed as a sign of declining traditions on the part of fans, players, the game, and Great Britain as a country; it is also the purported rise of showmanship, egoism, and aggression. When Manchester United concluded a worldwide marketing agreement with the New York Yankees, ridicule and derision abounded. The most hated and envied British team, which (in the eyes of many in Britain and, of course, United's countless enemies and enviers) practically embodies Americanization, was joining forces with its American counterpart not in an athletic but in a purely commercial undertaking. Even a relatively loose alliance, such as this was, between two obvious "Mr. Bigs" and "evil empires" amounted to nothing good and was prima facie evidence of "Americanization."

Barely a few years later, however, the very same Manchester United mutated into a sullied national icon that was being brutally victimized by an American ogre. When Malcolm Glazer and his sons, the owners of the Tampa Bay Buccaneers of the National Football League in the United States, assumed a majority position among Manchester United's shareholders, this most expensive and most desired sports entity in the world transformed into a local and helpless waif in the eyes of millions of Britons and the club's fans, who used everything in their power—including boycotts and some violence—to ban the American monsters from owning the club. In the battle with Americans, even mighty—and formerly chastised and envied—Manchester United metamorphosed into a helpless victim. Not only were the Glazers vilified in the British media, but so were—to add fuel to the fire—American sports and sports fans: all they do is eat hot dogs and popcorn, but they have no passion for their sports, no true understanding and appreciation of them, and certainly no real loyalty to their teams. They do not identify with their teams, which are appropriately called "franchises" that move from city to city, unlike in Europe where teams are clubs and never dislodge from their moorings. American sports culture (just like during the World Cup or at any other instance of comparison) was depicted as lacking in tradition and history. American sports are not worthy of that name and are clearly inferior to football (i.e., soccer), which stupid Americans will never learn to appreciate. There can be no doubt that the Glazers were vilified mainly because they were Americans and thus a priori inauthentic usurpers of a sacred piece of English (and British and European and global) tradition. But it was not only the Glazers but their entire milieu, which in this case meant the world of American sports. We have a fine comparison to underline this point: When the Russian oil tycoon Roman Abramovich purchased the prominent London club Chelsea a few years prior to the Glazers' acquisition of Manchester United, there were some voices of apprehension but nothing close to the hatred and contempt that greeted the Glazers. Above all, nobody felt the need to vilify the Russian sports world. The difference lay in the simple fact that Abramovich was conversant with the language of football by dint of his being Russian, and thus an insider, whereas the Glazers were not by dint of their being American, thus clear outsiders. And this, for many Britons, way beyond soccer fans (or football supporters, to stay true to the context), was unforgivable. Sheer blasphemy!

Britain's Independent Television Commission prohibited Channel 4 from showing weekly broadcasts of the NBA and NFL to its expert-minded and increasingly interested public. In the manner of the kind of *dirigisme* and cultural protectionism typical of France, this commission held that Channel 4 was broadcasting too much "Americana" and that, instead of basketball and American football, British sports like track and field should be shown.[53]

Needless to say, British intellectuals and journalists also lament the Americanization of soccer broadcasts: The commentators, it is said, wear funny jackets, use odd expressions, and speak in a strange language; there are too many trifles on the screen during the broadcast; and—worst of all—they are communicating far too many statistics meaning absolutely nothing for a game like soccer (unlike American sports).[54] Even Geoff Hurst, the man who became so (in)-famous in Germany and remains a hero in England for scoring the controversial winning goal against the (then West) German team at the 1966 World Cup final match in Wembley Stadium, was no longer able to endure the alleged Americanization of British soccer broadcasts. "Indeed," wrote the *Herald*, "so disillusioned had he [Hurst] become with TV soccer that he watched most of the last World Cup with the sound turned down, deploring the 'Americanisation' of British sport."[55] And when David Beckham, the superstar captain of England's national football team, has a bad game, he obviously does so in the eyes of English sports writers because he plays like a "quarterback" in American football, or perhaps also because his club team, Real Madrid, has naturally become totally "Americanized," according to key voices in the Spanish soccer world.[56]

A characteristic "damned if you do, damned if you don't" scenario emerged in the course of the British Open golf championship in the past few years. When, for the ninth time over the previous eleven years, yet another American walked away with the highly coveted Claret Jug trophy, many Britons talked irritably about U.S. dominance of their country's premier golf tournament, the oldest "major" in the world. Yet, at the same time, many complaints were voiced, particularly in 2004, about the scanty presence of American golfers at this tournament, which some members of the British golf public regarded as a snub against the event. When the Americans don't come, they exhibit arrogance by their aloofness. When they do come and win too much, they exhibit arrogance by their domination.

Two related decisions by the International Olympic Committee (IOC) in the summer of 2005 underline this damned if you do, damned if you don't syndrome besetting Americans in sports in the Europeans' mind: The IOC abolished women's softball from the Olympic Games starting in 2012 because the American women had been much too dominant in all three Olympics in which this sport was officially contested. At the same time, men's baseball was also abolished beginning with the 2012 games in good part because U.S.-based Major League Baseball was not going to suspend play during the summer and release its players to participate in the Olympics, thus weakening baseball competition at the Olympics to the point of rendering it second class at best. Thus, American men too weak; American women too strong; result: both had to go. While all votes of the IOC are secret and we thus cannot know who voted which way, all experts agree that these two sports were eliminated from the Olympics primarily by dint of a heavy European opposition to both. It is worthy of mention that Europeans hold 110 seats on the 180-seat IOC.[57]

In the context of this segment, a word about Lance Armstrong is in order. There can be no doubt that Armstrong came to be immensely respected by many European cycling fans for his unique achievement. Winning an unprecedented seven consecutive Tour de France races for anybody, let alone a cancer survivor, will result in such respect. But it is equally clear that Armstrong was far from liked by the world of European cycling. Indeed, he was constantly questioned, doubted, mocked, vilified. To be sure, some of that hailed from the welcomed human trait of disliking a constant winner—Mr. Big—in anything. But here we have a number of counterexamples in whose case this did not pertain. The legendary Belgian rider Eddy Merckx met with no such hostility in the 1970s, nor did the great French rider Bernard Hinault in the 1980s, or Armstrong's immediate predecessor, the Basque Miguel Indurain in the 1990s. None of their amazing feats were constantly doubted for being possibly (or probably) tainted by illegal doping, a very common occurrence in the sport of cycling, and part of its culture. No French publication ever called Merckx the Belgian ogre or Indurain the Spanish (or Basque) ogre. Yet, a quick Internet search for "ogre Americain" will reveal the impressive frequency with which Lance Armstrong was named just that, surely not a term of endearment. Moreover, the fact that confessed dopers like the hugely popular Richard Virenque never lost the love of the fans proves that the transgression of doping in cycling (rightly or wrongly) does not define acceptance of, affection toward, and respect for any athlete by the public and the fans. So the antipathy toward Armstrong, resulting in the mighty French sports paper *L'Equipe*'s veritable witch-hunt against him, had to have an additional factor, and that was Armstrong's being American, thus an outsider to the world of top-level professional cycling, yet also a citizen of disdained and feared Mr. Big, which was to triumph in yet another domain in which it had not played a role before and now was in the process of usurping, with Armstrong leading the way. While nowhere close to the animosities that confronted Armstrong's cycling career at the Tour de France, his compatriot Greg LeMond's successes at the Tour de France in the late 1980s met with similar sentiments of irritation, disdain, and hostility on the part of the European cycling powers— purely because LeMond was an American, thus an outsider from an emotionally charged place. Put differently, Armstrong's being American was not a sufficient but a necessary condition for the animosity directed at him by Europe's sports world, which went much beyond the French and also included, among others, the Germans and the Italians.

To be sure, the lukewarm clapping accompanied by prolific booing of the American team's entrance into the stadium at the opening ceremony of the Olympic Games in Athens in 2004 could be attributed to the world's and the Greek hosts' massive disapproval of the Iraq War. But when in many events spectators singled out American participants for an added level of derision and hostility, and when the Greek media blamed the Americans and American-led conspiracies for the banning of two Greek track stars from the competition because of their staged and self-inflicted motorcycle accidents to prevent themselves from undergoing drug tests, clearly more than the Greek public's opposition to America's Iraq War was at play.

It was not by chance that the United States Olympic Committee went to great length to instruct all American athletes before the games how to temper their exuberance in case of victory. This was not only in response to the tasteless antics of the victorious 100-meter United States relay team at the Sydney games in 2000 that justifiably incurred the anger of millions of viewers. Rather, it was in recognition of the massive Greek and global antipathy that America continues to engender, which is unique. Not by coincidence, such pretournament instructions were also unprecedented in the annals of any international sporting event.

## "Americanization" of Everything, "American Conditions" Everywhere: Long Live the Antonym!

### Work

"Americanization" connotes every kind of deterioration in the European world of work—from stress through job insecurity, from disqualification through work intensification, from "flexibility" through "mobility"—and is a synonym for all things negative in this very complex entity of a rapidly changing capitalism. Europeans complain about the "Americanization" of virtually every aspect of their world of work. This has a number of dimensions of which I will mention only a few: People criticize an alleged decline in workmanship and quality of European products, for which they blame the increased competition that "Americanization" exacts from them. Speed becomes crucial, which in turn leads to a diminished quality of the final product. Furthermore, there is also an increasing loss in the pride in one's work and one's product, which again bespeaks an increasing "Americanization." And, the quantity of work is constantly expanding, particularly for managers and others in leading positions. The oxymoron "working vacation" has entered the European vernacular, which again testifies to an "Americanization" of Europe's work life. European managers are taking ever fewer vacations, and when they do take them, their vacation time is basically useless since the managers just keep thinking about work all the time and are even working on their holidays. Yet, rarely, if ever, have I read anything about a purported "Japanization" or—of increasing relevance—"Chinazation" of European work life in the context of decreasing vacations and leisure time and growing pressure on managers. And yet, being on the job with little time off is practiced and extolled far more prominently in those two countries than it is in America. Apparently, fewer and fewer European managers identify themselves primarily as fathers, mothers, neighbors, and friends. Their identity is increasingly shaped by their job. Americanization allows no flexibility on this count. Yet, in the related area of labor markets, Americanization is tantamount to an excessive and destructive "flexibility" featuring a hire-and-fire mentality in which job security and social solidarity have massively eroded. "Americanization" always implies the weakening of organized labor on the shop floor, in the labor market, and in the political arena and allows the flourishing of neoliberal policies that always favor capital over labor. American unions are decried as pathetically weak, yet, at the same time, as unreasonably controlling and powerful. American workers are seen as unqualified and lazy, but also as rate busters who work much too hard: too complacent and too industrious, displeasing all the same.

Europeans depict work and workmanship in America as inferior, yet also as a challenge to which the Europeans will inevitably have to respond and which they need to take seriously. And yet again, America dictates, and Europe simply has no choice in the matter. Take the world of accounting, hardly a hotbed of system-challenging radicalism: There is an "Americanization" of accounting norms that are constructed to favor "American domination."[58] To the author of this article in one of France's leading business papers, Europe had already surrendered to a total American victory in this realm. Claude Bébéar, the chairman of AXA, the French insurance company, and one of France's (and Europe's) most powerful businessmen, equated the imposition of American accounting rules on Europe to the despotic fanaticism of the ayatollahs.[59]

Daimler, the legendary Stuttgart automaker, would apparently never have succeeded at taking over Chrysler, according to a view common in Germany, if the managers in Stuttgart had not converted their balance sheets years earlier to the American GAAP system.[60] In German eyes, therefore, Daimler succeeded only because it had already become a quasi-American firm, or at least thoroughly Americanized, even before it had purchased Chrysler. Every global player either has to be Americanized or lose. "The Lex Americana rules the world, because nobody is as good as the United States when it comes to understanding what matters for globalization: mobility, speed, transparency, high interest yields on capital, and a shot of brutality. ... The Stuttgarters fit in with Chrysler, because Daimler has been the most American of all German businesses."[61] The German and European view is that globalization equals Americanization and has little to do with capitalism, thus rendering European business not an accomplice to American business in their joint battle for market domination in an increasingly competitive global economy, but its victim.

Sooner or later, almost every problem in the European working world is either branded with the label "Americanization" or blamed on the culprit of Americanization—or both. I do not wish to be misunderstood here. As someone close to the trade union movement since my youth, I find the conditions bemoaned in many of these articles scandalous. It is not my intention to diminish genuine grievances, but rather to make it clear that the concept of "Americanization" (or even "American conditions") is used as a label, a stigma, and adds little in terms of explanation or analysis. How and why is the increase in stress in Europe "American"? What exactly is "American" about this? Have American firms introduced these trends into Europe? Is it really more stressful to have a job with Ford in Cologne than it is with Volkswagen in Wolfsburg? There are many problems that cry out for discussion here, and many issues that need to be illuminated. But blaming everything on "Americanization" is, of course, easier and (above all) much more popular. "Americanization" becomes a complacent shorthand expression that, while doing nothing to explain complex processes, goes a long way toward offering everyone concerned a welcome bogeyman. Not one of the numerous articles I read on the deteriorating situation of work in Europe would have lost even a bit of its expressive powers if it had avoided using the expression "Americanization" or replaced it with the much more appropriate concept of "capitalism." But this has somehow become a dirty and condescending term that only old-fashioned Marxists now use. Furthermore it is much too abstract and universal to mobilize emotions. That can apparently be accomplished much more easily by using "Americanization." Capitalism and its ills are abstract entities that require a face and personalization. Those are conveniently provided by labeling everything negative as "American" or "Americanization."

### Higher Education

The conservative Cologne sociologist Erwin K. Scheuch, spokesman for the equally conservative Bund Freiheit der Wissenschaft (Federation for Academic Freedom, founded in Bad Godesberg in 1970), has been warning against Americanization in German universities. In his lecture "Model America"—in which he told his audience, among other things, that at most fifty of the more than two thousand institutions called "universities" in the United States really deserved the label—Scheuch advocated blocking any attempt to replace the German system of teaching with the principle of courses for credit.[62] Scheuch viewed the introduction of performance-oriented salaries for professors as the very height of Americanization. This innovation would, according to the professor, destroy Germany's "collegial structures." Scheuch's views are by no means rare in German university circles, and even in the general discourse. When, in an article about the American higher education system I wrote for the magazine *Spiegel Spezial*, I praised the seriousness with which teaching is viewed in America and also (in contrast to the situation in Germany) evaluated by students, I received numerous letters of protest from my German colleagues.[65] "We are not, thank God, in America, where universities are just upgraded [secondary] schools," one furious colleague wrote me. That students might be allowed to evaluate their professors' teaching was rejected by almost all my German colleagues as a bad American habit that commercialized the university and damaged professorial and scholarly autonomy. And my friend and colleague Hans Weiler, an outstanding expert on comparative university and educational policy, long-time professor at Stanford, and the founding rector of the innovative Viadrina University in Frankfurt an der Oder, repeatedly told me how careful he had to be about expressing his reform proposals so that they would not be seen as American, which would have led to their being stigmatized a priori and not taken seriously. It was not so much that the proposals themselves elicited resistance, but rather the fact—or even the mere suspicion—that this might be an instance of something "American." And since Weiler—being identified as an American—had to deal with this inherent stigmatization, he had to use circumscribed language lest his suggestions be seen as a priori illegitimate.

The German and European fascination with Harvard and Stanford is the exact equivalent of the European fascination with Woody Allen and a few select Americans: Harvard and Stanford are regarded as decidedly "un-American" and basically "European," which is also (of course) how Scheuch characterized Harvard in his lecture, as an atypical American university.

In 1999 the French intellectual and cultural establishment, led by then Minister of Education Claude Allègre, worried about the hegemonic ambitions of American universities in Europe. There were two dimensions to this concern: first, the privatization of higher education in France and in Europe, which—though still in its infancy at the time, and not much further along today—was portrayed as about to displace the well-established public education system that upper-class European males at least had enjoyed for over two centuries. In addition, however, Allègre and others in France worried about the increased number of American universities creating programs, centers, and campuses in Europe. "The Americans install their universities all over the world. All follow the same curricular model; this is a catastrophe."[64]

A glance across the English Channel shows that all these negative themes are also afloat in England: "Bubblegum University's funny ways are becoming familiar in colleges over here. The huge range and exotic combinations of courses, the spoon-feeding mode of classroom teaching, the obsession with grades, the general acceptance that many students have to take jobs to see them through college . . . these have become standard features of universitas Britannica. The latest big issue, to seal the Americanisation of British higher education, is the switch to the semester system."[65] N.b.: Bubblegum University and, of course, the purported lowering of traditional standards. It can hardly get any more stigmatizing than this. Per usual, the article never even attempts to explain what exactly the problem might be with semesters (as opposed to trimesters), just like it does not bother to elaborate on the assumed ills of all the other alleged negative items that it lists.

Another instance of creeping Americanization seems to occur when British universities start engaging in that despicable American custom of fund-raising. During the friendly invasion of Great Britain by GIs in the course of World War II, they were usually characterized as "overfed, oversexed, and over here." In spite of the massive withdrawal of American military personnel from Great Britain in the 1990s, there were still twice as many American citizens (at over 200,000) living in Great Britain as ten years earlier. And this time it was managers, fund-raisers, and other professions alien to the British and causing them to characterize the new "Yanks," like the increasingly less common GIs, as "overpaid, oversexed, and over here." Under the headline "The Americans Who Are Running Britain," an article in the *Observer* asserts: "First it was burgers and movies. Now Uncle Sam has a finger in everything British," from the soprano at the Royal Opera House to the peace negotiator in Northern Ireland, from the manager of the new British Airways subsidiary Go to the fund-raiser for Oxford University's Lincoln College. A "counter-colonisation" on the part of American managers and luminaries "is in progress."[66]

It is only to be expected that European conservatives would make fun of American feminism, multiculturalism, affirmative action, and all the reforms affected by these movements that are allegedly ruling the best universities in the United States. There is a bevy of material that mocks these reforms under the rubric of "political correctness." They warn against the takeover of American universities by feminist agitators who issue decrees forbidding flirting and would try to punish men who express compliments to women. "The cult of political correctness is seeping evilly from American university campuses," warned Bernard Levin in an article headlined (so that there could be no doubt about his attitude) "All Joe McCarthy's Children Now."[67] In the article Levin relates horror stories about universities across the entire American continent in which a supposedly new left-wing McCarthyism is using methods and ideas like those of the infamous right-wing senator from Wisconsin in the 1950s. Another angry, sarcastic article in the *Times* has a professor of literature at Columbia University in New York encourage his students to present Shakespeare, in the manner of political correctness, as an anti-Semite and racist. This, according to the article, is happening at the same time that Georgetown University has made it possible to get a degree in English literature without having read a single word of Chaucer, Milton, or Shakespeare, those "dead white European males."[68]

Article after article warns about the decline of American universities in which ideological commissars have supposedly seized the curricula, and who see their job as replacing Western civilization with a politically correct multiculturalism. Once again: Damned if you do, damned if you don't. While Europeans, as a rule, have complained about the arrogance and elitism of American universities, now they are reproaching them for the exact opposite: that their achievements are being destroyed by the unqualified in the name of political correctness.

However, Europe's left-wing liberals have just as much trouble as Europe's conservatives tolerating the themes that are part of this complex. While the thrust of their criticism is different, the tenor is surprisingly similar. During the Clinton-Lewinsky crisis, many

European leftists regarded the critical position of some American feminists toward Clinton as laughable. Of course, puritanism was (again) to blame, only now this was coming from the "American Left" because it was being articulated by radical women's rights advocates.[69] Even during the controversy about Janet Jackson's exposure of her right nipple at the Super Bowl half-time show in 2004, left-wing liberal commentators in Europe saw the puritanism of American feminists at work; their permanent struggle against the objectification of women as sex objects was providing grist for the mill of traditional conservative male puritans.[70] And, in the *Guardian*, Ian Katz made fun of reforms in the language of the New Testament undertaken by some radical feminist and egalitarian circles in America. The Christian Bible's "Son of Man" had mutated into "the human one," and right hand of God is simply excised from the text so that left-handed people do not feel discriminated against.[71] That many American progressives can—and do—relate to religion and not thereby be ipso facto reactionary fundamentalists is something their European counterparts find completely incomprehensible and yet another reason to mock America as strange and worse.

### The Media

This sphere offers an endless bonanza for the inveighing of an "Americanization" and "American conditions" on every conceivable level. Of course, the European media have experienced an inevitable process of increased commercialization on account of Americanization. European media have allegedly become shallower, emptier, sillier, chattier, more violent, more commercialized, more sensational, only on account of Americanization. Televised hearings from the Bundestag featuring Foreign Minister Joschka Fischer as the main witness in the so-called Visa Affair constituted an equally crass case of Americanization as did the coverage from a Miami courtroom of the divorce war between Boris Becker and his wife.[72] So do the large salaries that popular TV anchors garner in Britain and increasingly on the Continent as well.[73] Rendering news anchors, sports commentators, and meteorologists into stars also serves as prima facie evidence for Americanization.[74] Commercialization of the structure, form, and even language of once tasteful radio programs, of course, can only be attributed to Americanization.[75] Introducing one-hour factual reports and news features on television (similar to CBS's *60 Minutes*) is a consequence of Americanization.[76] Of course, Americanization leads to the conveying of too little news, on the one hand, and way too much news, on the other, the much-bemoaned CNN syndrome that allegedly trivializes the news by its 24/7 ubiquity. This Americanization then leads to an alleged growth of a mixture of "news and newspeak," a completely oversimplified vocabulary communicating way too many details with an overabundance of graphics and other visual gimmicks that at best communicate obfuscating details at the cost of clarity and depth. The whole package is geared to sound and look smart instead of being so—in short, it feigns a pseudo-complexity when it is little but show.

All of this hails from an Americanization of the European public that entails an increased commercialization and superficiality at the cost of true substance and genuine civic culture that it allegedly possessed prior to its inevitable succumbing to America's evil ways. Of course, it all involves an alleged loss of indigenous authenticity and a feared subversion of local identity. Thus, that most British of institutions, the BBC, instituted a media policy at the beginning of the 1990s explicitly dedicated to importing fewer programs from abroad (meaning America) and openly emphasizing its British character against what was supposedly its perilously increasing American image.[77] For me, the height of hypocrisy has been the Europeans' frontal attack against the banality of American "reality shows," which, according to many critics and people of any taste, have overstepped the boundaries of tastelessness. These attacks are completely justified, but they have one small problem: "Reality shows" are a purely European invention. To present this media form, imported into the United States from Europe, as an undesirable Americanization of Europe's public sphere can only be described as chutzpah.[78]

## Health

The European body seems to be suffering from an irresistible attack emanating from two opposing corners. In the 1980s and 1990s, the American "health craze" invaded Europe and imposed its inescapable will on helpless Europeans. All of a sudden, Europeans had to jog too much, exercise beyond their comfort, and become beholden to fitness centers whose mirrors and fancy equipment became the new temples of a quasi-religious obsession with the body. Europeans, in short, became victims of the American culture of superficial looks that emphasized external appearances of the body over soundness of mind and depth of character. This "health craze" rendered nutrition gurus like Dr. Atkins and Weight Watchers, with their regimented dietary rules, into arbiters of how people ought to live their lives. Above all, so goes the European mantra, these rigid rules and obsessions with slimness and an alleged health deprived people of the ability to take pleasure in eating and living. "The problem is that we have become Americanized: in addition to jeans, coca-cola, hamburgers with cholesterol, they [the Americans] push us toward a healthy diet, to be skinny, young, brilliant, intelligent, and puritan in the sense of the dinosaurs from Big Brother."[79] Oh, how times change. Barely a few years later, television and radio talk shows and newspaper articles in Europe are replete with information about the fattening of Europe, which—how could it be otherwise—is also attributed to an "Americanization" just like the health craze of yore. Suddenly, everybody blamed the McDonaldization of European diets for the alleged disappearance of local culinary cultures, the increase of Europeans' girth, and the decrease in the quality of their health and life-styles.[80] "The Americanisation of our bodies," writes Christina Odone, "once meant importing" fitness. But "today, especially outside the metropolitan areas, the Americanisation of our bodies means obesity. The British Heart Foundation calculates that 17 percent of men and 21 percent of women here are obese (46 percent of men and 32 percent of women are merely overweight)."[81]

The same applies to Germany, supposedly. Here, too, there is the threat of "American conditions," one Internet health magazine warns. "64 percent of Americans weigh too much, and here at home the figure is 60 percent. Only among the super-fat is the U.S. ahead: There every third person is obese, while in Germany it is every fifth person. But Germany's lagging behind the U.S. on obesity is no reason to sound the all-clear signal yet: Current figures in Germany correspond roughly to those of the U.S. ten years ago."[82] Two reasons are chiefly given for this deplorable state of affairs: first, of course, it is the presence of American fast-food chains in Europe; second, it is the American culture of "sitting" and "not moving," in which people are perched for hours in front of their television screens and computers. When they move, it is only in their cars. The jogging craze and fitness mania that "Americanization" had imposed on Europe barely a decade before has long been forgotten.

Damned if you do, damned if you don't: Americans are either workout freaks and health nuts or couch potatoes and junk-food maniacs, but in either of these they inevitably impose their bad habits on helpless Europeans. One way or another, they are a menace to Europe and the European body. The fact that obesity in both Europe and America is chiefly a class-specific phenomenon—obese people disproportionately inhabit the lower rungs of the social scale on both sides of the Atlantic—appears hardly a matter for reflection and pales in comparison to the ubiquitous mention of the sole culprit: the "Americanization" of European life.

To Europeans, Americans are hypochondriacs who rely much too heavily on drugs as a cure-all to their ailments and woes. Indeed, in France and in Portugal—to mention but two countries—the medical profession is deeply skeptical of such pediatric illnesses as attention deficit disorder and blames the American medical establishment for exaggerating, if not indeed inventing, such problems for a twofold purpose: to boost the sales of psychopharmacological products, and to provide an easy (but erroneous) fix. "We [in Portugal] use fewer antidepressants than the Americans. . . . Portuguese teens spend more time with their families while American teens are granted more independence than is necessary."[83]

The reduction of tobacco smoking—surely one of the few domains in which the United States has in fact made a progressive contribution in the world—has experienced particularly scathing criticism, ridicule, and opposition by the Europeans, including the European Left. Even though European officials, just like their American counterparts, long ago recognized the dangers of smoking tobacco and have implemented measures to reduce it drastically, German politicians and health experts want to make certain that this be done without introducing any unwanted "American conditions" anywhere in the country, including Berlin. Thus, "U.S.-American conditions with the strictest possible anti-smoker-regulations are, however, not being called for in Berlin—neither by the [German] Non-Smokers' Association nor by experts in the health administration."[84] More should be done in Germany for nonsmokers, but under no circumstances are German smokers to be treated as gruffly as they are in the United States. Among the British, too (not to mention French views on the subject), many of the well-worn negative characteristics associated with America and Americans emerge in discussions about the American campaign against smoking: intolerance, religiosity, fanaticism, media manipulation, hypocrisy (in the sense of simultaneous toleration, even promotion, of other health-damaging activities like junk food), love of weapons (constant word-plays on "fire" as a verb and noun, meaning both lighting up a cigarette and shooting). Europeans find it particularly irksome that America's intolerant policing of cigarette smoking has been most vigorously pursued by members of the 1960s' generation of former hippies and paragons of the counterculture in whose bastions smoking is punished by fines and citations.[85] Many Europeans find the fining of people for smoking in public, just like the existence of programs to help smokers be weaned off smoking, the epitome of Americanization: intrusive, arrogant, repressive.[86] New York City's ban of smoking in public buildings caused a bevy of Europe-wide commentaries about America's "exaggerated Puritanism," "tobacco dry laws," and "new prohibition," to mention just a few of the typical epithets.[87] "Our body, at the end, is ours and only we have the right to abuse it with stress, everyday arguments, and tobacco."[88] Europeans resent America's healthy campaign against cigarette smoking just as much as they resent America's penchant for junk food, both of which they experience as equally unwelcome intrusions into their autonomy and a threat to their sovereignty.

## Law and the Judicial System

The "Americanization" of many aspects of the legal world and the administration of justice in Europe is also raising anxiety. The view articulated by Germany's former Justice Minister Hertha Däubler-Gmelin that the United States has a "lousy" legal system is widely shared in European intellectual circles.[89] Of course, the existence of the death penalty in a number of American states plays a major role in this perception, but there is much more to this: Europeans regard numerous aspects of the American administration of justice as bad, irresponsible, alternately—and simultaneously—too brutal and too lax, and always dominated by money-grubbing lawyers, sensational media, and irresponsible jurors. The huge penalties that America's large tobacco companies had to pay some plaintiffs who had sued these companies for damages incurred during a lifetime of smoking were prima facie evidence to many Europeans of a legal system gone wild and controlled by unscrupulous lawyers who have created a culture of a "claims mentality" and a rapacious litigiousness. In Germany, "Americanizing the claims mentality" comes in for widespread criticism. Because accident victims in Germany feel poorly compensated, according to attorney Ronald Schmid, they increasingly try getting gigantic compensation claims. As a model for this there are the so-called victims' attorneys, who extort exorbitant sums for accident victims of all kinds. Naturally, they are almost all Americans, though they can always count on the assistance of an increasing number of German associates and imitators. What is at stake here, apparently, is not so much the principle as the supposedly aggressive and uncouth manner of the Americans and their German imitators, whose ways run roughshod over the traditional collegiality that allegedly has hitherto informed the interaction among Germany's lawyers. To quote one such voice among many: "In order to avoid any misunderstandings: This is not at all about condemning attorneys who make it their business to represent the interests of victims and their surviving dependents. That is a noble task of the bar. It is simply a matter of their kinds of methods. And to that extent American conditions and habits may not and should not be adopted by Germany."[90] The possibility of introducing courtroom television broadcasts into Germany is also seen as succumbing to "American conditions."[91]

In Great Britain, too, the role of television in court assumes the stigmatizing label of "Americanization."[92] Indeed, the fear of Americanizing British legal life is wide-ranging: from the menace of ever larger law firms, which in the London business world are almost assuming the dimensions of their New York or Chicago counterparts, to the growing presence of London affiliates of the major New York law firms; from the fees that top-flight attorneys routinely demand to the workloads that they and their colleagues have to cope with in these offices.[93] Another awful expression of Americanization, as many Britons see it, is the epidemic of lawsuits that has recently emerged in the U.K.: "The law used to be called an ass. Now it's a hungry vulture, with Britain apparently heading down the American road of litigation madness." In this brutal and commercialized— i.e., Americanized—world, the "advocatus diaboli" (devil's advocate) means exactly what it says: a lawyer working for Satan.[94]

The apparent growth of so-called specialist courts as part of "therapeutic justice" is also criticized in Great Britain, using the stigma of Americanization. "While the majority of expert opinion favours drug courts, some are concerned about the Americanisation of criminal justice. . . . [According to] Roger Howard, chief executive of drugs research charity DrugScope: 'It's part of a movement over there of therapeutic justice and the growth of specialist courts; mental health courts, domestic violence courts and even tobacco courts for teens. It may be culturally appropriate in the U.S. but the question is whether it is here.' "[95] The Americanization of sentencing is lamented as much as the Americanization of prisons. In brief, there is hardly any aspect of justice and its administration that escapes the stigma "Americanization" in the current British discussion.

Ditto in France. Students who have been expelled from secondary school or have incurred other punishments for transgressions they committed have begun to hire legal council to help them with their case. To the appalled school administrators and principals, this turn of events is "a social disease that betrays the growing importance of legal conflicts and the Americanization of social relationships between individuals."[96]

An even more egregious instance of the Americanization of French legal life—and of France's very morals—are the increasing incidents of young adults suing their parents for all kinds of perceived injustices, including their failure to pay for items desired by the child. While there were only thirty such cases in 1992, they ballooned to more than two thousand by 2003 in the wake of the Americanization of French life. One case, in which a young man sued his parents for money to attend a better business school than was available in his hometown, so upset one reporter that she wrote the following: "And this family does not live in Nevada or Ohio but in Indre-et-Loire [central France]." Lest there be any ambiguities, she adds a comment by the young man's mother that "I thought such things only existed in the United States or in the movies."[97]

And of course, to Portuguese—as to other West Europeans—the aggressiveness and puritan outlook of American feminists has further increased the litigiousness of American society by creating the new category of "assault" in the workplace. Now this Americanization was about to invade Europe. A Portuguese newspaper had the following to say under the headline "Golden Shelves": "Moreover, new labor law protects workers to an incredible degree. The margin of error for managers has been reduced significantly. And as if this were not enough, we have begun to be paranoid about 'assaults'. First was sexual assault, certainly an idea that began in the minds of American feminists and ended in the Oval Office. Across the entire world managers are made to fear being sued for making even the smallest flirtatious comments to employees."[98]

Many in the Vatican, Italy, and elsewhere in Europe attributed the sex abuse scandals besetting the Catholic Church in the Boston diocese and elsewhere in the United States to the litigiousness of the Americans and a mass hysteria about both sex and money. When a group of American Catholics protested in front of St. Peter's Basilica in Rome that Archbishop Bernard Law, Boston's former cardinal and a major culprit in the cover-up of these sex scandals, was bestowed the honor by the Vatican of reading mass, a group of Italian (and other European) counterdemonstrators heckled and mocked the Americans for being money-grubbing and litigious prudes.[99] In Catalonia, the debate about privatizing surveillance services in all prisons and courts occurred under the expected sobriquet of "Americanization." "We do not want an Americanization of Catalan prisons" since "the countries that have privatized their services do not guarantee prisoners' rights and duties. . . . The privatized security model of the United States is not appropriate to European security and culture."[100] The mere fact that the Spanish Supreme Court wanted to change the layout of the court rooms in which criminal trials were held so that the defendant would henceforth sit next to her or his council constituted, of course, an unwelcome "Americanization" of the trials and the judicial system as a whole. [101] The tendency to Americanize so many aspects of the European justice system is a direct consequence of the massive influence that American television exerts on Europeans, "some of whom have watched Ally MacBeal so much that their brains have softened."[102]

## Crime

With respect both to the rise in crime quantitatively as well as to its new qualitative dimension, American conditions are constantly being invoked all over Western Europe: "Yet again [in the case of car-jacking]," according to Edmund King of the Royal Automobile Club, "we are seeing the Americanisation of crime in this country and we would like to see the police take a more active role tackling this problem."[103] In Great Britain especially, every discussion about arming police with pistols or other guns takes place in the context of a purported Americanization: "We needed to do something to counteract a growing gun culture and the 'Americanisation' of

crime."[104] Even murder is viewed as something Americanized, especially when a killing is particularly brutal or apparently done without
motive. Gang wars in the London underworld are seen as leading
to "an Americanisation of violence . . . whereby gunmen are blasting
away to sort out a minor dispute as if they are playing the part in a
gangster movie. Firearms have replaced forearms."[105]

In Germany as well, needless to say, the tragic shooting spree at
an Erfurt secondary school in 2002 immediately led to a discussion
about "American conditions" in German schools. Across the political spectrum, the specter of the massacre at Columbine High School
in Littleton, Colorado, was pushed into the center of the political
debate about the Erfurt incident. Edmund Stoiber, the conservative
prime minister of Bavaria, called for a general regulation of Internet
content so that "violent videos" and "killer games" be forbidden:
"This is something we have to achieve on a worldwide scale even
though, of course, we face the problem that the Americans have a
completely different conception of freedom."[106] Stoiber's remarks
alluded to the Americans' purported deification of freedom that, as
mentioned in chapter 1 of this book, others have termed "freedom
Bolshevism." It remains wholly unclear just how this American conception of freedom (too much, too little?) differs from that of the
Germans and what this means for the issue at hand. But to go into
details would be too burdensome and completely unnecessary for
Stoiber. There was a lot of discussion about the pathological effect
of violent games, from the "Power Rangers" to the lifelike simula-
tions of war depicted on computer screens. Among the many thousands of games of this genre, one called "America's Army" was, of
course, especially emphasized. And, naturally, Hollywood had to
take the blame, starting with cult movies like *Friday the 13th* and
Oliver Stone's *Natural Born Killers*. Otherwise, Stone is held in high
esteem by European film critics and the cultural elite as a director
who drastically depicts the hypocrisy and brutality of everyday life
in America.

Even the German police union issued another warning about
"American conditions" at German schools in the aftermath of the
Erfurt tragedy. In a press release, it said: "The German Police Union

demands more security in German schools. There now exist those 'American conditions we always warned against,' said the federal vice-chairman of the union, Wendt. . . . This also means increasing security standards 'up to and including uniformed guard personnel.' " Although the police now wanted to protect its officers, if need be, "by carrying protective vests and, of course, a weapon," and to allow them ("in order to be able to react quickly") to handle their weapons outside their holsters and search persons and vehicles with weapons drawn, things would not be taking a turn for the worst, the police official reassured the German public: "But there will not be rigorously intervening 'sheriffs' here at home, because the police will remain public-friendly."[107] And public-friendliness is, as we know, as un-American as violence is American. In a long interview, the chair of the Police Union, Thomas Mohr, issued a reassurance that German police would not try to introduce American conditions under any circumstances.[108]

After the tragedy at Erfurt hardly anyone mentioned the catastrophe that happened in 1996 in the Scottish town of Dunblane, where a youth councillor had murdered sixteen children and a teacher. Not that "record"-setting ought ever to matter in tragedies like this, but the fact is that three more people died in Dunblane than was the case at Columbine. Nobody in Germany mentioned this tragedy, and nobody talked about a "Britishization" of German schools, German violence, or German youth. Conversely, the British media constantly featured the "Americanisation" of British youth culture as the main reason for the terrible incident in Dunblane. The fact that the Columbine incident could not be brought into play, because it happened three years after the Dunblane tragedy, did not prevent anybody discussing the Scottish tragedy from invoking America as a general bogeyman in this case as well.

But not only in Germany is Dunblane as good as unknown. After a similar incident in the Parisian suburb of Nanterre in March 2002, the media, municipal administration, and citizens talked exclusively about America, Americanization, and "American conditions." " 'This isn't happening here. It's like America, not France. It's a pure nightmare,' said Germaine, a council secretary in her 40s, as police escorted relatives through the underground car-park into the building where the bodies of eight council members still lay in the meeting chamber."[109]

When it comes to violence and criminality, "Americanization" has played a central role in European discussions and notions since the 1920s. To this day, Europeans associate Chicago with gangsters. They regarded leather-jacketed rowdies in the 1950s as wannabe Americans in the same way as the motorcycle gangs of the 1960s and subsequent decades. A documentary about "Kicking for Dunblane" would be totally unthinkable in Europe; *Bowling for Columbine*, however, became an icon of European anti-Americanism.

### Miscellaneous

European holidays are allegedly increasingly Americanized, with Santa Claus displacing the Virgin Mary and Baby Jesus at Christmas, with the semipagan Halloween becoming prominent in places where a few years ago it was totally unknown, with birthday celebrations supplanting "name day" festivities of yore.[110] The American-style celebration of Halloween—costumes, candy, parties—has been growing in popularity with youth all over Europe in recent years. This, in turn, has led European elites to inveigh against this import as yet another threat to the very survival of European culture. "The Associated Press did a sweep of Europe and turned up people like Hans Kohler, the mayor of the Austrian town of Ranksweil, who called Halloween 'a bad habit.' He and the mayors of eight neighboring villages have organized a boycott of the event. A Swedish folklorist told the AP that Halloween was . . . an 'unnecessary, bad American custom' and a Catholic priest in Italy said that carved pumpkins symbolized 'emptiness.' "[111] American cities are characterized in Europe as "models of postmodern consumption" and "ungovernable juggernauts" (in German, the word *Moloch*—evoking the tyrannical Semitic god to whom the Canaanites sacrificed children—is used) that inflate what is already a "flagrant use of space" even further. German, British, and other city planners warn against an "Americanization" of European cities,[112] whose inner cities are becoming dilapidated, and where one can go shopping only by driving to gigantic shopping centers—controlled by Wal-Mart (and similar big companies)—on the city outskirts. The entire urban world is becoming Americanized. "Over-sized and over here" is the way one British observer paraphrased that catchphrase already mentioned, but now in the context of a lament about British cities. "I belong with those who lament the creeping Yankification of our culture. Now that town centres throughout Britain (Europe, even) have been homogenised by means of hamburger joints, neon-lit bars, regulation bollards, street furniture et al., Americanisation is moving out of town and making great inroads into retailing at the expense of well-established outlets."[113]

In Germany, "American conditions" also seem to prevail with respect to the budget for drugs and medicine as well as to pot-smoking kids; to the city of Leipzig, which has been "Americanized" by intercity express trains and a new central railway station; to the placement of signs regulating things that ought to be self-evident, to protect companies from law suits; to social clubs that are losing their names because of the "trend toward Americanization"; and in the animal kingdom.

That last point deserves to be covered in somewhat greater detail. "Americanization in the animal kingdom" was invoked by a schoolboy from Hamburg who wrote this letter to the *Hamburger Abendblatt*:

> A tranquil piece of wooded land. Brown squirrels are jumping merrily from branch to branch. Yet suddenly a black squirrel shoots by and chases the brown fellow members of its species. This is not a made-up story—I saw it myself. The first black squirrels were brought in from America. Ever since, there have been more and more of them. Previously, one saw only a few isolated black squirrels, but in the meantime they have become almost as numerous as the European squirrels. They are displacing the brown ones of which we have grown so fond—Americanization in the animal kingdom.[114]

The Americanization of European squirrels is hardly more eccentric than the supposed Americanization of the European weather that people were talking about during the great heat wave in the summer of 2003 all over Europe, and especially in France, where thousands of old and infirm people died during the traditional holiday month of August while they were sitting in their overheated urban apartments and neglected by their relatives at the beaches. During my stay in Europe that year, nobody told me that this summer with its record temperatures was similar to a typical summer in North America, which would have been entirely correct. All I heard was complaints that European weather was somehow becoming Americanized, and that the heat wave in Europe was linked to the refusal of the United States to sign the Kyoto Protocol on climate change (undoubtedly an irresponsible step in the wrong direction). There was nothing I was able to learn about the Americanization of European weather from the especially gruff, rainy, and unseasonably cool summer of 2004. On the cold side of things, apparently, what is required to earn the moniker of "American" or "Americanized" is an especially severe winter at several degrees below freezing with intense snowstorms such as much of Europe experienced during the winter of 2005–06.

For many European commentators and their intellectual public, America furnishes a kind of Orwellian society that obeys the dictates of a puritanical culture, is being kept under surveillance by increasingly rigid government regulations, has totally succumbed to the uninhibited requirements of the market, and therefore also has no consciousness about social welfare whatsoever. In many Europeans' eyes America is simultaneously prudish and lecherous, home both to an unbridled individualism and to collective conformism; it bears the legacy of both Harvard (educating the scions of the elite) and Hollywood (producing trash for the masses). More and more Europeans increasingly view America as a civilization different from their own and, in any event, inferior.[115]

## Schadenfreude

September 11 added something new to the anti-American mixture, a previously rather underrepresented feeling, namely, schadenfreude. In America today it is still thought that the Bush administration, with its aggressive unilateralism and irresponsible policies, scared away the Europeans, who had demonstrated their good will toward the United States immediately after September 11. Never before has the gap between the views of European elites and masses emerged more clearly than after the assault of September 11. On the whole, public opinion in Europe immediately after the attack was characterized by profound sympathy with the Americans and compassion for the victims. But even then there were signs that neither one of these sentiments was deep-seated or likely to last long.[116] Nevertheless, the great majority of the European public stood on America's side, both in their hearts and minds, from September 11 through early October 2001. This was not the case, emotionally or intellectually, among the cultural elite.

Ground Zero was still burning as the first reports and analyses from the highbrow media were already starting to deliver all those arguments, objections, suspicions, conspiracy theories, and barely concealed expressions of joy that became common knowledge in the ensuing period: that the Americans had deserved this assault (the constant expression of the sentiment "they had it coming to them"); that they were finally receiving a long overdue punishment for all their misdeeds of the past, from Vietnam to globalization, from the extermination of the Indians to the bombing of Dresden; that the whole thing was really no big deal because many more Americans lost their lives every year in traffic accidents; that the destruction of the Twin Towers benefited the New York skyline aesthetically; that it could only be advantageous now that these phallic symbols of male, Western arrogance were finally gone; that the Israeli Mossad was behind all of this (hence, all the Jews rumored to have stayed away from work that day because they had supposedly been warned in advance); that the entire event was a phantom, a lie, a joke or bagatelle (the worldwide banner "9/11 is a joke"); that it had been staged by the American government, which was only looking for an excuse for its imperialist plans (after all, the Reichstag fire in February 1933, something frequently alluded to in Germany, had ultimately contributed to the consolidation of the Nazi dictatorship); that

George W. Bush and Osama bin Laden were quite similar with regard to their mentality and their (chiefly religious) fanaticism, just as (more generally) a United States governed by Christian conservatives was no longer any kind of real democracy, but rather a regime basically identical to those of theocratic Islamists. While there can be no doubt that the salience of religion in American public and private life markedly differentiates the United States from contemporary Europe, here, too, European ignorance about—or more likely ill will toward—America needs mention: Equating America's religiosity with that of Islamic fundamentalists by dint of having the "Battle Hymn of the Republic" intoned in Washington, DC's National Cathedral during the memorial service one week after the crimes of 9/11—as a number of European radio and television commentators did—has to be interpreted as anti-American. Moreover, Europeans often invoke the American habit of saying "God bless you" as prima facie evidence for religion's fundamentalist bent and massive control of public life in the United States. Interestingly, I have never heard any European interpret the South German and Austrian (basically Catholic) custom of using the ubiquitous salutation of *Grüss Gott* (short for *Grüss Dich Gott* or *Grüss Sie Gott*—may God greet you); or the totally common *Pfirti* (short for *Möge Dich Gott führen*—may God guide you) as evidence for religion's stifling salience in these cultures.

One could read views like the ones just mentioned about the fanaticism of religion in America and the other points mentioned about 9/11 not only in marginal journals of the extreme Left or Right, but in many mainstream periodicals in every West European country. One can find numerous examples showing how important European intellectuals and elites greeted American suffering with unconcealed schadenfreude.

For the philosopher Jean Baudrillard, the destruction of the Twin Towers was "the absolute event, the 'mother' of all events." It fulfilled a long-desired dream, and the "fantastic pictures" of the planes flying into the Twin Towers brought "immense joy" to "our" hearts. "We" had all, "without exception," dreamed about the attack on the Twin Towers for years. The whole thing was a dramatic realization of the "terrorist notion" that inevitably "resides" in all of us and provides all of us with a psychologically redeeming answer to the dominance of the environment surrounding us, which is ruled by the hegemonic power of the United States. The terrorists gave us a "gift" with their actions that disrupted the "discourse" of the "banality of American everyday life." In doing so, "they [the assailants] *did* it, but we *wished* for it."[117]

The composer Karlheinz Stockhausen praised the imagination and precision that went into the assaults on the Twin Towers and called this crime "the greatest work of art imaginable for the whole cosmos."[118] And the Italian Nobel Prize winner Dario Fo expressed his joy this way: "The great speculators wallow in an economy that every year kills tens of millions of people with poverty—so what is 20,000 dead in New York? Regardless of who carried out the massacre, this violence is the legitimate daughter of the culture of violence, hunger and inhumane exploitation."[119]

And European intellectuals continued to rave about this for months on end. Two years after September 11, 2001, Geoffrey Wheatcroft made the effort to take a second look at and comment on what had been written (above all) in the British press. He was struck by three things: the way the crime had been trivialized and relativized, the condemnation of the United States as the real guilty party, and the immense number of important British intellectuals, writers, poets, journalists, and composers who weighed in on this subject. Even more than how he was struck by the trivialization of the catastrophe and the effort to shift blame onto America, Wheatcroft was shocked by the sheer nonsense emitted (above all) by poets, writers, and artists. Hence his title: "Two Years of Gibberish." Wheatcroft, a left-liberal intellectual and journalist, ended his investigation with the tragic words: "If the old Leninist left was buried politically in the rubble of the Berlin wall, the literary-academic intelligentsia disappeared morally in the ashes of ground zero."[120]

The active and routine perusal of German periodicals and relevant analyses by Andreas Hess, Lars Rensmann, Elliot Neaman, and Henryk Broder make it clear that German-speaking intellectuals—just as in Great Britain, if not even more so—as well as literary figures translated into German, such as Arundhati Roy and Slavoj Zizek, were vehement about their public expressions concerning September 11 and its consequences.[121] There were, of course, exceptions like the novelist Peter Schneider, who characterized the mostly anti-American reaction of his colleagues (in a November 2001 article in the liberal weekly *Die Zeit*) as "an almost unbearable intonation of moral superiority."[122] But the vast majority of statements were more critical and more negative toward the United States than they were toward the Jihaddists.

Even some of the positions taken by European intellectuals that seemed pro-American at first glance turned out to be "Trojan horses" on closer examination. This was the case, for example, with the widely praised commentary made by Jean-Marie Colombani, "Nous sommes tous Américains" (We are all Americans) in *Le Monde* on September 13, 2001. Purportedly a major statement of solidarity with the United States, it turns out on closer reading to be the exact opposite. Although Colombani views the attacks on the Twin Towers and on Washington, DC, as criminal acts and condemns them much more harshly than do many other European intellectuals, he simultaneously accuses the Americans of being the progenitors of Osama bin Laden and thus the godfathers of Jihaddist terrorism. As early as December 2001, in an open letter to "our American friends," Colombani retracted the scanty sympathy he had earlier shown for the victims in New York, Washington, DC, and Pennsylvania. In this letter he accused the United States—with its aggressiveness, unilateralism, and religiosity—of being the mirror image of the Jihaddists and therefore of bearing the blame for its own suffering. Exactly one year to the day after September 11, 2001, Colombani had absolutely no problem letting the cat out of the bag and showing his true colors. On September 12, 2002, he wrote in *Le Monde*: "The reflex of solidarity from last year has been deluged by a wave that would have everyone in the world believe we have all become anti-Americans."[123] German Defense Minister Peter Struck's almost identical words to Colombani's at a session of the German Bundestag on September 12, 2001 ("Today we are all Americans") were viewed by the great majority of the German literati and intellectuals as laughable, irritating, and totally undesirable. In the population at large, opinion was split. According to a survey from the Allensbach public opinion research institute, 47 percent agreed with Struck's statement, while 42 percent rejected it.[124]

By the end of 2001, bookstores in Paris, Berlin, and London were already displaying numerous publications where the tendency was to take joy in the attack of September 11. In France, Thierry Meyssan's *11 Septembre 2001: L'Effroyable Imposture* (September 11, 2001: The Awful Imposture), which treated the American government as pulling the wires behind this crime, climbed to the top of the charts and became a solid bestseller.[125] The same applies to Mathias Broecker's German hit, *Verschwörungen, Verschwörungstheorien und die Geheimnisse des 11.9.* (Conspiracies, Conspiracy Theories, and the Secrets of 9/11), which put forward an argument quite similar to Meyssan's book, was rung up at the cash register 130,000 times in less than eight months, and stayed on various bestseller lists quite a bit longer than its French counterpart.[126] The German journalist Tobias Jaecker compiled a detailed study of the many anti-Semitic conspiracy theories that proliferated in Europe after 9/11 and continue unabated.[127]

Opinion surveys make it clear that this high-volume schadenfreude rapidly spread from European intellectuals and elites to a considerable portion of the population. According to surveys, one-third of Germans under the age of thirty had become convinced by the summer of 2003 that the American government had ordered the assaults on New York and Washington. Over 20 percent of all Germans, according to the same survey, shared this view.[128]

Naturally, a substantial portion of normal human schadenfreude resonated along with all of this. All of us are happy when the big guy—regardless of the context—gets hit on the head. As mentioned earlier, everybody—except for those immediately affected—experiences satisfaction when "Mr. Big" stumbles or falls. Whether it is the New York Yankees, the Los Angeles Lakers, Manchester United, or Harvard—everybody is overjoyed when these giants lose, because they are both envied and feared, and they are seen as arrogant to boot simply for existing and having been winners for so long.

One could also detect a similar Europe-wide schadenfreude in the immediate wake of the disaster wrought by Hurricane Katrina in early September 2005. Following the British, French, German, and Austrian television news, listening to radio shows, reading the letters to the editors of major daily newspapers, and perusing the Internet, one could not help but come away with the impression that many Europeans once again harbored a not-so-hidden joy, a serves-them-right attitude following this disaster. Witnessing the pathetically inept and socially unjust response by American authorities to this tragedy, the Europeans' views rightfully mutated into anger, disbelief, and ridicule. But that is not what I am criticizing here. I indict the indisputable tone of schadenfreude that emerged in Western Europe the very next day after the hurricane hit the New Orleans area before the ineptitude of the American rescue efforts became evident.

In the case of European schadenfreude concerning Hurricane Katrina and also the September 11 crime and catastrophe, though, there clearly enters an additional element to the perception and the response that needs to be considered: old-established anti-Americanism. To illustrate this point, permit me to submit the following telling counterfactual: had the Air France Airbus A-300 Flight 8969 crashed into the Eiffel Tower in Paris on December 24, 1994, as the Groupe Islamique Armée (GIA) wanted it to, I doubt very much that any—let alone many—American intellectuals would have written lengthy pieces in prestigious publications like the *New York Times* or *Washington Post* by, say, December 26 and 27 all but exculpating this crime by invoking France's many military and political missteps as well as its atrocities, from the Vendée to the Paris Commune, from Indochina to Algeria. Nor would they have invoked all kinds of conspiracy theories involving the French government, the Israeli Mossad, or any of the other agents so often mentioned in connection with 9/11. I also doubt very much that books purporting that such a crime was actually planned and executed by the French president—had this terrible tragedy become reality—would have been written by American intellectuals, let alone become bestsellers in the United States. But all of this has indeed happened in Europe, particularly among social groups from whom one would least expect it by dint of their intelligence and education. Clearly, antipathy, as has often been the case, trumps either and both.

American (and European) intellectuals would have mourned the destruction of the Eiffel Tower and viewed it, not as a just act of revenge against modernity or even as an esthetic improvement of the Parisian skyline and a justified destruction of a phallic symbol of French power. The literati would have mourned the thousands of French victims and paid them the kind of respect that they never granted the perished at these three American sites.

But American and European intellectuals, of course, have a completely different relationship with France from that they have with America. A serious British journalist in a serious daily newspaper would never have written the following words on France in the same way one did, in all earnestness, concerning America: "We are enslaved by our interest in America and Americana. We try not to be, pretend not to be, but we can't disengage."[129] And other intellectuals have argued that Americanization and America's culture industry have usurped and stolen Europe's very own history, and thus the core of its identity. For example, the well-known German film director Edgar Reitz stated explicitly that by making the television series *Holocaust*, Americans robbed Germans of their rightful history.[130] And this is precisely the point. If one lets the numerous illustrations in this chapter pass by in review, the thread of the story becomes apparent: It is the feeling of constant self-incapacitation that Europeans must somehow endure, the feeling that they are inevitably condemned to be America's victims, to be permanent minors under America's tutelage, to be ruled by an entity that they have consistently regarded as their cultural and moral inferior. Europeans have long ago failed to remain the masters of their own destiny where America is concerned; they are inevitably and helplessly "enslaved" to it.

## CHAPTER 4

# The Massive Waning of America's Image in the Eyes of Europe and the World

So what? Why and how does it matter that these multifaceted derisions of and ubiquitous irritations with America and all things American have become part of daily discourse in most of West Europe's media? Do talk and sentiment have any real consequences in action?

Indeed, Peter J. Katzenstein and Robert O. Keohane argue in a major forthcoming volume that they basically do not.[1] In a very perceptive chapter entitled "The Political Consequences of Anti-Americanism," Keohane and Katzenstein investigate a number of areas in which one would assume that anti-American attitudes on the part of Europeans and others could have easily led to direct actions in policies and concrete behavior. The authors first look at the struggle against terrorism, which they subdivide into two sections, on anti-Americanism being a potential breeding ground for terrorists and counterterrorist government policies. In neither do they find any serious evidence of anti-American attitudes having had an effect on concrete policies, behavior, or actions. Keohane and Katzenstein then proceed to analyze the world of "soft power"—particularly that of diplomacy. Here, too, they conclude that anti-American attitudes and opinions have scant, if any, effect on policies and actions. Lastly, they investigate boycotts of American name-brand products and anti-Americanism's possible ramifications on tourism to the United States. Again, their verdict is unequivocal: There are no visible, palpable, or measurable adverse effects at all. To be sure, Katzenstein and Keohane in no way mean to use these examples to deny or denigrate the existence of anti-Americanism in Europe and the world. But they conclude that its effects on actual behavior and policies (other than in a few limited cases in Latin America, the Turkish parliament's decision of March 1, 2003, not to let American forces attack Iraq from Turkish territory, and Canadian Prime Minister Paul Martin's refusal to have Canada commit to being integrated into the North American Ballistic Missile Defense) are either demonstrably nonexistent or so tenuous that they are tantamount to being nonexistent. True enough, though one would be hard put to interpret America's standing virtually all by itself in UNESCO's passing a new convention on cultural diversity, designed to combat the homogenizing effect of cultural globalization as being totally devoid of a certain opposition—perhaps even antipathy—to the United States, particularly by the convention's major protagonists, Canada and France.[2] Moreover, the International Olympic Committee's elimination of men's baseball and women's softball from the 2012 Olympic Games may again not be conclusively attributed to any overt anti-Americanism on the part of a majority of the delegates. But surely, the atmosphere as a whole lent itself in that global forum—just like in UNESCO's—to the taking of such concrete actions and the formulations of such clear policies. Lastly, Keohane and Katzenstein introduce fascinating data from the soft-drink industry, among other consumer goods items, to demonstrate that Cadbury-Schweppes, arguably Europe's most prominent competitors to America's Coca Cola and Pepsi Cola, actually lost market share to its American counterparts in 2003–04, the height of anti-American feelings and attitudes in Europe. Still, I really think it unlikely that the French government would have intervened to prohibit the acquisition of the famous yogurt maker Groupe Danone had Cadbury-Schweppes been interested in purchasing it rather than PepsiCo. Nor do I think it likely that Cadbury-Schweppes would have been called the equivalent pejorative of, among others, *ogre Americain*, whose rapacious acts against a French cultural icon had to be stymied by any means possible, including political intervention and state interdiction.[3] We have encountered this term in connection with Lance Armstrong, but it has become part of the French vernacular—and always with "Americain" as a qualifier. Thus, native French speakers and denizens of Paris have confirmed my limited impression of never having encountered an "ogre" bearing a different nationality than American. There simply does not seem to exist any other *ogrerie* in contemporary France than "*à l'Americaine*." Philippe Roger, undoubtedly France's foremost expert on anti-Americanism in that country, went even further in his response to my presentation of this issue at a conference on anti-Americanism at Princeton University in November 2005. He argued that the linkage between *ogrerie* (ogreness)—in other words size being associated exclusively negatively with such things as rapaciousness, terror, and danger—and America reaches well into the nineteenth century in French discourse.

To be sure, nixing women's softball and men's baseball from the Olympic Games, inveighing against PepsiCo, buying Adidas instead of Nike shoes, and many of the examples that Katzenstein and Keohane consider and that I raise to challenge their assertion really remain in the realm of the trivial. One can solidly argue that in areas that really matter, European-American cooperation continues unabated. But once again, the tone makes the music and tones matter immensely because they define the context wherein content is shaped and implemented. Lastly, as we know so well from Steven Lukes and other students of political power, what matters often at least as much as the visible, measurable, and manifest expressions of discontent are its silent and latent counterparts, those that set a tone, an agenda, an atmosphere, but operate stealthily to "normal" senses of observation.[4] Thus, decisions *not* taken because of residues of anti-Americanism, policies *not* implemented because of an existing though silent antipathy toward America, might be as important as the visible expressions that we can measure and observe. "For example, did the French and German decisions not to back America in

Iraq simply reflect policy disagreements, or were the French and German leaders aware they could play to a growing anti-Americanism and so boost their strength?"[5]

But even if anti-Americanism's direct policy implications remain murky and subject to the examples one chooses, it does not mean that there exist no behavioral ones, such as the prolific burning of American flags, the destruction of property related to the American government (American cultural centers and "Amerika Häuser" in Germany, for example) or to American companies (bulldozing of a McDonald's being merely the best-known case), and the derision and teasing of American visitors in many settings. At this juncture, anti-Americanism has yet to be harnessed by policymakers for concrete purposes, even though that, too, has already happened, as attested to by the two examples mentioned in the preceding chapter: Gerhard Schröder's successful electoral campaign of 2002 (also mentioned by Keohane and Katzenstein), and Jörg Haider's inveighing against Vienna's alleged mutation into Chicago, both of which preceded the Iraq War. European policymakers may very well continue for the foreseeable future to cooperate with Americans in fighting terrorism, though there have been many instances in the past in which this cooperation has been rocky at best and fraught with irritation on the part of many a European government, often accompanied by outright refusal to share information with the Americans. Surely, it must be relevant for a number of dimensions in this cooperation that at the very same time many of these European policymakers consider America equally as dangerous as the terrorists, if not more so. Simply put, the United States is much too big and much too important for Europeans to have their acutely felt and openly articulated continentwide anti-Americanism interfere with their interests. European business executives to whom the American market remains absolutely essential for the success of their firms will clearly not implement any policies hailing from their disdain for Americans that might in any way hinder their companies' successful operations in the United States. These businessmen will continue to express their contempt for Americans, to ridicule them for their alleged lack of culture, to insist that Americans do not speak proper

English, but they surely will never let these sentiments and prejudices interfere with their successful operations in the United States. Thus, anti-Americanism's policy implications will remain muted as long as Europeans need America, be this in politics or the economy. Antipathies, though substantial, will not be allowed to interfere with interests; expressive sentiments will always remain subordinate to instrumental considerations. "Anti-Americanism, it seems, often stops where it might hurt: people like to inveigh against the United States but then go on buying the same brands and looking for means to send their kids to be educated here."[6]

Still, it matters that teenagers in Saudi Arabia, Bahrain, South Korea, Mexico, China, Taiwan, Lebanon, Pakistan, Nigeria, and Argentina have come to despise America *and* the American people despite—or precisely because of—their being eager consumers of American culture. Indeed, the DeFleurs' study, which carefully documents this hatred among this little-surveyed group, blames the American media.[7] The study also includes teenagers from two European countries, Spain and Italy, whose views of Americans may not be quite as massively negative as those of their counterparts in Saudi Arabia, Bahrain, South Korea, Lebanon, Mexico, and China, but who nevertheless harbor many more negative feelings toward Americans than positive ones. At least Italian teenagers—together with Argentinians—are the only ones among the surveyed who as a group do not consider American women to be sexually immoral. And Spanish as well as Italian youth are the only respondents who seem to believe that Americans have strong family values. For many German youth, particularly in the eastern parts of that country, there is absolutely nothing for which to thank the Americans, whom they view to be governed by a crypto-fascist system headed by a "second Hitler."[8] And a study of textbooks commonly used in social studies and history classes in France's secondary schools shows a near unanimity with which terrorism is depicted in these curricula as an understandable, even forgivable, reaction of the weak against the evils of American power and American globalization.[9] In their much-discussed book *Élèves sous influence* (Students under the Influence), Barbara Lefebvre and Ève Bonnivard provide a bevy of

examples of rampant anti-Americanism deeply entrenched in
French history books. They suggest two possible explanations for
this: First, they believe that this anti-Americanism appeals to
teachers, who, as a group, have long cultivated left-leaning political
views that have been consistently inimical to most things American.
Second, the tone of the textbooks goes to great length not to insult
or alienate the Muslim student population, which has been particularly vocal in defending terrorism as a justified act of resistance
against non-Muslim invaders, meaning, of course, almost exclusively the United States and Israel. Lefebvre and Bonnivard argue
that the United States has become a major scapegoat in the representation of French secondary school textbooks. By criticizing and
rejecting American influence, the French are trying to forge a new
cohesion beyond religious and sectarian differences. Then, by portraying the United States as the main danger to world peace, the
history and social studies textbooks relativize the importance of
other dangers, in particular the salience of violent Islamic fundamentalism. Lastly, and this is what the authors regard as their main
finding, France is trying to define its very identity as a vanguard in
the fight against American supremacy. Their conclusion: While the
textbooks present the United States as a caricature, France has
reached a stage wherein its self-perception and self-definition as an
anti-America have become central to its politics and public life.[10]
Little surprise then that French teenagers at the country's elite secondary schools demonstrate nothing but contempt and hatred for
the United States and Americans.[11] Thus, the wearing of blue jeans,
listening to hip hop, and hanging out at McDo's in no way inocu-
lates young people against becoming anti-American; quite the contrary. Indeed, expanding beyond the DeFleurs' concentration on
American media, one can safely say that it is American consumer
culture writ large that serves as a major instigator for this pervasive
antipathy. And surely this will have consequences of some kind in
the future. Already there are some indications in this direction.
Thus, it is the young, the wealthier, and the better educated, in
short, the elites—especially in Europe, but also in much of the rest
of the world, with the notable exception of the United States, the

Philippines, India, and Japan—who have the most pronounced desire among all their respective countries' respondents to have Europe be stronger and more influential in the world than the United States.[12] The report states:

> Looking at variations by age is especially significant, as the attitudes of young people compared to older people suggest possible future trends. Indeed, all the striking findings of the study appear to be more pronounced among young people. Young people (18–29) are more supportive of Europe becoming more influential than the US (60%) than those 60 or more (51%). Excluding Europeans, 56 percent of young people are supportive, as compared to 45% of older people. . . . Education is also an important variable, as those who are educated are likely to be better informed. Here, too, the striking findings of the study are more pronounced at higher educational levels. Those with relatively high levels of education are more likely to have a positive view of Europe becoming more influential than the US (63%) than are those with lower levels of education (53%). . . . Income followed a pattern quite similar to education. Those with higher levels of income were more likely to have a positive view of Europe becoming more influential than the US; to have a positive view of the influence of Europe, of France, Russia, and Britain; and to have a negative view of the influence of the US.[13]

Doug Miller, President of GlobeScan, concludes: "Our research shows that Europe's star has risen as America's reputation has declined under the Bush Administration. Americans really must worry when it is the wealthy of the world and the youth of the world that are the most upset with them."[14] Since this book focuses on Western Europe, here are the overall results from the relevant countries: Spain—with 81 percent of its respondents preferring a more influential Europe in world affairs than the United States—leads all countries, followed by Germany at 79 percent, Italy at 76 percent, France at 70 percent, and Britain at 66 percent. In other words, our five European countries (Austria and Portugal were not included in the study) are the clear leaders of the pack in wanting Europe to surpass the United States as a global player. The most enthusiasm for greater European influence at the cost of America's (other than among the five European countries) existed among America's neighbors—Mexico at 66 percent and Canada at 63 percent—followed by China (66 percent), South Africa (63 percent), Australia (62 percent), and Russia (60 percent).[15] According to this study, and surely very much in the context of being perceived as America's most prominent rival and outspoken opponent, France has become the most highly regarded individual country in the eyes of the GlobeScan study respondents. France's most enthusiastic supporters were its continental neighbors Germany (77 percent), Italy (73 percent), and Spain (67 percent). Britain—not surprisingly—weighed in at a much less emphatic 53 percent. Only in the United States did a clear majority of the respondents (52 percent) view France's global influence mainly as negative instead of positive. (In all cases the population of the country being evaluated was excluded from the totals.)

The gist of these findings has been replicated by other studies conducted in 2004 and 2005. In a large survey about the world's perception of America published by the Pew Research Center in June 2005, the publics of sixteen nations were asked to give favorability ratings of five major nations—the United States, Germany, China, Japan, and France. The United States fared the worst among the group. "In just six of the 16 countries surveyed did the United States attract a favorable rating of 50% or above. By contrast, China received that level of favorability rating from 11 countries, while Japan, Germany and France each received that high of a mark from 13 countries."[16] Other than in the five Muslim countries of Turkey, Pakistan, Lebanon, Jordan, and Indonesia, where the favorability rating of the United States can only be described as abysmal, thus solidly confirming the *New York Times* columnist Thomas Friedman's characterization of America's standing in the Muslim world as "radioactive," the United States garnered far and away its lowest scores in the West European countries of Spain, France, and Germany. The results in Britain were appreciably better, but nowhere close to the positive marks that the United States obtained in Poland and, especially, India, which in this study and others seems to be the only country in the world (except Israel, of course) in which there still exists a genuinely broad-based affection for America. This study excluded Italy and—like most—also Austria and Portugal.

In addition to France's benefiting immensely from America's loss of popularity, prestige, and affect in the world, so do China and, to nobody's surprise but the Germans', Germany. Indeed, among all the West European nations surveyed by Pew, Germany garnered the highest favorability rating of any of the five leading nations (United States, France, China, Japan, and Germany) covered by the survey. Telling of the Germans' fifty-year-long post-Holocaust ambivalence to nationalism and national pride, the Germans had a much lower view and esteem of themselves than does the rest of the world. Among Western European nations, Germany had by far the most tentative assessment of its global popularity. Only about half (51 percent) of Germans said their country is generally liked, and nearly as many (43 percent) indicated that it is generally disliked.

> Particularly striking are the differences between the self-assessments and global assessments of neighbors Germany and France. Eight-in-ten French believe the world likes their country; while only about half of Germans think the world likes theirs. But Germany's favorability ratings exceed those of France in 10 of the 16 survey countries. In fact, even the French give Germany a higher favorability rating (89%) than they give their own country (74%). The Germans, however, return the favor, giving France a 78% favorability rating, higher than the 64% they give their own country.[17]

Even in a new survey that awards twenty-five countries a quarterly "brand index" very much analogous to what has been given to products for decades, the United States slipped from its initial fourth spot that it shared with Germany in the spring of 2005 to eleventh place by August of that same year.[18] The nations that superseded the United States were Australia, Canada, Switzerland, the United Kingdom, Sweden, Italy, Germany, the Netherlands, France, and New Zealand. A German reporter summarized the survey's findings in the following manner:

> Public relations and advertising are inadequate venues to boost one's ranking on this list. The easiest and most rewarding arena wherein

one will have success is that of culture, because culture is by and large quite value neutral. In this realm, the United States will always perform poorly. Even though American popular culture still enjoys considerable desirability in the world, there is the inherently growing danger that with this culture's over-saturating the planet its popularity will lead to an inevitable backlash of increasing dislike and resistance. And "American culture" to the world means solely popular culture since American high culture, according to Anholt's study, remains for all intents and purposes completely unknown and uninteresting to the world. Moreover, the United States has recently neglected to continue its formerly successful policies of cultural diplomacy with which it celebrated immense successes during the Cold War.[19]

Clearly, entities such as Europe, Germany, and France have benefited objectively from the white heat of global and European anti-Americanism by having their profile and power increase at the cost of America's. One would be hard put to imagine a scenario in which any of these actively discouraged (or desisted from) what has—even if inadvertently—proved to be a beneficial development to them.

There is no question that shortly after 9/11 there emerged in Europe—and the world—a convergence between the traditional antipathies toward America harbored by elites for decades, if not centuries, and a popular sentiment that has never before been so decidedly negative against America. While pro- and anti-Americanism have waxed and waned in the public opinion of European countries since 1945, there has never been such consistency, duration, pervasiveness and intensity in the negative views toward the United States among Western Europeans as in the epoch beginning shortly after 9/11 with America's military engagements in Afghanistan in the fall of 2001 and culminating with its war against Iraq in March 2003. To be sure, far and away most of the antipathy from all quarters and on all levels is directed at the American president, George W. Bush. By his policies, habitus, demeanor, and entire being, Bush represents to Europeans the quintessential ugly American: arrogant, uncouth, uncultured, ignorant, inconsiderate, and aggressive. On a lower step in the hierarchy of antipathies comes American policy, followed by the American government and then the American people. Of course, millions in the world and Western Europe still differentiate between the American government and the American people (i.e., Americans), but there can be no doubt that the barrage of hostility, contempt, and derision that has been incessantly directed at the American president, American policy, and the American government has inevitably "bled over" onto the American people. Many Western Europeans still see Americans as "hardworking," "inventive," and "honest," but a majority or a plurality also perceive them as "violent" and "greedy." Fewer Western Europeans than respondents in Muslim countries see Americans as "immoral," but on the whole "the United States remains broadly disliked in most [of the 16] countries surveyed, and opinion of the American people is not as positive as it once was. The magnitude of America's image problem is such that even popular U.S. policies have done little to repair it."[20] In other words, what the DeFleurs call the "dual pattern"—the clear demarcation and differentiation in attitudes between a country's government, leaders, and policies, on the one hand, and its ordinary people and citizens, on the other—which they fail to find among teenagers' views of America in the twelve countries of their study—seems as well to have weakened considerably, if not yet totally disappeared, in the publics of the West European countries comprising the focus of this book.

The sentiment expressed in a lengthy letter to the *Financial Times*, certainly not an anti-American newspaper by any stretch of the imagination, under the telling title "A Common Language Should Not Blind Us to the Reality of a Deepening Transatlantic Gulf" encapsulates the growing irritation on the part of Europeans with Americans much beyond the policies of the American government and expresses Europeans' desire to distance themselves from Americans:

> There are massive entrenched differences between the societies [the U.S. and U.K.] and their values, whereas the lack of a common language in Europe leads some monolingual Anglo-Saxons to presume social and political differences between, for example, the Germans

and the British, which scarcely exist compared with the transatlantic gulf. Europeans do not (ordinarily) carry guns, do not routinely execute prisoners, do not have Chapter 11 bankruptcy proceedings, monster homes, cars that guzzle fuel on the US scale, virtually universal male circumcision nor—above all—an appalling level of economic inequality between the super-rich and a working class whose real living standards have scarcely risen in 30 years. Europeans generally have "socialist" medical, educational and welfare systems, that enjoy broad popular support, as do higher income tax levels, and are among the reasons for superior life expectancy and public health in much of Europe. Europeans are deeply attached to their railways and do not regard public transportation as something only for social outcasts. European societies are humanist and secular in their predominant values while organised religion plays a role in US society otherwise only equaled in Muslim societies.[21]

The tone and content of this letter find ample evidence in survey data that clearly replicate this sentiment. What lends this development an added irony is the fact that precisely when a majority of West European respondents clearly wants to loosen, if not sever, its ties with the United States, Americans, in turn, wish to maintain, even enhance, their alliance with Europe and Europeans. To wit: Whereas 66 percent of Americans favored a continuation of a close partnership with Europe in the spring of 2005, which represented an 11 percent increase from the spring of 2004, only 43 percent of Spaniards, 42 percent of Britons, 39 percent of Germans, and 26 percent of French expressed a reciprocal desire vis-à-vis the United States.[22]

It is interesting that while Europeans have become increasingly irritated with Americans for what they perceive as their excessive religiosity, the Muslim world despises Americans for what it perceives as their wanton secularism. If Europeans ridicule American prudery (no topless bathing for women, restricted sexual mores, no nudity on network television, no legalized prostitution, to mention but a few items), the Muslim world regards America as the epitome of debauchery and purveyor of an unfettered secular permissiveness featuring sex, drugs, and rock and roll. If the Muslims' antipathy toward Americans on this dimension closely resembles that of the old European Right and conservatives, than its contemporary European counterpart bears strong affinities toward the European Left's dislike of America. Too religious for one group, too secular for the other—damned if you do, damned if you don't.

Public opinion surveys are much too complex and nuanced phenomena to lend themselves to generalized conclusions and sweeping summaries. They are sophisticated statistical instruments wherein details often matter as much as overall findings. Still, even a cursory perusal merely of the titles of the fine series published by the Pew Research Center for the People and the Press on this book's core topic makes it clear that dislike and mistrust of America by Europeans and the world have informed key aspects of public discourse since 9/11.

A careful reading of the studies themselves will reveal a clear progression: What commences with an open antipathy toward George W. Bush soon mutates into a profound distrust of American policy, only to spill over into a serious skepticism about the American people and their values. Here are the titles of the studies and their publication dates: "Bush Unpopular in Europe, Seen as Unilateralist" (August 15, 2001); "America Admired, yet Its New Vulnerability Seen as a Good Thing Say Opinion Leaders. Little Support for Expanding War on Terrorism" (December 19, 2001); "What the World Thinks in 2002: How Global Publics View Their Lives, Their Countries, The World, America" (December 4, 2002); "Among Wealthy Nations . . . U.S. Stands Alone in Its Embrace of Religion" (December 19, 2002); "America's Image Further Erodes, Europeans Want Weaker Ties" (March 18, 2003); "Views of a Changing World, War with Iraq Further Divides Global Publics (June 15, 2003); "Anti-Americanism: Causes and Characteristics" (December 10, 2003); "A Year after Iraq War, Mistrust of America in Europe Even Higher, Muslim Anger Persists" (March 16, 2004); and "American Character Gets Mixed Reviews: U.S. Image Up Slightly, but Still Negative" (June 23, 2005). Seconded by other opinion polls commissioned and/or conducted by the BBC, the German Marshall Fund of the United States, and the Compagnia di San Paolo/Fundação Luso-Americana, to mention just three prominent institutions engaged in such studies, the evidence, I believe, is unmistakable: Eu-

ropeans, like the rest of the world, want to disengage from America.
They want to distance themselves from American politics, mores,
habits, language, culture, food. The acute outburst of Euroskepti-
cism that torpedoed the acceptance of the European Constitution by
the French and the Dutch publics in the spring of 2005 and created
a serious setback for the European project had absolutely no bearing
on the Europeans' overwhelming desire to increase their independence from the United States on matters of security, diplomacy, and
all aspects of international relations. Indeed, as argued in the preceding chapter, the defeat of the proconstitution forces, in France in
particular, can be interpreted as prima facie evidence of the strength
of those political currents to which a European opposition to all
things American has become a politically defining credo.

Nothing describes a general, amorphous, yet pervasive global—
and European—opposition to the United States better than the data
garnered in response to the question: "Right now, the U.S. has the
most powerful military capability in the world. Would you like to
see the U.S. remain the only military superpower or would it be
better if [Europe (ask in all countries outside of Europe)/ the EU
(ask in Europe)], China, or another country became as powerful as
the U.S.?" In literally every single one of the fifteen countries surveyed—except the United States, of course, where 63 percent of
the respondents wished to see the status quo maintained—a decisive
majority wanted to have another country as powerful as the United
States in the world. France led the way among all countries with
85 percent (superseding even Russia with 74 percent), followed by
Germany with 73 percent, the Netherlands with 71 percent, Spain
with 69 percent, and Britain with 58 percent. Tellingly, there was
massive disagreement as to who this new challenger to America's
global power should be. Thus, it is clear that anti-Americanism is
an integral part of an amorphous European and global opposition
to America as "Mr. Big" whom everybody wants to see fall on its
face and cut to size. It is simply undeniable that anti-Americanism
has become a very potent and increasingly legitimate political currency around the world. "They hate us, they really hate us" ex-
claimed the title of a book review in *The New York Times* featuring

two books on anti-Americanism.[23] One of the books analyzed in detail the Pew surveys that were so briefly summarized in this chapter plus other evidence showing the growing depth and breadth of anti-American feelings in virtually all parts of the world. Its senior author is Andrew Kohut, the president of the Pew Research Center.[24] Indeed, in a study summarizing data from 2006—thus not included in the book—Kohut and his colleagues at Pew demonstrate how America's global image has slipped even further (The Pew Global Attitudes Project, "America's Image Slips, But Allies Share U.S. Concern over Iran, Hamas," June 13, 2006). The other book, written by Julia Sweig, argues essentially that if the twentieth century came to be known as the "American century," the twenty-first might very well becoome the "anti-American century."[25] In short, anti-Americanism is a major force which will not fade anytime soon. Europeans perceive America increasingly as a burden, as an unpleasant associate, and as an overbearing competitor rather than as a friend, ally, and protector. At a time of steadily growing competition with the United States, anti-Americanism is in the process of becoming an ideology that helps substantiate an identity for Europe as a growing power bloc. As I will argue in chapter 6, anti-Americanism might very well also contribute to the launching of a common European identity on the levels of sentiment and emotion, if not those of intellect and interest. These developments have been precipitated by the persona and policies of George W. Bush, but they were created by neither. The white heat of anti-Americanism and its "overdrive" phase, which we have been observing since October 2001, might very well abate beginning on January 20, 2009. But they will not disappear or even attain the status quo ante 9/11, let alone the era before the fall of the Berlin Wall. Massive joint interests, as represented particularly by the intertwined economies of these two continents, will never permit the fraying of transatlantic relations. But they will remain rocky and fraught with tensions and recriminations of which anti-Americanism will constitute an integral and quotidian part. Before I proceed to a discussion of anti-Americanism's role in the formation of a European identity, a few words about anti-Americanism's twin—anti-Semitism—are in order. We turn our attention to that topic in chapter 5.

*CHAPTER 5*

------------------------------------------------------

# "Twin Brothers": European Anti-Semitism and Anti-Americanism

Anyone who deals even marginally with anti-Americanism has to be struck by its closeness to the prominent topic of anti-Semitism.[1] I have always viewed the two as close relatives or (to put the point even more figuratively) as first cousins. But my research for the project leading to this book convinced me that the relationship between these two phenomena is even closer than is the case among cousins. André Glucksmann's characterization of the two as "twin brothers" seems more apt. Glucksmann, like myself, sees contemporary anti-Semitism as, among other things, a consequence of as well as a necessary corollary to anti-Americanism and both as essential ingredients of a Europe-wide hatred with a pedigreed history.[2] He writes about the current situation in France and Europe:

> One plus two plus three: From the extreme Left to the extreme Right, everyone in French politics—simple activists, members of parliament, trade unionists, cabinet ministers, and the head of state in unison—is raving against the intervention in Iraq: "Bush equals Sharon equals murderers" is the chant from the street. "Sharon equals Bush equals disregard for international law" is the pronouncement from the salons. The rise of anti-Semitism is really not a result of the Intifada, but rather a twin brother of the wave of anti-Americanism that

has sloshed up onto the coasts of Europe since September 11 and flooded the continent since the Iraq war.[3]

A central theme of this chapter is to discern one of the main characteristics of anti-Semitism in Europe today: its status as an epiphenomenon of anti-Americanism. This feature is, I believe, perhaps the most important component of the "new" anti-Semitism. It is a recent addition to stereotypes reviving both traditional anti-Semitism and the specific element of that decades-old hostility to Israel directed against the existence of an entire country in its capacity as a "collective Jew."

European anti-Semitism, of course, predates anti-Americanism by more than a thousand years. And, of course, there are major differences between these two phenomena at every conceivable level. The most important such difference is the fact that European anti-Semitism motivated the brutal, systematic murder of millions of innocent people and humiliated, ostracized, persecuted, and oppressed people for centuries. In contrast, anti-Americanism, even in its most aggressive, most hate-filled form—with the few exceptions of individual terrorist attacks (and leaving aside conflicts between states in various wars, which I am not including here)—hardly ever led to a loss of human life and was largely restricted to property damage in the form of "America Houses" destroyed or American flags burned for symbolic reasons. Put simply, millions of Jews in Europe were killed, humiliated, mistreated, demeaned, and shunned solely because they were Jews whereas few, if any, Americans ever experienced anywhere near this kind of hardship only on account of their being American. This is an all-or-nothing difference, which places these two European phenomena in completely different explanatory realms and indicates that there is a fundamentally different quality, indeed a principally different status, to anti-Americanism and anti-Semitism.

But this does not mean that the two cannot be analyzed and discussed together, especially since they have gone hand in hand with each other since at least the early nineteenth century. Let us put it this way: One can easily write about European anti-Semitism without ever talking about anti-Americanism. The converse, I maintain, is impossible.

## Anti-Semitism—a European Phenomenon

Just as with anti-Americanism, when it comes to anti-Semitism I am firmly convinced that, in principle, there are (or were) no country-specific differences within Europe, even if, from time to time, different countries produce specific intensities and expressions that motivate different forms of social violence and are also partly manifested in different functions. European anti-Semitism's conceptual structures, its symbolic language, and its essential content have been remarkably similar in Europe both diachronically and synchronically. To be sure, countries—even regions, social groups, and cultures within countries—differed in terms of their motivations for and implementations of anti-Semitism. To give one current example, German postwar anti-Semitism has always been associated with a special defense mechanism against a sense of guilt; that is, prejudices and irritations have been expressed against Jews, among other reasons, because Jews embody a constant reminder of past national crimes and therefore of a feeling of "national shame" that can impede Germans' unbroken identification with their nation. This phenomenon does not alter the content of German anti-Semitism one bit and renders it identical to Romanian or French anti-Semitism. However, its motives are obviously specific to Germany—to be more precise still, the former *West* Germany. One might mention other such country-specific nuances in the manifestations of anti-Semitism across Europe even though conceptually, emotionally, historically, structurally, and content-wise anti-Semitism was and is a wholly pan-European construct.

It is precisely for this reason that the Nazis were so successful in carrying out the extermination of the Jews, although the murder of European Jews emanated from Germany and has to be seen against the background of a specific German constellation, and of Germany's prewar political culture and hegemonic self-image as a "blood nation." In addition, of course, without the Wehrmacht and the entire apparatus of a modern industrial state, there could never have been such a quick and efficient effort at sorting out millions of people from their societies across an entire continent, deporting them to death camps, and then—often within a matter of hours—killing them with industrial precision and logic. But the project of exterminating the Jews was basically just the logical apex, the compelling goal, of a brutal European anti-Semitism that had lasted at least a millennium. The Shoah was, at the same time, the culmination of a European process of repeatedly mobilized and institutionalized degradation, exclusion, and persecution of Jews that had been the common property of everyday culture on the continent since 1010 at the latest.[4] If anti-Semitism had been exclusively—or even just primarily—a German phenomenon rather than the established common property of Europe that it was, the Nazis would never have received so much support for their genocide from the populations of those countries occupied by or allied with them.

Obviously, there were different degrees of cooperation and participation, as well as resistance, something Hannah Arendt had already described in detail in her book *Eichmann in Jerusalem*[5]: Just as with anti-Americanism, there have always been country- and time-specific variations in the manifestation of European anti-Semitism, which sometimes appeared stronger in Great Britain, and then in France; initially vehement in Spain, later in Poland, Russia, Romania, Hungary, Austria, and Germany. At first its foundation was chiefly religious and economic; then, starting with the Spanish Inquisition, clearly racist components were added. (The political dimension of anti-Semitism was ubiquitous.) There is not a single country in Europe—not Ireland in the West, not the Scandinavian countries in the North, Italy and Greece in the South, not the Ukraine and Russia in the East—in which anti-Semitism has not, over the centuries, assumed a significant role in a very concrete manner in the everyday life of its citizens. Regardless of whether the hegemonic religion has been Roman Catholic, Protestant, or Greek Orthodox, whether the modes of production were mainly agrarian or industrial, or whether politics was shaped by a feudal aristocracy or a parliamentary-oriented bourgeoisie, they all knew and used anti-Semitism. Of course, there were enormous differences between the lethal violence of pogroms in czarist Russia and the snobbish ostracism of London clubs that refused to accept Jewish members. But these were differences in the manifestation and exercise of this prejudice and hatred, not in its conception and essence.

Already in the seventeenth century, well before the establishment of the American republic, the divergent paths that religion took in these two settings—and that still differentiate the United States from Europe perhaps more than any other single social, political, or cultural factor[6]—also had a major bearing on the development of anti-Semitism in these two respective societies, as well as on its role in their relationship with each other. Whereas Europe's religious life continued to be ruled by a deeply anti-Semitic Catholic Church in the continent's geographic center and its south, a state-oriented, equally anti-Semitic Protestantism mainly of the Lutheran variety in its north (though one would need to differentiate the vehemence of anti-Semitism practiced by German Lutheranism as opposed to its much milder Danish and Swedish variants), and a structurally very similar Orthodoxy in its eastern regions, America's religious life featured two characteristics that Europe never had, and the ramifications of which Europeans fail to comprehend to this day: First, religion in America was decentralized and local. The search for political freedom in America was—as Tocqueville so well understood, in contrast to other Europeans of his time and so many of Europe's current elites—inextricably tied to the search for religious freedom, thus giving religion and religious vocabulary in American politics a significantly different meaning from what both have had in Europe. Second, it featured a Protestantism that professed its great admiration for the Jews, indeed, one that saw itself as a close relative of the Jews, whose ancient writings and customs it extolled. This, after all, was the world in which biblical names such as Elijah, Jeremiah, Jeddediah, and Josiah became commonplace. The point is that from well before the founding of the American republic, the framework wherein people related to Jews and Judaism was profoundly different in America from what it had been in Europe. Be it Arthur Herzberg, Seymour Martin Lipset, Ben Halpern, or Marshall Sklare, and most of all Irving Howe, all experts trying to explain the experience of Jews in the United States via an explicit comparison to its counterpart in Europe come to one overarching conclusion: put succinctly, in the words of one of Ben Halpern's fine articles, "America is different." Despite the uninterrupted—sometimes vehement—existence of anti-Semitism throughout the history of the United States, very few Jewish individuals in America were ever murdered solely because they were Jews, and no mass killings of Jews at the hands of their non-Jewish neighbors ever occurred in America, which few, if any, European countries can claim in their history.[7] Indeed, there is simply no contest as to where the Jews met with greater acceptance, security, even appreciation between America and Europe. "To find evidence of serious anti-Semitism in America for much of the time Jews have lived here, you need to put on knee pads, and go searching in the nooks and crannies of history," wrote David Klinghoffer in reviewing two books on anti-Semitism in America.[8]

It was not until the late nineteenth century—coinciding precisely and not by accident with the rise of what became known as "political anti-Semitism"[9]—that anti-Semitism began to accompany European anti-Americanism in a systematic and regular manner and these two isms became the twins in European thought that they remain today. It was the fear and critique of capitalism that brought these two resentments together. America and the Jews were seen as paragons of modernity: money-driven, profit-hungry, urban, universalistic, individualistic, mobile, rootless, and hostile to established traditions and values. That it was anxiety caused by this modernity that linked Jews and Americans at this juncture of European resentment is best borne out by the fact that Jewish immigration to the United States had not yet reached the large numbers that it would twenty years later, and that American power in the world was still rather ephemeral. In other words, it was not the actually existing United States and its Jews that were feared and disdained, but the combination of Judaism and Americanism as concepts and social trends. After World War I, the view of the Jews as rulers of America became pronounced. It was at this juncture that the notions of Jewish Wall Street, Jewish Hollywood, Jewish jazz, in other words, of a thoroughly "Jewified" America, became commonplace. It was at this time that all the forerunners for current codes, such as the "East Coast," were permanently established. From then on, Jews and America became incxtricably intertwined, not only as representatives of modernity but also as holders of actual power. America was powerful and the Jews in it even more so. One of the standard staples of European anti-Semitism has always been to impute much more power to Jews than they actually have. Moreover, what makes this putative power even more potent is that it is believed to be clandestine and cliquish. With America's strength massively growing after World War I, power as a unifying notion between Jews and America became more pronounced and also lasting. The hostile perception of this alleged link became absolutely integral to National Socialism.

Things appeared to change after the end of World War II, the Holocaust, the establishment of Israel, and the Cold War. American power, though still massively resented, became a much-needed protector against the Soviet Union, its allies, and Communism. Probably for the first time in over a thousand years, the Holocaust rendered overt anti-Semitism socially unacceptable among Europe's elites. And Jews for the very first time in nearly two thousand years actually attained real power by dint of running a state. While these structural changes substantially altered the tone and the substance of the discourse about Jews and America in Europe, the two remained as intertwined as ever.

It is certainly also no accident that a massive intervention into Europe by the United States—for the second time in the course of the last century—was required in order to make the pan-European language of anti-Semitism that had prevailed for a millennium unacceptable, both socially and politically. I am not arguing that the United States in any manner intervened in Europe to impede or alleviate European anti-Semitism. But the defeat of European fascism and German National Socialism by the Red Army and the Western powers dominated by the American armed forces led for the first time in Europe's history to political regimes and a hege-

monic discourse in which anti-Semitism became basically illegitimate. This post-Holocaust concordance lasted almost exactly fifty
years. In my view it is therefore no accident that anti-Semitism in
some form or another is showing its face again in Europe just at
the time when the United States is in the process of withdrawing
politically and militarily from Europe. Again, the correlation between a gradual reappearance of certain anti-Semitic tropes in Europe's acceptable discourse and the disengagement of the United
States from the continent might be tangential and epiphenomenal—
just as was the pushing of anti-Semitism to Western Europe's discursive fringes with America's reentry into Europe following its destruction of fascism and National Socialism as just mentioned—but
it most certainly is not spurious. I do not know if I would go as far
as Jean-Claude Milner, who views the destruction of the Jews as
a necessary condition for European unification, and, by extension,
European unification itself as the result of this singular crime. However, I have no doubt that anti-Semitism is assuming an important
European function—as a pan-European discourse steeped in tradition, and (above all) as an important ingredient in the European
emotional repertoire—just when the establishment of a new European proto- or quasi-state has become (and is likely to remain) a
political reality in Europe's everyday life.[10]

## Anti-Americanism and Anti-Semitism as Joint Symbols

A visit to virtually any sizable public protest, conference, convention, or gathering of any kind that featured antiglobalization as one
of its themes focused virtually all its criticism and anger toward the
United States. This indeed makes sense since without any question
the United States has been first among equals in this—partly—new
stage of capitalism currently known as globalization. Two related
phenomena in this milieu are striking: first, the virtual absence of
any criticism, let alone venom that is reserved for the United States,
for any of its major capitalist partners and competitors in this global-

ization process; second, the centrality of Israel as the protesters' co-target with the United States. Why is this so?

Why do Britain, Germany, France, Canada, Italy—the other members of the Group of Eight (G8), including Europe, which enjoys an added seat at this club's table—or China and increasingly India, for that matter, not engender anywhere near the anger among the protestors that they have regularly exhibited toward the United States, and well before the advent of the Bush administration? Why is the number of American flags burned and defaced at these occasions massively outnumbering that of German, Italian, French, or European flags, which I—in my limited experience, to be sure—have never seen abused on any of these occasions? Concomitantly, what is the reason behind the burning and defiling of Israeli flags at these gatherings, in fewer numbers than the abuse of American flags, but still? Why is Israel such a prominent object of vilification at these meetings and demonstrations? Surely, countries like Germany, France, Canada—not to mention Europe—are much bigger players in the globalization process than is Israel. Why not protest against Saudi Arabia or any of the oil-exporting countries that, arguably, play a much greater role in the global economy than does Israel?

When José Bové, a figurehead of the antiglobalization movement, visited Palestinians in Ramallah in the spring of 2002—instead of traveling to Gujarat, where many more Muslims had been killed in pogroms by Hindu mobs—the primary concern was not to demonstrate solidarity with an oppressed people. As the reincarnation of Pierre Poujade, the right-wing populist defender of small shopkeepers and other "modernization losers" in France of the 1950s, and the media-savvy representative of a global Poujadism, Bové's political disposition includes populist elements much closer to the convictions of French protofascism than to the Left (whether old or new). But none of these traditions is what drove Bové toward Ramallah and made him—like other opponents of globalization—a fierce enemy of Israel. Unlike Poujade's anti-Semitism, which was solely driven by the classic European Right's disdain for Jews as soulless capitalists and brutal modernizers, Bové—at least to my knowledge—has never uttered anything that could even vaguely be termed anti-Semitic. So Bové's primary driving force in this matter was a deeply held antipathy toward Israel that emanates first and foremost with Israel's association with the United States, the world's evil globalizer and builder of McDonald's restaurants, one of which Bové bulldozed to the ground, making him instantly a perennial favorite of the antiglobalization movement worldwide. It was decidedly not anti-Semitism in its conventional sense. It is Israel's power sui generis and its close relations with the United States that have rendered this one Near Eastern country into the covillain for many globalization opponents. Yet, the West European Left's hatred for Israel did not remain self-contained. As I will argue, it has indeed been the anti-Zionism of the European Left, emanating from the Six-Day War of 1967, that has been the most prolific mediator between anti-Americanism and anti-Semitism.

There is no need here to delve more deeply into the emergence of the atrocious anti-Semitism that accompanied international meetings in Durban, Porto Alegre, and Davos. But the golden calf incident in Davos in January 2003 deserves brief mention of a tone that has become endemic in this milieu. That this is the case is best attested to by a need for some "attac" members in Austria and Germany to take an open stance against the pervasive anti-Semitism among its ranks in which the Davos event—among others—appears as a case in point and which links the self-identified left-radical "attac" uncomfortably close to the world of anti-Semitic tropes traditionally more common among the radical Right.[11]

At the Davos demonstration one participant wore a Donald Rumsfeld mask over his head and a yellow six-pointed star with the label "Sheriff" on his chest, while his colleague, equipped with an Ariel Sharon mask, was swinging a club. These two characters were accompanied by one group of demonstrators disguised as "capitalist pigs" and another masquerading as "pig priests." The whole ensemble was dancing around the golden calf. "It is interesting," writes Marcus Hammerschmitt,

> that an ensemble patched together from Carnival costumes (in part, with clear references to animals), the golden calf, a Star of David

straight out of Nazi propaganda, and some masks of politicians is so
brazenly used to mark the enemy, because the demonstrators assume
that the message is already understood: Jewish Americans, or American Jews, worship money and gold and protect it with (animalistic)
power, as only they know how.

Simultaneously confusing and clear, both unfathomably deep and
barbarically simple, as only authentic credentials of anti-Semitic
mania can be, this procession reveals not only the abysmal stupidity of
the demonstrators, but also the relationship (seldom clearer) between
anti-Semitism and anti-Americanism: The idiots of Davos, who probably still see themselves as leftists, stick onto the person portraying
Rumsfield (in lovely conformity with Iraqi government newspapers)
the yellow star and inscribe the star with the word "Sheriff" in order
to dispel any last doubts about their idiocy: For them, everything is
one and the same, Americans are Jews, all Jews are like Sharon, a Star
of David is the same as the star on a sheriff's badge, the golden calf is
a Jewish calf, it's all the same. The onlookers, so they suspect, will
certainly understand just what and who is intended; the main point is
that the demon dancing around the idol has a signet.[12]

It took merely three years for some of these sentiments to traverse
the seemingly massive gap between the demonstrators' snowy fields
and the posh digs inhabited by the world's movers and shakers. At
the Davos conference in January 2006, a two-page article headlined
"Boycott Israel" was published in the conference's official magazine,
*Global Agenda*. It denounced Zionism as a "19th century style chauvinistic, ethnocentric . . . nationalistic response to prevalent European chauvinistic, ethnocentric nationalisms" and viewed it as a
"now-outdated European colonial model." The article ended with
an appeal for a "global civil society" that needed to arise as a "movement against Zionism" and "against Israeli Apartheid."[13] To be sure,
Klaus Schwab, the founder of the Davos conclave, rejected this
article's content in the strongest possible terms and offered a public apology at the forum's full session for its publication. Still,
one would be hard put to imagine finding a comparable article
in this magazine on any of the other ills befalling the world's poor
and oppressed.

Lest the reader think that this overlap between overt anti-Americanism and anti-Semitism remains confined to the most extreme elements of the left, here are two examples from the jewel of Europe's established social democracy. In his perfectly justified defense of the "German model," Franz Müntefering, chairman of the SPD, invoked an analogy of American hedge funds to "locust firms" that descend anonymously upon innocent, well-meaning German companies only to strip them of their assets and suck them dry. The SPD's "locust" campaign of April 2005 met with great popularity among the party's rank and file as well as the public at large. Müntefering's remarks were reinforced by an article in one of Germany's leading left-liberal magazines, *Stern*, in which seven of these "locust firms" were listed by name, some of them recognizably Jewish.[14]

Not to be outdone, Germany's most prominent labor union, IG Metall, featured an article on the same subject in the May 2005 issue of its magazine *metall*. Titled "U.S. Firmen in Deutschland: Die Aussauger" (U.S. Companies in Germany: The [Blood]suckers), the cover depicts a mosquito doffing an Uncle Sam–like hat with the American flag, grinning ravenously under its huge nose, revealing a gold-filled tooth. It carries an American-style attaché case and is ready to descend upon the hapless German economy. The article inside the magazine carries the title "Die Plünderer sind da" (The Plunderers Are Here).

In the fifty-seven-year history of *metall*, there has never been a more successful issue than this one featuring a barely disguised anti-Semitic cover and a thinly veiled anti-Semitic feature article. Although, in both the SPD's locust campaign and IG Metall's mosquito followup, anti-Semitism had to be conveyed somewhat subtly, this was not the case with anti-Americanism.[15] Whereas the caricatures' noses were only moderately crooked and the gold teeth only visible upon a close look, the symbols of the American flag and Uncle Sam–like top hats are unmistakable.

The fact that the new anti-Semitism based on hostility toward Israel goes hand in hand with anti-Americanism among major portions of the European Left is confirmed by the first report on anti-Semitism in fifteen European countries published by the European

Union Monitoring Centre on Racism and Xenophobia (Europäische Stelle zur Beobachtung von Rassismus und Fremdenfeindlichkeit) in Vienna. In the analytical section of the report, before
the data from the individual country studies are presented, the text
entitled "EUMC Report on Anti-Semitism" says unambiguously
that the European Left's acute antipathy toward Israel is partially
concealing anti-Semitism in both tone and content, and that these
emotions cannot be separated from aversion to America.[16]

> The supposedly close ties between the U.S. and Israel have contrib-
> uted additional motives to growing anti-Semitic attitudes that one
> finds on the radical Left. . . . The United States of America are also
> attacked most severely by the peace movement, the antiglobalization
> movement, and some developing countries. Elements of the radical
> Right join in and categorize the U.S. as an imperial power acting
> as Israel's protector. Thus, for example, many people in German-
> speaking countries especially use the term "East Coast" as a synonym
> for a supposedly total Jewish influence on the U.S. and its politics.
> Sympathizers with these extremes immediately understand the
> meaning of this word without additional explanations. They can use
> it incessantly without running the danger of violating any antidis-
> crimination laws in a particular state. This example makes it clear
> how closely anti-Americanism and anti-Semitism are bound up with
> each other.[17]

The kind of anti-Semitism linked to the struggle against globalization represents a meeting point between the Right and Left of a
kind that has not existed so openly since the heyday of National
Bolshevism. The intensity of hatred against Israel has not least of
all to do with a perception of Israel as America's proxy, as a de facto
constituent of the United States—as well as vice versa. One can rail
against Israel because it is powerful and belongs to an even greater
power, the United States. But one can also rail against Israel because
it happens to be a Jewish state. Before I delineate the key features
in my view that render anti-Semitism, in both its old-fashioned and
current manifestations, an integral part of anti-Americanism, a brief
presentation of what I mean to constitute anti-Semitism is in order.

## Some Conceptual Contours of Anti-Semitism, Anti-Zionism, and Their Interaction with Each Other and with Anti-Americanism

As a preamble to my short presentation on the essential ingredients of anti-Semitism, permit me to state that I take Jean Paul Sartre's dictum about anti-Semitism at face value: Anti-Semitism is rarely, if ever, the Jews' problem. Instead, they are merely the constant recipients of its hatred, though never its cause. The definition of such a complex phenomenon as anti-Semitism is actually quite simple: It is a persistent prejudice against individual Jews and the Jewish people as a collective that reaches many disparate areas of social life, that faults Jews for ills that they did not commit, that blames Jews for wrongs in the world, that is—like anti-Americanism—antonymous: Jews are too strong and too weak; too rich and too poor; too radical and too conservative; too assimilated and universalistic, but also too sectarian, clubby, and particularistic. Above all, anti-Semitism is an obsession that blames all Jews for evil deeds, dangerous acts, and subversive behavior independent of how each individual Jew—or even Jews as a collective—behaves in reality. Because of their detrimental character and role in society, anti-Semites want Jews changed, converted, in some fashion "tamed," or— if these Jewish traits are deemed incorrigible—deported, expelled, or annihilated.

Conceptually and in principle, anti-Semitism, anti-Zionism, and criticizing Israel have absolutely nothing to do with each other. Anti-Semitism is a prejudice against all Jews. By contrast, the other two are political points of view. Criticizing Israel's policies comprises open disagreement and vocal disapproval of strategies and tactics employed by the Israeli government in any field of state action. Anti-Zionism denies the appropriateness of the need or desire for the Jewish people to articulate their political will and identity in the form of a state anywhere, but particularly where it has been located since 1948. Surely, the Bundists of Eastern Europe of the late nineteenth and the first half of the twentieth century, who were bitter opponents of the Zionists and their vision of a Jewish state, were in no way anti-Semitic but clearly anti-Zionist. Today, too, it is possible to take positions against the existence of the state of Israel without thus being ipso facto anti-Semitic. The (in)famous epigones of the legendary Rabbi Joel Teitelbaum from the Romanian-Hungarian town of Satu Mare/Szatmar (hence known to this day as "Satmars") deny the existence of Israel. The Neturei Karta group of ultra-orthodox Jews allies itself with some of Israel's most implacable foes; nonetheless, I would not classify them as anti-Semitic, even though (as I said at the beginning of this book), being a Jew does not a priori exempt someone from anti-Semitism. In fact there are Jews who are anti-Semitic, alongside many others whose world view is anti-Zionist, and then there are yet others who are both. Anti-Zionism per se bears absolutely no ill feelings toward Jews either as individuals or as a collective.

But as Mitchell Cohen argues, "the overlap between anti-Semitic and anti-Zionist discourses today is considerable, and it is especially striking at a time when many intellectuals, notably the post-modernist Left and post-colonial theorists, base their work on the very notion of 'discourse,' contending that clusters of assumptions, embedded in our languages and cultures, pre-select how we think about the world, and mesh the production of knowledge and power."[18]

Indeed, there exists an anti-Zionism that in fact either is anti-Semitic or functions as a vehicle and a protective cover for anti-Semitism. By the first I mean the anti-Zionism that avails itself of anti-Semitism's classical themes to stigmatize—and demonize—the current state of Israel or any sovereign construct for Jews. Commonly used contemporary tropes like Israelis (and Jews) as Nazis, Israelis (and Jews) as Christ killers, as usurers, bloodsuckers, exploiters, wild animals, and subhumans fit this bill of a clearly anti-Semitic anti-Zionism. In this form of anti-Zionism, all the historical ingredients used to demonize Jews are simply transferred to the state of Israel, which—in the standard diction of anti-Semitism—behaves Jewlike by grasping for global power (the theme of globalization), exhibiting Old Testament–like (pre-Christian) vengefulness of "an eye for an eye and a tooth for a tooth" kind, bamboozles the world as cunning Jews are wont to do, extorts money from hapless victims who have been fooled into seeing the Jews as victims, exhibits capitalist greed, and, of course, indulges in constant brutality toward the weak. Israel thus becomes a sort of new Jew, a collective Jew among the world's nations. Anti-Zionism mutates into a magical construct that massively exaggerates the actual power of Israel and Jews and imputes motives and capabilities that are nonsensical in the real world but all the more potent in an imagined one. The actual fear on the part of some Chileans and Argentines that Israel and the Jews might well occupy Patagonia for a new Jewish homeland is to give one egregious but not exceptional example of this mental construct.

But there is a second—and related—dimension in which a heavy dosage of anti-Zionism, though not in and of itself anti-Semitic, contributes to the reentry of anti-Semitism into discursive respectability. By constantly singling out Israel in a disproportionate manner and by having rendered the term "Zionism" into a pejorative expression, European publics can rightfully wonder whether this awful stuff that guides Jews in Israel might not actually have *some* relationship to Jews in Europe and the world. After all, most Jews in the world do support Israel in some manner, and cliquish as Jews are believed to be, surely this Zionism must have some ill connections to Jews outside of Israel. Enter the old—and revived—anti-Semitism. Anti-Zionism facilitates the acceptability of an anti-Semitic discourse. It renders anti-Semitism excusable. It nibbles away at anti-Semitism's marginality in Europe's post-Holocaust norms. In short, anti-Zionism offers a convenient cover and a vehicle for the reemergence of anti-Semitic sentiments in a world where these lay dormant though—surely—were never moribund.

The question of whether there is a non-anti-Semitic anti-Zionism among the European public—a European anti-Zionism that singles out this one small state in the Middle East in order to call its existence into question in a fundamental way—is, alas, largely a theoretical one. Today it is hard to find examples in European public opinion of a non-anti-Semitic singling out of Israel, the Jewish state, for exclusion from the community of nations.

As a very cautiously worded study by the European Union Monitoring Centre on Racism and Xenophobia states: "It needs to be carefully observed whether a double morality is being construed in which Israel is judged according to entirely different standards as are other states, whether false historical parallels are drawn (like the comparison to National Socialism), and whether anti-Semitic myths and stereotypes are being used in order to characterize Israeli policy."[19] One of the finest empirical studies on precisely this point— to ascertain to what degree there is an actual overlap between anti-Semitic and anti-Israeli attitudes among Europeans, in this case Germans—was conducted by Andreas Zick and Beate Kuepper.[20] The researchers posed questions designed to test the level of the respondents' anti-Semitism and what they determined to be anti-Semitic criticisms of Israel. Among these were such staples as the myth of excessive Jewish influence; the Jews deserve the hatred and persecution that they face on account of their actions; the Jews use the Holocaust for their own enrichment and their advantage; the Jews identify more with Israel than with Germany; the Jews behave in Israel just like the Nazis behaved toward the Jews in the Third Reich. They then also constructed a measure in which they assessed the respondents' criticism of Israeli policies that could in no way be construed as anti-Semitic. Among these were statements such as "I get furious when I think how the Israelis treat the Palestinians"; and "It is unjust that the Israelis take away the Palestinians' land." The study's sobering finding reaches the following conclusion: Only 11 percent of the respondents disagreed with all seven indicators of anti-Semitism, and 4 percent agreed with all. By extension, 89 percent of the respondents agreed with at least one of the indicators. Most important, however, was the finding that 90 percent of those respondents who agreed with the totally non-anti-Semitic criticisms of Israeli policy also agreed with at least one of the seven indicators of anti-Semitism. The authors conclude that a totally non-anti-Semitic criticism of Israel is certainly conceptually possible but empirically rather rare. Above all, as the title of their study indicates (" 'it is their own fault if one dislikes them' or how one dismantles one's prejudices"), the hostility toward Israel does not so much serve as a criticism of its policies but rather as a shill to shed one's antipathies toward Jews and give these old feelings a new legitimacy.

Of course, there are also plenty of anti-Semites who neither criticize policies of the Israeli government nor openly challenge Israel's right to exist. Conceptually, the lines of demarcation are rather clear and easy to understand, but in practice there are always overlapping and opaque grey zones that make the entire situation complicated and highly charged. The various actors' intentions and the nuances of their actions are often the only indicators allowing any evaluation of their respective positions. And even with the most meticulous attention to everyone participating in the discourse, there are inevitably misinterpretations and misunderstandings. This is hardly likely to change in the future, for the simple reason that the complex "Israel" cannot be completely decoupled from the complex "Jews," and also (and especially) because the latter, like the culturally and historically layered "images of Jews" embedded in European consciousness, is not so easily negated as an integral component of Europe's (and America's) history. The *New York Times* columnist Thomas Friedman contributed these wise words to the discourse about the American Left's complex relationship to Israel at the country's elite universities: "Criticizing Israel is not anti-Semitic, and it is harmful to assert as much. But singling out Israel for scolding . . . is anti-Semitic, and not admitting so is dishonest."[21]

In what follows, I proceed from the assumption that, in Europe, Jews are frequently what people have in mind when they strike out at Israel, and that this is by no means restricted to those anti-Semitic anti-Zionists who deny Jews and Israel a right to existence and demonize them in toto. In this context I find one of the Reverend Martin Luther King Jr.'s statements about the manifest and hidden dimensions of anti-Zionism in the West as valid today as it was in the late 1960s: "When people criticize Zionists, they mean Jews; you are talking anti-Semitism."[22] When it comes to anti-Zionism and hostility toward Israel, we have long been dealing with a new, legitimated form of anti-Semitism that is coded and, rather than being stuck with the stigma of Jew-baiting, conveys moral nobility, a sense of moral superiority toward the alleged perpetrators de jour, America and Israel.

The substance and tone of public debates really matter. These debates create "frames" that influence political behavior and can also contribute to enduring elements of political culture. Debates shift the boundaries of legitimate discursive space in politics since they define the realm of acceptable terms and sanction those who violate them. Debates also shape language and create new code words for old ideas, including prejudices and antipathies. Above all, the ensuing changes in discursive space alter how elites and ordinary citizens discuss and then think about a topic. Thus, the tone of these debates reflects broader ideological shifts in politics and society.[23]

## Anti-Semitism and Israel in the European Discourse

Here are a few key ingredients that—in my view—exhibit anti-Semitic dimensions in the criticisms of Israel. They thus go beyond the first category of anti-Zionism, which does not see the creation of a Jewish state as a political option (or solution) for the Jewish people, and constitute the second version of anti-Zionism, in which anti-Semitic tropes are used to delegitimate Israel directly or—conversely—to use anti-Zionism as a convenient cover and vehicle for the reentry of a certain anti-Semitic discourse from Europe's political fringes to its mainstream.

1. The disproportional nature of the quantity and quality of criticism of Israel compared with other countries—the phenomenon of "singling out" and the problem of double standards.
2. The pejorative inclusion of Israel in protests and issues that—like those against the International Monetary Fund in Washington or the already-mentioned annual meetings in Davos—have nothing to do prima facie with Israel. Here, of course, we are dealing with an attendant symptom of anti-Americanism, for the main target of these actions is always the United States. Jews and Americans as the global capitalists, as the Wall Street financiers who suck the world dry: Israel in this case becomes the collective Jew whose oppressive and conspiratorial power via capitalism and imperialism is omnipresent and omnipotent.

3. The constant comparison and equation of Israel with Nazism and the crimes of the Holocaust, the murder of six million Jews like the accompanying demonizing of Israeli actions by invoking Auschwitz with regularity. The rapid accumulation of analogies between Israelis and Nazis in a broad variety of texts in newspapers and journals; it has become standard operating procedure in this new discourse among the British and Continental left-liberal milieu regarding Israel to equate the Star of David with the swastika or with SS runes in caricatures or on posters and placards, and to depict Sharon as Hitler or a Nazi.[24] In Portugal the prominent Nobel Prize winner for literature, José Saramago, compared the Israeli blockade of the Palestinian city Ramallah with Auschwitz.[25]

4. The utilization of classic anti-Semitic depictions and stereotypes like Christ-killing or ritual murder, of pronounced "Jewish" characteristics like hooked noses, hunched backs, and Stars of David.[26] The massive growth of caricatures, cartoons, and other depictions that use the Star of David—incidentally an ancient religious symbol, analogous to the cross, and not a political symbol—to designate Israeli soldiers, tanks, airplanes, and other military equipment and aggressive actions. Brief descriptions of three cartoons—from Britain, Italy, and Greece—should convey this point clearly. All three papers are highly respected publications in their respective countries: On January 27, 2003, the *Independent* in Britain published a cartoon showing Ariel Sharon eating a baby. The newspaper's caricature was modeled on Francisco Goya's world-famous painting of Saturn devouring his own children. In spite of protests, the commission that handles complaints against the press in Great Britain found that there was nothing wrong with the cartoon. Not only that, but the drawing was awarded the "Political Cartoon of the Year" prize for 2003 by the Political Cartoon Society of the United Kingdom. On April 3, 2002, in the reputable Turin newspaper *La Stampa*, there appeared a cartoon clearly alluding to the old anti-Semitic prejudice about Jews as Christ-killers. We see an Israeli tank—designated, of course, by a large Star of David on its turret—whose gun is fixed on a manger in which a small boy with a halo is saying: "They can't possibly be coming in order to kill me a second time." A cartoon

from April 7, 2002, in the newspaper *Ethnos*, close to the pan-Helle-nist Socialist party PASOK, showed two Israeli soldiers in Nazi uniforms with Stars of David on their helmets. They are stabbing daggers into the bodies of small children, from which blood is spurting. One soldier says to the other: "Don't feel guilty, my brother, we weren't in Auschwitz and Dachau in order to suffer, but to learn." Frequently there are similar cartoons in other newspapers from the PASOK camp, such as *Eleftherotypia*, *Avriani*, and *Ta Nea*. All four papers have trotted out stories reflecting the exact verbal equivalents of the images in those cartoons. *Eleftherotypia* talks about "Israeli Nazis" and *Ta Nea* sees the Israelis as "worthy successors of Hitler."

An integral part of any denunciation and stigmatization is their constant denial by those that practice it. Very few racists ever admit that they are racist; and few of the voices that use any of these anti-Semitic tropes to denounce and stigmatize Israel will ever admit to harboring anything but the most benign views of Jews as individuals and the Jewish people. This, as we shall later see, is particularly true in today's virtuous Europe. Being an anti-Semite puts one clearly beyond the pale of the acceptable; being anti-Israeli places one at the core of the current empathies and sympathies among millions of Europeans.

## Characteristics of an "Acceptable" Anti-Semitism in Contemporary Europe

1. There exists a steady trivialization of anti-Semitism in today's Europe: Anti-Semitism, what is that, after all? "You are being oversensitive, touchy, paranoid," one often hears in reply from people who would never be as forgiving with any other kind of prejudice and hatred. This monster doesn't even exist, and if there are occasional encroachments, then these are just a few isolated incidents of property damage by errant youngsters. The fuss about anti-Semitism is either Jewish hysteria or—worse and more probable—a Jewish conspiracy in order to deny and choke off justified and much-needed criticism of Israel.

Here is one relatively useful gauge of the Europe-wide situation on anti-Semitism: There are a few European countries—Finland, Ireland, Portugal, and Luxemburg—where there has been practically no violence against Jewish persons or institutions. Jewish citizens and Israeli offices have received threatening and abusive letters, e-mails, and telephone calls in these countries, but otherwise there have been no major incidents. Then there is—on the diametrically opposite pole—a group of states in which there has been considerable, and steadily growing, violence against both Jewish people and institutions. This group is led by France, followed by Belgium and Holland. Germany, Sweden, and Great Britain fall in between these two poles, although in these countries, as in the previous group, there has been a great deal of verbal aggression against Jews. Finally, there is a group including Spain, Greece, Italy, and Austria that has experienced far fewer acts of violence than France or Germany, but where the media and the public tolerate and even cultivate an especially blatant anti-Semitic discourse. Anti-Semitic views in these countries are also widespread and considered legitimate among the population at large.[27]

2. Warding off guilt: Anti-Semitism was and is something done by the extreme Right. These new outrages are the machinations of neo-fascist groups. It is always the same right-wing radical youths, who cannot stand Muslims and Jews and attack them on occasion.

3. Sympathy with the perpetrators: We are dealing with poorly integrated youngsters from the bleak concrete deserts of the Parisian suburbs and their British counterparts, whose lives were ruined by the dominant order. This is the only way to understand their outrages against Jews and Jewish institutions; by no means is one entitled to situate these perpetrators in proximity to fascism or stigmatize them as the heirs to Vichy or other former right-wing regimes.[28]

## Israel, Anti-Semitism, and the European
## Left-Liberal Discourse

By the late 1960s, Israel became little more than an extension of American power to many, especially on Europe's political Left. Is-

rael was disliked, especially by the Left, not so much because it was
Jewish but because it was American. And as such it was powerful.
This in no way means to exculpate some of the radical European
Left's hatred for Israel on purely anti-Semitic grounds. Martin
Kloke's detailed study on the German Left's anti-Semitism has irre-
futably been corroborated by Wolfgang Kraushaar's work on the
"Tupamaros West Berlin," Europe's first urban guerilla group, that
had planted a bomb in West Berlin's Jewish Community Center to
explode on November 9, 1969, during that center's commemoration
festivities for Kristallnacht's thirty-first anniversary when the center
was packed with hundreds of Jewish men, women, and children.[29]
The attempt failed merely due to a technical glitch. As Kraushaar
documents, the leader of the Tupamaros West Berlin used openly
anti-Semitic language of the foulest sort, and anti-Semitism was indeed part of this milieu's quotidian discourse. What failed in West
Berlin succeeded one year later in the Jewish old-age home in Munich in which seven members died in the fire-bombing of that institution. And Ulrike Meinhof's (still an iconic figure to many European leftists and progressives) open rejoicing at the slaughtering of
the Israeli athletes at the Munich Olympic Games two years later
also bore straightforward anti-Semitic tropes.

America and the Jews were always suspect and hated among the
European Right and by conservatives as representatives of an unstoppable modernity. But this is not the chief tenor of hostility toward Israel in today's European public. Naturally, traditional anti-
Semitic stereotypes are always seeping into the mix when Israel is
portrayed as a particularly evil and deceptive power, and when it is
repeatedly held responsible for a "conflagration" in the Middle East
and for terrible, "genocidal" crimes, which are often called to mind
in the media using key words ("Sabra and Shatila," "Jenin") that
function as symbolic representations of or ciphers for Israel's purportedly essentialist, incorrigible maliciousness.[30] It is worth won-
dering, in the context of these ubiquitously known and recognized
concepts, why it is that the former two are the only still remembered
massacres of many such events in the decade-long Lebanese civil
war, and why the latter's depiction of the Israeli Army's massacre of

thousands of Palestinian civilians, so widely reported by the European media, has long been exposed as a fraud. Europeans also increasingly resort to traditional anti-Semitic images to delegitimate and demonize Israel on behalf of "appeasement," of accommodation, of reasonableness, of countering a bellicose agent that not only oppresses a weaker Third World nation but that—just like the United States—actively endangers Europeans' well-being. So there is also a self-interested motive among Europeans to criticize Israel, not only an altruistic one.[31]

There is an additional reason why the anti-Israeli discourse in Europe is much more attributable to the Left than to the Right. The Right, especially because of the illegitimacy of National Socialism and fascism in European public opinion, has long behaved far more circumspectly with respect to its depiction of Jews and Israel than has the Left. Because classical anti-Semitism was usually associated with the Right, the Left enjoyed a kind of bonus or free ride on matters relating to Jews and Israel. Unlike the Right, the Left could take the liberty of being anti-Israeli and (in part) even anti-Semitic. This bonus gave it the chance to establish an anti-Israeli discourse that has now become part of a widespread and accepted linguistic usage. Because of its general acceptability and legitimacy, left-wing criticism of Israel and left-wing anti-Semitism are far more relevant and alarming than what one finds on the Right, which has barely changed over the years. Today's neo-Nazis are ugly and unpleasant, yet they continue to remain well beyond the bounds of what is respectable in the European discourse. The Left's anti-Semitism does not usually break clear and universally recognizable taboos. Left anti-Semitism does not often talk about world Jewish conspiracy and the Protocols of the Elders of Zion; or Jews as Christ-killers; or Jews as blood suckers; or Jews as capitalists; or Jews as racial polluters; nor does it deny the Holocaust in a straightforward manner. Left anti-Semitism does not derive from a clear and conscious hatred of Jews. Rather, it emanates from a particular understanding of global imperialism and of the role of Israel, Zionism, and Jews within this bigger picture, wherein the United States plays an absolutely central role.

> Left anti-Semitism is like institutionalized racism. It does not depend
> on the psychological state of individuals. . . . Rather it is a property
> of the politics, policies, campaigns and ideas themselves. As with in-
> stitutionalized racism, those who stand accused rebut those accusa-
> tions with statements about their own personal opposition to anti-
> Semitism. They thereby miss the point—the point being that politi-
> cal positions are not necessarily motivated by anti-Semitism but that
> they are in themselves anti-Semitic, irrespective of personal feelings
> and motivations. Because left anti-Semitism is almost never open and
> clear, and because it is institutionalized amongst parts of the left,
> rather than being the result of subjective racisms, it is sometimes
> difficult to spot.

And it is almost always successfully denied.[32]

Anti-Semitism always played a definite part in the Left's—particularly New Left's—obsessive disdain for Israel, beginning with the
Six-Day War of 1967. But precisely the fact that this antipathy went
into overdrive in 1967, after Israel ostensibly mutated overnight
from a small and encircled victim to a conquering giant, testifies to
the fact that Israel's power became the Left's major target of dislike.
This primarily leftist discourse gradually assumed a hegemonic presence in much of Western Europe's elite perception of Israel over the
past forty years. It is by virtue of this shift in power that contemporary Europeans dislike Israel so intensely and why their current anti-
Semitism assumes a different veneer from the traditional one that
dominated Europe for one thousand years. Most Europeans do not
frown on Israel mainly because of its Jewish identity (although "Zionism," which refers primarily to the identity of the Jewish state, is
viewed in the European Left as decidedly negative and "reactionary,"
if it is not regarded as a special swear word associated closely with
concepts like "imperialism" and "colonialism"). Instead, Israel comes
in for disapproval owing to its power and its political disposition,
which (in the eyes of these Europeans) it shares with the United
States in a way that is increasingly remote from Europe. Israel is
regarded as nationalistic, religious (and therefore backward-looking
and regressive), particularistic, attached to realpolitik, unilateral, and
playing according to political rules that Europeans (who glorify

themselves as postnationalist, secular, universalist, and multilateral) have allegedly and self-promotingly long since abandoned.

As Mark Lilla has argued, contemporary Europe's supposedly postnational elites dislike states that behave the way European states used to before 1945: assertively, unilaterally, particularistically, real-politikally—all of which pertain to Israel's conduct in the world, as well as to America's, especially under the aegis of the Bush administration.[33] In this connection, Europeans equate the United States and Israel with the bad old pre-1945 Europe that they believe they have long since left behind owing to their successful labors of overcoming the past. Ironically, all the people who were so outraged at Donald Rumsfeld's disparaging remarks about "old Europe"—and who saw themselves compelled to reject his category of the "new Europe"—actually identify themselves as "new Europeans" in that they equate Israelis and Americans with the flawed "old Europe" they purportedly left behind in 1945.

To be sure, this postnationalism pertains only to intra-European dimensions and to any kind of bellicose interaction among European states. War among European states truly is unthinkable, surely an impressive accomplishment. But to call France's policies postnational really misses the point. Indeed, by every conceivable measure, France continues to pursue its highly national interests as it always did. It merely uses the postnational veneer as a convenient smoke-screen to pursue its realpolitik, which—over the past fifteen years—has been mainly directed against the United States. The same pertains to Germany, particularly under the Red-Green coalition of the Schröder government. Germany, too, uses the postnational ideology to justify the pursuit of its highly nationalistic policies. If the (West) Europeans were genuinely so postnationalist, why then would the French and the British not relinquish their permanent seats in the United Nation's Security Council and have them replaced by a genuinely postnational European seat? Instead, Germany seeks to join the council in an act of old-style nationalism. The alleged post-nationalism of the West Europeans extends mainly to the Paris-Madrid-Berlin-Moscow axis, whose primary purpose is to oppose the United States in every possible forum.

The fact that current European anti-Semitism has changed is best demonstrated by the fact that the very people who are ostensibly appalled by anti-Semitic incidents in their own countries are also often Israel's most ruthless critics. That they then often resort to characterizations of Israel's essence and its very existence—as opposed to its policies—in eerily similar terms and tone to the old-fashioned European anti-Semitism of yore attests not to the end of European anti-Semitism but merely its mutation from what Daniel Goldhagen called the Shylock Jew (which is unacceptable in contemporary Europe) to the Rambo Jew (a highly legitimate perception).[34] And we all know how much Rambo has become a synonym for America and Americans in European discourse of the past two decades. The tough Jew in the form of the omnipotent Israeli has led to a new twist on the longstanding interaction between anti-Semitism and anti-Americanism: If in former times it was the almighty United States that basically used powerful Israel as its puppet in its "imperialist" and "neocolonial" designs, then we witnessed a reversal, especially in the context of the Iraq War of 2003, in which an all-powerful Israel and its "East Coast" minions, Jewish "neoconservatives," and Leo Strauss epigones were alleged to have co-opted American power for their own purposes. As mentioned in chapter 1, anti-Americanism has been perhaps the only prejudice in Europe that correlates positively with the respondents' level of education and social position precisely because it is not perceived as such. One can legitimately voice this prejudice because it inevitably also expresses a critique of—often even an opposition to—a very powerful actor, who, adding insult to injury in the eyes of the Western world's postcolonialist Left, is a Western entity in the middle of Third World peoples. With the latter assuming for the Western Left the role of the subject of history in lieu of the long-abandoned and much-maligned proletariat, Israel's position as a bogeyman for this milieu has remained rather overdetermined since 1967. Being prejudiced against the powerful has an entirely different social acceptability than being prejudiced against the weak. And this is the position to which the new European anti-Semitism has mutated. While it has become illegitimate in the post-Holocaust world to express ha-

tred for powerless Jews—meaning Jews currently living in Europe—
it has become all the more acceptable to express antipathy toward
powerful Jews. The former is obvious anti-Semitism, which one can
only express in the pub or on the Internet, in other words apart from
acceptable public discourse. The latter has become a badge of honor
and constitutes legitimate speech. One of the legacies of the late
1960s has been the important fact that acceptable discourse does
not permit derision and chiding of the weak, be that women, the
physically challenged, ethnic minorities, or animals. Accepted discourse toward the weak has—as the testimony of a compassion informing public life in advanced industrial democracies that is unprecedented and a clear sign of social progress—truly changed in
the public spheres of all advanced industrial democracies. Exactly
the opposite pertains to the strong. Criticizing, deriding, and attacking them not only have become acceptable; indeed, they have
become commendable, a clear code of belonging to the socially desired group of progressives. Thus, deriding the Jews is not tolerated
because the Jews are weak; deriding Israel is praiseworthy because
Israel is strong.

Jews in Europe have become contested space by dint of what Salomon Korn sees as a "power triangle of anti-Semitism" that seems to
reveal elements of what might at least be an evolving reality in the
continent's political chemistry: "The Islamic anti-Semitism that is
pressing forward from southern Europe at the same time as the 'classic' anti-Semitism seeping in from eastern Europe will initiate a
'pincer movement' that will presumably intensify the secondary or
'guilt-reflex' anti-Semitism already present in western Europe. The
outcome might possibly be a kind of 'power triangle of anti-Semitism'—a reciprocally reinforcing alliance of distinct forms of animosity toward Jews."[35]

## The Two European Anti-Semitisms

There are several reasons for the presence of, and interaction between, the two European anti-Semitisms:[36]

1. The disappearance of communism as an enemy and a perceived threat, and thus the need to accord absolute primacy to the task of containing, even defeating, this perceived ill.

2. Indeed, with the disappearance of communism and the major task at hand to begin coming to terms with that past, anti-Semitism has made its steady appearance in a number of East European countries where the old adage of Jews = Bolsheviks has been revived. Somehow, the anti-Semitic dimensions of Communist regimes—the Doctors' Plot in the Soviet Union, the Rajk trial in Hungary, the Pauker trial in Romania, the Slansky trial in Czechoslovakia, and the Merker affair in East Germany, to mention but the most obvious ones—come up much more rarely when compared to the constant mention of the disproportionate presence of Jews among the Communist elites. Interestingly, the anti-Semitism witnessed in contemporary Eastern Europe is of the classic kind—a continuation of the standard negative tropes, but quite devoid of its anti-Israel and anti-American component so prominent in the western half of the European continent. Precisely because the East European countries do not exhibit nearly the acuteness in anti-Americanism as do those in the West, contemporary anti-Semitism does not have one of its major linkages and arenas in Eastern Europe that it so richly enjoys in the West.

3. Because of communism's defeat, the substantially decreased need for the United States as a protector. This fostered the resurgence of an already present anti-Americanism, of which the intellectuals and the political classes have been the most avid carriers. As is well known, with manifest anti-Americanism, anti-Semitism has rarely been far behind.

4. What makes them so related is their characterization as the quintessential expressions of modernity. With a massive critique of modernity afoot in Europe—just as in the United States and elsewhere—there emerges yet another piece of the puzzle that might explain a necessary, albeit not a sufficient, reason for the rise in anti-Semitism in Europe.

5. Modernity is, of course, also associated with "Europe," with Brussels, with this new central power of a newly constituting state in this

fascinating process of state building before our very eyes. As we know from history, all state-building processes are very painful. Inevitably, there are clear winners and clear losers, and the losers do not fade easily.

The debate about a European identity, about what will constitute the soul, the flesh and blood of this new entity—never mind its skeleton, which is now being gradually put into place—has just begun. We have no idea what shape it will take, where it will go, who will lead it, who will be the winners and losers. In a sense, "Europe" in its modernist persona represents a quasi-America to its skeptics and opponents: distant, impersonal, market driven, dismissive of tradition, large, undemocratic. It is thus not a coincidence that there is a convergence in virtually every European country between its far Left and far Right in their dismissal of "Europe" as a project. Not surprisingly, many of the arguments that these groups use in their opposition to Europe bear a great resemblance to those that they deploy in their opposition to America.

What is quite clear is that the enemies of the European statebuilding process—on both the Right and the Left—have mustered tropes from the past that certainly have not compellingly been antiSemitic per se, but that feature themes which, historically speaking, have not been the most favorable to Jews.

6. Everything that I said about "Europe" in point 5 pertains to the whole issue of "globalization," a process that has been with us most certainly since the advent of capitalism and the "discovery" of the Americas in the late fifteenth century, and that has had many more vastly greater leaps in its history than the one we are currently experiencing, some of which—like the one from 1890 until 1920—changed human existence much more profoundly than anything that we are witnessing today (Fordist mass production, the automobile, the airplane, antibiotics, the radio, women entering the public arena via the franchise, a major step no matter how limited we view it as today [and correctly so], World War I as the most important hiatus between the old, essentially feudal, world and the new capitalist world of what Eric Hobsbawm has aptly called the "short twentieth century"). That one of the major responses to this massive transfor-

mation was the "age of fascism" should not surprise us in hindsight but should give us pause as to what collective social formations and political manifestations might be still awaiting us in response to the globalization phase that we are currently experiencing.

7. Europe's multiculturalism. This has basically two dimensions:

a. The simple fact that as a consequence of the post-Yalta world, borders have opened up and population shifts have occurred that Europeans never expected and that exacerbated the earlier immigrations waves of the 1960s and 1970s, which these states could contain under the guise that these workers were merely "guests" or "temporary." In the 1990s the whole question of identity and citizenship—of permanent inclusion and exclusion—became central. This changed the tenor of the debate completely. Suddenly, the multiculturalism that these Europeans enjoyed in terms of the growing diversity of their culinary possibilities mutated into a nasty contest over identity, citizenship, permanence, language, ethnicity, religion—the hot buttons of politics.

b. The empirical reality that a large number of these new immigrants hailed from the Muslim world: Turkey (but also Arab countries and Iran) in Germany; the Magreb (Algeria, Tunisia, Morocco) in France; Pakistan and the Arab world in Britain; Kurds in Sweden; Albanians in Italy; Moroccans in Spain. While these immigrants awakened first and foremost a nasty strain of xenophobia in all European countries against themselves, they also have triggered a massive, twofold reemergence of anti-Semitism: first, on the part of those who hate these newcomers and wish them ill (this is the European anti-Semitism of old, "your father's anti-Semitism," so to speak); second, on the part of those who are the targets of this hatred who happen to be from cultures where anti-Semitism has attained a major presence mainly—though not exclusively—by dint of the Arab-Israeli conflict.

It is not that Muslim anti-Semites and European anti-Semites suddenly discovered their mutual love for each other—although that has happened, too, and is increasingly becoming common in certain right-wing circles in Germany and elsewhere in Europe where radical rightists seek out radical Islamists as allies even though they hate each other, but in the hierarchy of their respective hatreds that of Jews and Americans receives respective pride of place, thus fostering this otherwise bizarre alliance—but that anti-Semitism has yet another voice in these plural and democratic societies where such voices have often reached very receptive audiences. By having to adjudicate far-away conflicts on their own soil—that is, when the Middle East conflict is suddenly carried out in the middle of Hamburg, London, or Paris—these European states invariably and inevitably are drawn into disputes that willy-nilly involve Jews yet again. And their populations do not like it.

### Anti-Israeli Discourse as a Facilitator for a New "Uninhibitedness" toward Jews in Europe: A Lowering of the Threshold of Shame

Surely one needs to mention Israel's often deeply problematic policies and frequently objectionable actions in the occupied territories as irritants to most European publics, elite as well as mass. But here, too, the line between completely legitimate criticisms of policies and the much more worrisome questioning of Israel's very existence needs to be strictly delineated. Alas, it is increasingly less so in the commentaries of the European public. All of this occurs in a discursive context wherein the late Daniel Bernard, the French ambassador in London at the time, blithely called Israel a "shitty little country" (in refined company) and then, as André Glucksmann reported, "added the remark: Why should the world be brought to the brink of a Third World War because of this country? The ambassador, formerly spokesman for one of President Mitterrand's foreign ministers, was criticized by the British press, but no apology was forthcoming. His remarks about the 'shitty little country' were not repudiated as unacceptable. ... He ended his career as French ambassador in Algeria, in other words, at an important and reputable posting."[37]

While one could chalk up Bernard's comments, made at a private dinner party, as "anti-Semitism of the remark,"[38] the British journalist Deborrah Orr's approving article on the French ambassador's comments published in the respectable British daily the *Independent* bespeaks a public flaunting of an attitude with an impunity, even pride, that one would be hard pressed to witness toward any other country in the world, and that the author clearly knows enjoys legitimacy among her readership: "Ever since I went to Israel on holiday, I've considered it to be a shitty little country too. And I was under the impression that even Israelis thought this. I mean, if they thought Israel was small but perfectly formed, surely they wouldn't be hell-bent on making it bigger, come what may. . . . In my experience Israel is shitty and little. What's more, the daily trauma it undergoes in defending its right to exist is the main thing that makes the place so shitty." Not only is the three-time usage of this scatological term part of the author's disdain for Israel, but she continues her offensive (in both senses of the term) by dragging in the issue of anti-Semitism—just for good measure and to stake out her territory: "I'm fed up with being called an anti-Semite. And the more fed up I get, the more anti-Semitic I sound." Moreover, if the Jews "continue to insist that everyone with a word to say against Israel is an anti-Semite, [they are] going to find one day that the world is once more divided neatly between anti-Semites and Jews."[39]

The gauntlet is thrown. Everywhere in Europe the mantra is voiced that any criticism of Israel is being stymied by the Jews by calling it anti-Semitic. In an article addressing the growing tolerance and usage of anti-Semitic tropes in the British media under the guise of having the right to criticize Israel, and the concomitant inveighing against an alleged McCarthyism on the part of Jews and their minions against all who do so, Melanie Phillips examines the growth of anti-Semitism in Great Britain, which she attributes almost exclusively to the "Sharon-hating Left" and not to the usual right-wing radicals. Phillips describes how hostile and irritated the dominant discourse has become among the British intelligentsia when its members talk about the "vastly exaggerated" warnings concerning a new anti-Semitism, and how the stigma of a "new McCarthyism" is bestowed on this phenomenon (a witch-hunt intended to muzzle criticism of Israel and brand anyone daring to criticize Israel as an anti-Semite). Phillips herself was then accused, along with other British Jews, of trying to exert control over the public debate about Israel and Jews in the U.K. Phillips describes British dons who organize boycotts against Israeli colleagues and universities but would never dream of undertaking similar measures against Kuwait (which expelled 350,000 Palestinians in 1991) or Jordan (which murdered tens of thousands of Palestinians) or Syria (which, a year after Phillips wrote her article, still militarily occupied and politically controlled vast parts of Lebanon). She ended her article with the infamous statement of South African Archbishop Desmond Tutu, who said that people were too afraid of forthrightly identifying the power of the Jewish lobby in America:

> "So what," Tutu asked. "The apartheid regime was very powerful, but it does not exist any longer. Hitler, Mussolini, Stalin, Pinochet, Milosevic, and Idi Amin were all quite powerful, but in the end they all met their demise." So Jews, according to Tutu, not only have enormous power, but they are to be equated with these tyrants. Apparently their power was not great enough to prevent Tutu from publishing such an ignominious opinion and thereby charging up even more hatred against the Jews. But, of course, Jews who call this attitude by its rightful name are the new McCarthyites.[40]

In an issue of the *Independent*, Marie Woolf wrote about some politicians' warnings against the growing virus of anti-Semitism in Great Britain.[41] Former Minister Stephen Bryers had said that "the dividing line between legitimate criticism of the Israeli government and demonizing and dehumanizing Jews has been crossed, and that there is a double standard" for judging Jews and Israel according to completely different criteria from all the other nations of the world. Woolf quotes Labour MP James Purnell, who was shocked at the caricatures and cartoons about Israel and Jews. He added astutely that the Holocaust had proved to be a good vaccination shot against the virus of anti-Semitism for sixty years, but that now—owing to the alliance policy of the radical Left, "which has gotten involved

with some extremely dubious elements"—it was losing its effective-
ness: "During the anti-war demonstrations there were really frightening pictures of people who dressed up as suicide bombers and
carried slogans equating the Star of David with the swastika. The
apparent incorporation of these symbols by anti-war Leftists is absolutely incredible." The visibly shocked Purnell could have observed
identical scenes at similar demonstrations in Berlin, Paris, Rome,
Stockholm, Athens, and many other European cities. They are the
symbols of the current European peace movement, which has not,
even for a single moment, really distanced itself from this imagery
in an explicit and decisive way.

While such things are nothing new in the worlds of the extreme
Right and Left in Europe and have been commonplace since the
Six-Day War in June 1967, they were not part of Europe's accepted
political discourse until the 1990s. After all, many people have been
rightfully upset with many a country's policies. But in virtually no
case has that led to the questioning of the very worth of that country's existence. Slobodan Milosevic's Yugoslavia became the bogeyman of Europe's publics (certainly after the slaughter of 7,500 Bosnian Muslim men in Srebrenica), but even this atrocity never led
any British, French, German, or Italian diplomats or journalists
writing for these countries' papers of record to question the very
right of Yugoslavia to exist as a country. Put crudely, it is becoming
clearer by the day that the post-Auschwitz moratorium is gradually
coming to an end. The Jews are not "off limits" anymore in Europe.[42] This development reinforces my view that among all the
prejudices that have beset European history, anti-Semitism has constantly assumed a place all its own. It is related to racism but yet
different from it, furnishing a category all by itself. And it is back
with a vengeance in acceptable European discourse. "Der Ton
macht die Musik," the tone makes the music. Seldom has this been
clearer than in the case of contemporary Europe's irritation with
Israel and Jews, which can never be analyzed by itself but must be
done in a comparative context. To come back to my earlier example
of Deborah Orr's using scatological language in a major British
newspaper: Would she have used such terms to describe *any* other

country in the world? Would her editors at the *Independent* have allowed such blatantly insulting terms in a report about any other country but Israel? I really doubt this to be the case. There is an added edge, an additional enthusiasm, in the voice and passion of Israel's detractors that one simply cannot see in the case of any other country in the world, with the possible exception of the United States. But even in America's case the hatred rarely extends to a constant doubting of the legitimacy of the country's very existence. America is perhaps simply too big for expressions such as "I hate Bush, but I do not mind America's existence," something that one encounters on a daily basis with Israel, where the country's existence is constantly questioned, and ultimately opposed.

This fits in with the hegemonic self-perception Europeans currently have of themselves as paragons of world peace. Anyone who has followed the tone of the European media's reporting on the Near East conflict since the beginning of the second Intifada in September 2000 would hardly be surprised. And this tone comes not from the Right but from the Left. Here it suffices to mention just a few examples of this reporting's selective language: The BBC always talks about violent attacks by the IRA or the Basque ETA using the words "terrorists" or "terrorism," but it never uses these terms for bomb attacks by Hamas or Islamic Jihad against Israeli civilians. Instead, expressions like "resistance," "opposition," "struggle," "militants," "radicals," "activists," or "extremists" are used. The acts of violence are described using the passive voice or in an impersonal manner, such as "a bomb was placed" or "they attacked a bus." Israelis, by contrast, are portrayed as operative actors: They "murder," "kill," "destroy," and "attack"—and are also given adjectives like "brutal," "gruesome," and "merciless." In the German media Israelis "murder," "shoot," "liquidate," or even "execute" Palestinians, while (by contrast) Israeli victims merely "meet their death." To most journalists it is not even clear, as Antje Kraschinski has written in the *Frankfurter Rundschau*, "that they are [stirring up] the notion of a Jewish God of vengeance with their permanent use of the word 're-taliation' [Vergeltung]." Even worse, the concept of "preventive strike" actually used by the Israelis often gets translated as "retaliation." The press gladly divides Israelis into "good" and "evil." On the "good" side are conscientious objectors, peace activists, and leftist politicians; "evil" are Jewish settlers, conservative Jews, the Orthodox, and the Likud party. And why are "Irish terrorists" designated as such when Hamas members are called "extremists," "activists," or "radicals"?[43] Language describing Palestinian military actions is always couched in much more neutral terms than is the case with Israeli measures. Invariably, Palestinian suicide bombers were "nationalists" who acted out of "desperation," whereas Israeli retaliation was inevitably "vengeful" and "brutal." Interestingly, the German media have without any hesitation always depicted the Basque ETA and the Irish IRA actions in Spain and Britain, respectively, as "terrorist." The passion against Israel is simply disproportionate in its tone and its shrillness when compared to other agents of injustice.[44]

To the participants at a conference on "Anti-Semitism in the German Media and the Near East Conflict" (sponsored by two Social Democratic fora, the Moses-Mendelssohn-Zentrum at the University of Potsdam, and the political initiative Honestly Concerned), at least, it was clear that "the purported taboo about not being allowed to criticize Israel is just a myth."[45] In the broader German and European media landscape, however, this myth is constantly kept alive. It is a myth associated with the thesis (also eagerly put forward by large segments of Europe's leftist intelligentsia) that every marginal criticism of anti-Semitic elements in the Left's Israel discourse and of hostility toward Israel and "anti-Zionism" is always nothing more than an illegitimate charge of anti-Semitism, and that such accusations are launched by the "established media" and a "Zionist lobby" in an effort to "muzzle" critics of Israeli policy.[46]

The discourse in Great Britain's left-wing liberal media has become so one-sidedly anti-Israeli that some of the publications most responsible for this, such as the *Guardian*, the *Observer*, and the *Independent*, felt compelled to address the problem openly in at least a few sporadic articles. Thus the *Guardian* featured an editorial entitled "Our Dulled Nerve" saying that a new anti-Semitism is on the march around the globe. . . . All Jews are seen by extremists as legitimate targets. Here in Great Britain, ultra-Orthodox Jews were pelted with stones. They had absolutely no relation to Israel. There were even some among them who, for theological reasons, do not recognize the state of Israel. . . . Why are leftist liberals not sufficiently alarmed about the growth of anti-Semitism? In this year's anti-war demonstration in Paris, Jewish peace activists were beaten by demonstrators. There were less dramatic confrontations in the million-person march in London. It did not matter at all to the culprits that many Jewish writers and activists had been verbose in their opposition to the war. It also did not matter to them that many of these Jews criticized the policy of the current Israeli government toward the Palestinians. Their victims were selected only because they were Jews.[47]

The article ended with an almost laughably naive question that clearly shows how the *Guardian* either cannot or will not grasp this problem as an identity-shaping "wedge issue" for its left-liberal readerships: "Were left-liberals, who in earlier eras always endeavored to protect Jews against prejudice and bigotry, unable to rediscover their old values?" I am afraid that the answer to the question has to be a clear "no" because it is becoming increasingly obvious—in light of the current general discourse so hostile to Israel and the new, morally legitimated left-liberal anti-Zionism that, if not anti-Semitic sui generis, certainly facilitates the return of anti-Semitic tropes in acceptable British and European public life—that Jews qua Jews were never particularly important for the Left. Indeed, the Left always reserved its universalism for the Jews while applying the legitimacy of its identity politics to all other nationalities, particularly in the developing world.

A new tone has entered among European intellectuals in which criticizing Jews—not merely Israel and Israelis—has attained a certain urgency that reveals a particularly liberating dimension. One can almost hear the cries of relief: "Free at last, free at last, we are finally free of this damn Holocaust at last!" In this context Europeans posit that Jews, who created a culture of guilt and shame for

Europeans, and kept them from speaking their minds as they wished, now behave just like they did. The lid is off; Jews are legitimate targets yet again. End of what Germans call the *Schonzeit*—the closed (hunting) season.

This new "uninhibitedness"—an awkward, arguably inadequate, English translation of the German original *Unbefangenheit*—surely also informs the German discourse, especially since the ascent of Gerhard Schröder's chancellorship and the governing coalition of Social Democrats and Greens, a group of people who by dint of their party affiliations and their age clearly could never come close to being associated with anything resembling the far Right, let alone its National Socialist variant.

Just two weeks after the Bundestag election of September 27, 1998, in which those two parties barely defeated the conservative-liberal camp, the writer Martin Walser received the Peace Prize of the German Book Trade awarded annually at the Frankfurt Book Fair. It is customary for the recipient to give a speech in the city's most illustrious public forum, the famed Paulskirche.

Walser's address sparked the first "anti-Semitism dispute" in reunited Germany.[48] It has not been resolved to this day, and Walser continues to enjoy broad approval, recently for his highly popular novel *Tod eines Kritikers* (Death of a Critic) in which he basically reiterates his positions from the 1998 dispute.[49] The novel features a Jewish character who has the vilest traits of standard anti-Semitism—greedy, haughty, arrogant, oversexed, speaking in Polish-accented German—and is easily recognizable as a caricature of Marcel Reich-Ranicki, a well-known cultural critic of Polish Jewish origin.

Matthias N. Lorenz's book, *Auschwitz drängt uns auf einen Fleck* (Auschwitz Pushes Us onto One Spot), presents convincing evidence that Walser's work well beyond *Tod eines Kritikers*, beginning with his early plays and novels, bears major elements of anti-Semitism dating back to his seemingly left-wing beginnings in the early 1960s. Among other things, Lorenz reveals that Walser—in a speech honoring the late Victor Klemperer (professor of Romance literature in the former German Democratic Republic, an assimilated German Jew [married to a gentile woman] who survived the Nazi regime by staying in Berlin throughout the entire war and wrote about his life, which—in its two-volume publication—became one of the most successful and well-known testimonials of everyday life in National Socialist Berlin)—argued that the Holocaust would never have occurred had all German, and European, Jews assimilated as successfully as did Klemperer.[50] It should be noted that had Klemperer—despite his total assimilation—not been married to a German gentile woman, he, too, would have been sent to a death camp.

The fact that even Chancellor Schröder expressed solidarity with Walser during the 2002 election campaign[51] indicates the reversal that has occurred since Germany was reunited. In his speech on October 11, 1998, Walser referred to the constant recalling of Germany's crimes in the Holocaust as a "permanent representation of our shame." He deplored an "instrumentalization of our shame for current purposes" and a "negative nationalism" that was disseminated by "intellectuals" and "opinion soldiers." These, he claimed, used the memory of the Holocaust by holding it "at moral gunpoint" as a "means of intimidation deployable at any time" in order to hurt "all Germans"—by thwarting the Germans' national pride and self-satisfaction.[52] Walser, to be sure, was not the first to speak of the "Auschwitz cudgel," but he gave such notions his poetic blessing.[53]

One key aspect of this "uninhibitedness," particularly pronounced in Germany, but certainly not exclusive to it in Europe, is the concerted effort by many players in society, and not only on the political Right, to break taboos that have become part of Germany's (and Europe's) post-Holocaust discourse and in the process free themselves from what the journalist Henryk Broder has termed "secondary anti-Semitism" which may be distinguished from ordinary anti-Semitism (with which, however, it shares most of the usual stereotypes) by dint of its defense mechanisms against guilt. The phenomenon of "secondary anti-Semitism" was well described for the first time by Theodor W. Adorno and Max Horkheimer in their studies of the way postwar German society dealt with the Shoah. Because of the psychological mechanisms involved, Adorno and Horkheimer named this syndrome somewhat cumbersomely but all the more precisely "Schuldabwehrantisemitismus," which best translates into "anti-Semitism as a defense mechanism against guilt."[54]

The new uninhibitedness about Nazi history is by no means directed solely against depictions of the German extermination of European Jews. With increasing frequency, every aspect of critical history writing on National Socialism and its consequences is being disputed. This is demonstrated, for example, by the enormous success of the books written about the Allied bombing of German cities during World War II by the formerly left-wing author Jörg Friedrich, with titles like *The Fire* and *Fire Sites*.[55] Friedrich (once known and praised for his publications on the Nazi past of lawyers in the postwar Federal Republic[56]) and his publisher conceive of his book *The Fire* as a comprehensive work about the "campaign to exterminate German cities systematically planned and implemented by Britons and Americans." What this quote from the dust jacket signals is demonstrated by the book's content: The author is interested in drawing a linguistic equation between the Allies' war against Germany and the Germans' war against the rest of the world, especially the war of extermination on the eastern front and against the European Jews. In Friedrich's account, the air-raid shelters in which the German civilian population sought refuge become "crematoria," the bombing victims become the "exterminated," and the Royal Air Force's 5th Bomber Group becomes an *Einsatzgruppe* (the German name for the special task forces dedicated to rounding up and massacring Jews in occupied eastern Europe). The book, although vehemently criticized by some scholars because of its style, though much less for its content, enjoyed great popularity with the public and furnished additional evidence for the widening discourse of normalization. This happened at a time when Germany was governed by a Red-Green coalition that—as the Walser case shows—not only tolerated the trend but helped promote it.

By constantly bringing up the truly warped and ill-willed analogy of the Israelis with the Nazis, Europeans absolve themselves from any remorse and shame and thus experience a sense of liberation. If the Israelis were anywhere close to the Nazis and their genocidal deeds, the Palestinians would have ceased to exist decades ago. Thus the Israelis = Nazis analogy is not intended to describe Israel's deeply objectionable occupation policies. It is not meant to criticize Israel but to demonize it—to place it outside any discussion about actual politics and policies. Since the terms "Nazi" and "racist" have become internationally synonymous with ultimate evil, they form concepts beyond any discussion—one is a Nazi and a racist, case closed. This analogy does not only exculpate Europe from its own troubled past under the Nazis, but it also hurts the intended target—the Israelis directly, the Jews indirectly—by equating it with the very perpetrators who almost wiped it off the Earth in the most brutal genocide imaginable.

Most importantly, all of this needs to be viewed in a comparative context, in terms of both its tone as well as its substance: As to the former, what is important here is that no other vaguely comparable conflict has attained anywhere near the shrillness and acuity as that between Israelis and Palestinians. Nazifying Israel makes it possible to kill three birds with one stone: The first objective achieved is the delegitimation of Israel by associating it with the symbol of evil par excellence. Second, one can attack and humiliate the Jewish people by equating it with the perpetrators of the brutal genocide that nearly succeeded in exterminating the Jews completely. Finally, this malicious analogy between Israelis and Nazis frees Europeans of any remorse or shame for their history of a lethal anti-Semitism that lasted a solid millennium.

If one looks at two much more bloody—and geographically proximate—conflicts, the four succession wars following the dissolution of the former Yugoslavia and the Russian wars in Chechnya, neither of them has even vaguely created a tone of dismissal, bitterness, and contempt for the respective aggressors (the Serbs, the Croats, and the Russians) among Europe's intellectuals as have the Israelis. Oxford University dons would never have dreamt of banning Russians, Croats, Serbs, Chinese, Spaniards, Sudanese, or even Ulster Protestants from their laboratories. But this actually happened in May 2003 to a young Israeli scientist simply because he, like most Israeli citizens (men and women), had served in the Israeli Army. To be sure, after the Oxford University administration intervened, Professor Andrew Wilkie, who had blocked the already admitted Israeli doctoral candidate from access to his laboratory, was suspended without pay from the university for two months. He also resigned his position as "Fellow" of Pembroke College in the wake of this incident but did keep his post as Nuffield Professor of Pathology at Oxford University. But the message of the original decision to exclude Israelis from science could not have been clearer: In the pathology labs of Oxford's Pembroke College, at least, Israelis are not wanted.[57]

Norwegian veterinarians did not refuse to send DNA samples to institutes that requested them if they were in Russia, Serbia, or any other country that was engaged in a military conflict, or even in measures of undeniable repression and injustice. But they certainly did when a Jerusalem institute asked for such samples. The editor of the *Translator and Translation Studies Abstract*, published in Britain, did not summarily dismiss colleagues from the journal's editorial board because they belonged to nationalities whose countries were engaged in some form of conflict and injustice. However, Mona Baker, director of the Center for Translation and Intercultural Studies at the University of Manchester, did precisely that with two Israeli colleagues solely because of their nationality.[58] Lest there be any doubt, she made the reason for her decision crystal clear: "I can no longer live with the idea of cooperating with Israelis as such."[59] No European intellectuals and academics called for an organized boycott of Serbian, Croatian, or Russian institutions, including research and cultural links, as did 120 university professors from thirteen European countries in the case of Israel. And Britain's Association of University Teachers' (AUT) resolution to boycott Bar Ilan and Haifa Universities speaks volumes about the singling out of Israel as the world's sole miscreant. Adding insult to injury, this so-called boycott was really much closer to what is conventionally known as a "blacklist" since it stigmatized academics not only by their university affiliation and nationality but—worse still, if such a thing is possible—by their political beliefs. After all, the boycott statement made it totally clear that faculty members at these two institutions were exempt from the AUT's boycott if they were "conscientious Israeli academics and intellectuals opposed to their state's colonial and racist policies."[60] In other words, if they passed an ideological litmus test devised by the AUT, they were not to be boycotted. Even though the AUT's boycott resolution was ultimately aborted, exactly one year later the much larger National Association of Teachers in Further and Higher Education (NATFHE) launched a renewed effort in this direction. Even at the height of the boycott against South Africa's apartheid regime, the campaign never aimed at individuals, only institutions.

As previously mentioned, this noticeable change in European discourse hails much more from the Left than the Right. Thus, the BBC never admonished, let alone considered firing, the poet Tom Paulin as one of its regular commentators on culture after the latter had openly incited for the murder of Jews: "Brooklyn-born" Jewish settlers on the West Bank "should be shot dead" because "they are Nazis" and "I feel nothing but hatred for them."[61] Paulin, who teaches at Oxford, granted an interview to the Egyptian paper *Al-Ahram Weekly* in which he described Israel as a "historical obscenity" that "never had a right to exist" by way of clearing up any doubts about what his position might be. After the interview was published, of course, Paulin used the obligatory ploy in such circumstances, namely, by claiming that the paper had taken his statements out of context. His denial was not terribly credible: Over the years Paulin had been conspicuous for numerous anti-Israeli remarks and poems.[62]

Paulin, of course, is a solid man of the Left, not of the Right, and remains a respected member of Britain's cultural elite that sees itself as anti-fascist, anti-Nazi, and—of course—anti-anti-Semitic. Paulin is not an aberrant exception in this milieu. The *Guardian*, the *Observer*, the *Independent*, and the BBC, to mention a few British examples that have their counterparts in other European countries, did not develop their hostility toward Israel, Jews, and the United States under the influence of the right-wing extremist National Front.[63] It is by dint of this left-liberal voice, not the Right's old-style anti-Semitism, that 59 percent of Europeans view Israel as being the greatest threat to global peace, placing it first ahead of countries such as Iran, North Korea, the United States, Iraq, Afghanistan, and Pakistan, in that order.[64] China was mentioned by 30 percent, thus ranking it as number 13. Not surprisingly, Europeans had the best opinion of themselves, placing Europe as dead last in terms of representing any danger to world peace. Only 8 percent of the respondents listed the European Union or any of its members as threats to peace, with the Germans having the self-confidence (or might it be a bit of selfish arrogance) to list themselves dead last at 2 percent. The respondents in the Netherlands were particularly critical of Israel, viewing it as a threat to peace by a whopping 74 percent. The equivalent figure in Germany was 65 percent. In another survey, some 35 percent of Europeans believe that the Israeli Defense Forces intentionally target Palestinian civilians. In the same poll, 39 percent agreed that "Israel's treatment of Palestinians is similar to South Africa's treatment of blacks during the apartheid regime." And almost half of the European respondents felt that Israel was not an "open and democratic society."[65] Anybody following the European media's tone in covering the Israeli-Palestinian conflict since the second Intifada in September 2000 will not be surprised by these results. Once again, the origins of this hegemonic tone in Europe's acceptable discourse hail not from the Right but from the Left. And the tone set by elites and opinion leaders, such as journalists, really matters in terms of framing the acceptable contours of mass opinion.[66]

And this brings us to the difference in substance. It is rather evident that European intellectuals and political classes—as well as increasingly the general public—are not so much expressing their sympathies for suppressed Muslims or disadvantaged Arabs as they are their antipathies toward Israel and (not so indirectly) the Jews. This is best demonstrated by the following paradox: Precisely those Europeans who were the most silent during the Bosnian War's massive slaughter of Muslims at the hands mainly of Serbs but also Croats have been among the most vocal opponents of Israel. These people only raised their voices in the Bosnian War once the United States intervened. Because the United States entered the conflict on behalf of Muslims, many European intellectuals de facto rallied to the side of Slobodan Milosevic, who had engaged in mass murder of such Muslims. Thus, antipathy toward Israel and its accompanying anti-Semitism cannot be separated from a larger enmity toward the United States and what it represents. How else can one explain the attitude of Greek intellectuals, politicians, clergy, and public opinion—from Left to Right—all of whom were rabidly pro-Serbian, pro-Milosevic, and vehemently anti-Bosnian Muslim while at the same time they are among the most pro-Arab and pro-Palestinian Europeans? Anti-Israeli discourse has become so routine in everyday Greek public life that it now covers the entire political spectrum and shows up in almost every kind of imaginable forum. "In Greece," according to Moses Altsech, "anti-Semitism exists not just on the extreme Left and Right, but is completely embedded in Greece's mainstream. It shows up in the most diverse varieties and forums: in the context of religion, education and training, the application of justice and laws, and of course in the form of politically motivated anti-Semitism among all of the country's major political parties."[67] Needless to say, the thin dividing line between anti-Zionism and opposition to Israel, on the one hand, and anti-Semitism, on the other, is constantly being crossed. The boundary line is virtually as good as nonexistent. Greece is, moreover, an especially good illustration of my thesis that today's "new" anti-Semitism is closely allied with America and anti-Americanism. It is no accident that most of the anti-Israel demonstrations in Athens start out in front of the American Embassy and then proceed toward Israel's. Many Greeks still cannot forgive the Americans for having successfully supported right-wing militias against the Communist-led national liberation movement immediately after World War II. Greek rancor toward the United States is even greater, and more understandable, because of the crucial American role in supporting the military junta that ruled Greece from 1967 to 1974. This antipathy has never ebbed and has always remained acute, as is attested by the assassinations of American diplomats and officers, but also of civilians, over the last thirty plus years. The animosity experienced a new climax in the course of the wars in Bosnia and Kosovo, when the Greeks found themselves, for historical and religious reasons, virtually unanimously in Europe's pro-Serbian camp.

Although the Greek Jewish community is one of the oldest in Europe, Christian Greeks do not accept its members as Greeks, since at least a nominal tie to the Greek Orthodox church remains, to this day, a condition for membership in the Greek nation as far as most Greeks are concerned. The fact that Greeks do not accept Jews as equal members of their society is, admittedly, just the expression of a norm that remains in effect throughout Europe, in spite of proclamations of tolerance issued with regard to the Holocaust.[68] As in the rest of Europe, Jews are also associated with Israel in Greece. Negative attitudes toward Israel are often presented using manifestly anti-Semitic content and in unequivocally anti-Semitic form. Designating places with names like Dachau, Auschwitz, and Mauthausen is standard practice when reporting on Israeli policy in the occupied territories. The terms "Holocaust" and "genocide" have frequently been used since Israel's invasion of Lebanon in 1982, and since the second Intifada this language has worked its way into daily usage among the mainstream media when it comes to characterizing Israeli policy.

But this tone is by no means limited to PASOK and the Left. Politicians and journalists from the right-wing conservative Nea Demokratia party have made anti-Semitic remarks that—in contrast to those from the PASOK discourse—are not chiefly restricted to Israel, but instead also revive the timeworn themes of classical anti-Semitism. At a book presentation (where he was flanked on either side by the Greek minister of culture and education minister), the great Greek composer Mikis Theodorakis, who held a cabinet position in a short-lived Nea Demokratia–led coalition government during his phase of sympathizing with the Right, said that he regarded the Jews as "the root of all evil."[69] In a wide-ranging interview that Mikis Theodorakis granted *Haaretz* journalist Ari Shavit twenty-four hours before the start of the Olympic Games in Athens in the summer of 2004, Theodorakis was keen to maintain that he had not said Jews were the root of all evil, but rather that Jews could always be found at the root of all evil. In this interview Theodorakis gives voice to every standard anti-Semitic theme, both old and new: from the many Jewish Nobel Prize winners, which Theodorakis attributes to Jewish arrogance and aggressiveness, to the complete Judaization of America and the subservience of American politics to Jews; from Jews as unpatriotic people to the proudly repeated analogy between Israel and Nazi Germany. In this context Theodorakis raises a point that I had never read before in quite this way in any of my rather extensive readings about the different rationales for hatred of Israel and anti-Semitism: "After World War I the Germans were victims. They felt like victims. They also felt they were in the right to feel this way. Others had caused them grief, but they were in the right. This was the germination for Hitler. . . . Hitler said we will never be victims again. We will arm ourselves and we will avenge ourselves. Look where that led. Something like this could also easily happen with Israel."[70] In spite of the rather drastic political shift from Left to Right and then back to the Left again undertaken by Theodorakis, his name continues to be mentioned as a possible head of state for Greece. His reputation as a public intellectual, and not just a composer, remains stellar throughout Europe, where Theodorakis continues to be revered.

One Nea Demokratia politician denounced his PASOK rival as a "Judasse" and called Prime Minister Costas Simitis the "High Priest of Jewry." Some Nea Demokratia members held a joint celebration with retired army officers from the fascist organization Chrysi Avgi, which picked swastika-like runes in black, white, and red (the antirepublican colors of both imperial and Nazi Germany) as its symbol. The conservative weekly paper *To Vima* published a commentary by Archbishop Christodoulos, who accused the Jews of forcing the EU to stop using religious affiliation on personal identity cards.[71] A report from the Simon Wiesenthal Center in Los Angeles on anti-Semitism in Greece confirmed these observations and maintained that, in spite of repeated pleas to different Greek governments under socialist Prime Minister Costas Simitis and his conservative successor Kostas Karamanlis to do something against the rising tide of anti-Semitic graffiti and desecrations of Jewish graves and other

Jewish institutions, nothing ever happened.[72] Nor did repeated letters from the Greek Helsinki Monitoring Group beseeching Prime
Minister Simitis to have the graffiti saying "Death to the Jews" and
"Jews get out" removed from along the highway route (traveled by
thousands) between Corinth and Tripolis receive an answer or lead
to any serious political response.

The motivation that drives the liberal Left in Europe is dislike
and hatred of Israel and America, and not a genuine sympathy for
and identification with downtrodden Muslims. In every one of the
European countries under consideration here, surveys show that the
native European population despises its country's Muslim inhabitants much more than its Jewish fellow citizens. This fact is unfortunately used by some people—chiefly left-leaning politicians and intellectuals—to trivialize or deny the anti-Semitism that also exists.

It was not the slaughter of innocent Muslim women and children
in Bosnia that really riled the European Left. Instead, what mobilized thousands in the streets of Berlin, Paris, and Athens once the
much-belated step was taken to intervene on behalf of the brutalized
Muslims was once again the American bogeyman. And once again,
far Right and far Left met on matters relating to America and Jews.
No far Right in Europe has a nastier anti-Serbian history than the
German and Austrian, both of which have been long-time supporters of the most vicious anti-Serbian fascists in Croatia (the notorious
"Ustashe") and elsewhere (primarily Bosnia). Still, their hatred of
Serbs could not compete with their hatred of Americans, and once
the United States intervened against Serbs on behalf of the Bosnian
Muslims and their Kosovar coreligionists, German and Austrian
neo-Nazis and far rightists rallied to Milosevic's side in their unmiti-
gated opposition of NATO's American-led interventions. *Les extremes se touchent* on matters related to Jews and America yet again,
as they did so often throughout the twentieth century. The primary
force of mobilization here is anti-Americanism. One would be hard
pressed to arrive at any items in politics apart from anti-Semitism
and anti-Americanism in which there has been such a strong and
lasting concordance between the extreme Right and the extreme
Left in virtually every European country.

The Israeli psychologist Zvi Rex once said that the Germans will never forgive the Jews for Auschwitz. He could have added that the same pertains to the Americans' (and the Red Army's) defeat of National Socialism as well. It is hard to swallow the fact that Germany did not attain its now vaunted democratic culture, pacifism, and sense of virtue on its own but by dint of foreign powers vanquishing Hitler's dictatorship. And when both victors, in their very different ways, are perceived as clearly inferior to Germans—culturally, politically, in terms of bravery, valor, and perseverance of the troops, to name just a few pertinent items—the defeat stings all the more and, on some level, never was accepted. Adding insult to injury, both the Americans and the Soviets remained strongly identified with Jews and Jewry in the minds of Germans. But this issue goes far beyond the Germans and pertains to all of Europe. Here is Max Horkheimer's authoritative voice on this matter:

> America, regardless of its motives, saved Europe from complete enslavement. The response today from everywhere, not only in Germany, has been widespread and profound hostility toward America. There has been a great deal of puzzling over the origin of this. Resentment, envy, but also the errors made by the American government and its citizens, all play a role. It is especially startling to notice that everywhere where one finds anti-Americanism, anti-Semitism flourishes. The general malaise caused by cultural decline seeks a scapegoat, and for the aforementioned reasons, it finds the Americans, and, in America itself, once again the Jews who supposedly rule America.[73]

The surplus of enmity exhibited toward Israel by Europeans and the much greater coverage of Israel by the European media than any other conflict in the world, including those much closer to Europe, bespeak a qualitative dimension to this sentiment and attitude that borders on an obsession and reaches way beyond the conventional criticisms that are accorded to other political conflicts and disagreements. In prewar Europe, "good Jews"—if such a category was not an a priori oxymoron for most gentile Europeans—pertained at best only to converted and assimilated Jews. Today, for many

Europeans, "good Jews" are those that have explicitly shed their support for Israel.[74] In an interview in one of Hungary's leading intellectual journals, Imre Kertész, the Hungarian Nobel laureate, encapsulated this matter in the following poignant way: "A language I call Euro-anti-Semitism has developed. For a Euro-anti-Semite, it is not a contradiction to pay tribute to the memory of the victims of the Holocaust in one sentence and make anti-Semitic remarks in the next under the pretext of criticizing Israel."[75] The Europeans' enmity toward Israel cannot be detached from the Europeans' thousand-year hatred of the Jews and their shorter and much less lethal, but still palpable, antipathy toward America. And thus we are back to the three standard pillars of classical anti-Semitism and anti-Americanism: Jews, America, and modernity.

*CHAPTER 6*

------------------------------------------------

# Anti-Americanism: A Necessary and Welcomed Spark to Jump-start a European Identity?

**February 15, 2003**

Fundamentally, the European views about America have little to do with the real America but much to do with Europe. It is a completely open question which direction European anti-Americanism will take, because it is an equally open question as to what content and form the European project will assume. Still, it is one thing for European elites, artists, and intellectuals to have waged a longstanding culture war against America; enlisting the masses in their *Kulturkampf*, as seems to have happened since the end of the Cold War, 9/11, and the Iraq War in particular, is yet another. As indicated throughout this book, the Bush administrations' policies have produced a convergence between elite and mass opinion in Europe and elicited the mobilization of anti-American countervalues in the name of Europe. Hence, anti-Americanism has become an emotional, potent, and very real aspect of European identity formation. No mobilization on behalf of these European countervalues could have been more intense than during the enormous demonstrations of February 15, 2003. On that day, as never before in European history, millions of Europeans united publicly for a single purpose. From London to Rome, Paris to Madrid, Athens to Helsinki, everywhere Europeans from the most diverse political camps, age groups, and social classes coalesced in order to demonstrate their opposition to the impending attack on Iraq. In countries like Germany, France, and Greece, these marches turned into something like voluntary rallies in support of the demonstrators' own governments.

Never before had there been such perfect harmony among intellectuals, governments, and "the people" on such a broad foundation and in such an impressive international (or was this already the start of something national?) context. This rare congruence could happen only because of a clearly perceived common enemy for all parties: the United States of America. Indeed, some European intellectuals proclaimed this moment as the birthday of a united Europe. Like no other day in European history, February 15, 2003, united Europeans emotionally. Certainly the most forceful interpretation of this day, as a kind of European national holiday in the making, was offered by former French Finance Minister Dominique Strauss-Kahn: "On Saturday, February 15, 2003, a nation was born on the streets. This nation is the European nation."[1] Strauss-Kahn's article makes it clear that the only common attribute of this nation-in-the-making is its opposition to the United States. He leaves no doubt about his view that the gap between Europe and America is primarily derived from differences in values, identities, and (above all) the essence of these two continents. These kinds of differences, unlike political disagreements, do not allow for compromise. They cannot be bridged or negotiated. On May 31, 2003, Jürgen Habermas, Jacques Derrida, and other leading European intellectuals, plus the well-known American philosopher Richard Rorty, joined in the chorus of agreement about this new common baseline: For this group, the conflict over the war in Iraq represented the highly promising start of a consciously created European nation, in clear opposition to America.[2] It is characteristic of the symbolic meaning of this gigantic pan-European demonstration day that Habermas delivered his essay for the *Frankfurter Allgemeine Zeitung*—in all likelihood written earlier in the year—using the title "February 15." For some reason the editors of the newspaper must have opted for another title.[3] Many in Germany accorded this notable publication extravaganza a special pride of place since only an exceptional event—plus the unique prestige of Jürgen Habermas—could get the erstwhile rivals *Frankfurter Allgemeine Zeitung* and *Süddeutsche Zeitung* to collaborate so effectively and willingly.

Bespeaking Europe's lively debate culture, Habermas and his colleagues did not only meet with admiration and approval for their collective intervention, they were roundly criticized for their ideas and exhortations. Some objected to Habermas's rendering a unique situation under the Bush administration into a generalized depiction of America as a whole. Others reproached Habermas for having forgotten the American role in liberating Germany and Europe from the yoke of National Socialism. Some accused him of painting an excessively rosy picture of Europe; while others took him to task for projecting a glorified vision of the preunification Federal Republic's virtues onto an entire continent. By far the most profound criticism and greatest disappointment centered on the fact that Habermas and Derrida not only explicitly extolled a Franco-German "core" Europe, but that the entire offensive reeked of exclusion since no intellectuals from any of the Eastern European countries, the Low Countries, Scandinavia, or Britain were invited to voice their opinions as part of this unique event.

But nary two years after this euphoric publication event, the citizens of France—one of the two major pillars of core Europe—and of the Netherlands resoundingly rejected their own country's acceptance of the newly created European Constitution. While the causes for these two negative votes were many and are beyond the scope of this book, there seems little doubt that a serious disillusionment with the European Union—a sort of Euro-skepticism and Euro-fatigue, if not outright hostility to the Union's running of Europe, though not the idea and the project of Europe itself—had engulfed a large segment of the public in many West European countries following those heady days of the spring of 2003. But even in this temporary derailment of the European project, America's negative image played an important role. Both sides in the French contest constantly invoked America as a threat: In leading the pro-Constitution camp, President Chirac never tired to exhort his fellow citizens to vote for the acceptance of the Constitution since only via a strong and unified Europe could France resist the American juggernaut. Those opposed to the acceptance of the Constitution painted the European Union, the Brussels bureaucracy, the EU-induced reforms and all their purported ills as manifestations of an Americanized Europe that had to be opposed and resisted.

At this juncture, a brief excursus will prove helpful to Hannah Arendt's almost clairvoyant views on the theme of how America as Europe's "other" and European anti-Americanism might prove essential in producing a European identity that Arendt labeled "Europeanism." She attached a pejorative meaning to this term because she associated with it an identity formation based merely on a facile populist deployment of anti-Americanism appealing to negative forces such as resentment and exclusion. Arendt contrasted this to a positive European identity that—so she hoped—would arise from Europe's federated state structure and its ensuing cosmopolitan as well as genuinely postnationalist culture and inclusive values that would build on shared ground with America and its republican traditions.

## Hannah Arendt: Critique of Anti-American Europeanism

More than fifty years ago, on January 28, 1954, Arendt gave a lecture at a Princeton University conference entitled "The Image of America Abroad" that first appeared as a three-part series in the September 1954 issue of *Commonweal* but was only made accessible to today's readers some forty years later, as three chapters of her book *Essays in Understanding 1930–1954.*[4] Arendt opens her lecture with the thesis that the European notion of America, compared with Europeans' ideas about all their other ex-colonies, was always different, more intense, more complex, and more problem-laden. America—unique among European constructs outside Europe in being called (not by coincidence) the "New World"—always embodied an idea and something "other," something "alien," which had little to do with American reality but therefore all the more with European illusions, hopes, and anxieties unrelated to America. For Europeans, long before the political founding of the United States in 1776, America was simultaneously a dream and a nightmare. Above all, it was an image. "Without an image of America, no European colonist would ever have crossed the Ocean."[5]

Arendt ascribes to the European creation of the United States of America an exceptional importance. She writes: "The American republic owes its origins to the greatest adventure of European mankind, which, for the first time since the Crusades and at the height of the European nation-state system, embarked upon a common enterprise whose spirit proved to be stronger than all their national differences."[6] But America as the extraordinary product of a pan-European project could never deprive the Europeans of their fear of and aversion against their own creation. One of the reasons, in Arendt's view, was America's geographic, political, and even intellectual isolation from Europe and the world. This irritated Europeans and led them to regard their distance from America as much greater than it actually was. Indeed, speaking in 1954 at the height of the Cold War, when, according to conventional thought, America and Western Europe were allegedly at their closest and Europeans rejoiced in their relations and affinities across the Atlantic, Arendt emphasizes the exact opposite, namely, that "for a considerable segment of European opinion—by no means including only Communists or fellow travelers"—Russia and Asia, "both of which are being Europeanized through Marxism," are much closer than are the United States.[7] Once again, Arendt's analysis seems quite prescient concerning the Paris-Berlin-Madrid-Moscow axis in opposition to the United States, and European public opinion's viewing the United States much more warily than Russia or China. Arendt continues about Europe's discomfort with America:

> It is also true that the feeling was always present that the difference between the two continents was greater than national differences in Europe itself even if the actual figures did not bear this out. Still,

at some moment—presumably after America emerged from her long isolation and became once more a central preoccupation of Europe after the First World War—this difference between Europe and America changed its meaning and became qualitative instead of quantitative. It was no longer a question of better, but of altogether different conditions, of a nature which makes understanding well nigh impossible.[8]

But even more important for European displeasure with America, according to Arendt, was its wealth and its disproportional size (which I have described elsewhere in this book using Josef Joffe's characterization of "Mr. Big"). Arendt speaks mainly of differences in material wealth, but in the following passage she also says something that relates to what was already then experienced—and which today, of course, strikes European sensibilities even more flagrantly—as a power gap between Europe and the United States:

> There is a much more cogent reason, however, which also goes a long way toward explaining why Europe will so often pretend to find herself in closer kinship with non-European nations than with America; this is the stupendous wealth of the United States. . . . Like an invisible but very real Chinese wall, the wealth of the United States separates it from all other countries of the globe. . . . We all know from personal experience that friendship involves equality. Although friendship can be an equalizer of existing natural or economic inequalities, there is a limit beyond which such equalization is utterly impossible. In the words of Aristotle, no friendship could ever exist between a man and a god. The same holds true for the relationships between nations where the equalizing force of friendship does not operate. . . . Those who believe that this situation can be easily corrected by Marshall plans or Point Four programs are, I am afraid, mistaken. . . . Mistrust of American intentions, the fear of being pressured into unwanted political actions, suspicions of sinister motives when help is given without political strings attached—these things are natural enough and need no hostile propaganda to arouse them. But even more is involved. In this case, as in all beneficence, the prerogative of action and the sovereignty of decision rest with the

benefactor, and therefore, to cite Aristotle once more, it is only natural that the benefactor should love his beneficiaries more than he is loved by them. Where they have suffered passively, he has done something; they have become, as it were, his work.[9]

Arendt then characterizes the ungratefulness expressed toward every kind of generosity with the following apt words: "It has always been the misfortune of rich people to be alternately flattered and abused—and still remain unpopular, no matter how generous they are."[10]

Expanding Arendt's analysis beyond the theme of wealth to include that of power, we would gain an even more complete picture of the constant irritation and traditional antipathy Europeans hold against America. Especially in the current situation, in which Europe's prosperity—not least of all thanks to the military protection that the United States (in its own interest, needless to say) granted Europe for fifty years—is now fully equivalent to (if it does not in fact surpass) America's affluence, it is perhaps the Europeans' power deficit and not their prosperity deficit that is now the most important reason for their aversion to America. It remains to be seen, of course, if European antipathies toward the United States will diminish once Europe's power buildup, which is now fully apace and enjoying much legitimacy in the eyes of the European, indeed global—that is non-American—public, will in fact bestow the kind of power to the Europeans that they will accept as being America's equal. It could well be argued that on the dimensions of ever-important "soft" power, Europe has become America's equal and might in fact be in the process of surpassing it in the foreseeable future. But for Europe to deploy any of its power—hard or soft—effectively, it will need a common sentiment, a unifying identity of some kind. And here, too, Arendt's words are enlightening.

At the end of her lecture's first section, Arendt takes a more precise look at the relationship between anti-Americanism and pan-European nationalism. She says there:

In Europe, it [anti-Americanism] is well on the way to becoming a new *ism*. Anti-Americanism, its negative emptiness not withstanding, threatens to become the content of a European movement. If it is true that each nationalism (though, of course, not the birth of every nation) begins with a real or fabricated common enemy, then the current image of America in Europe may well become the beginning of a new pan-European nationalism. Our hope that the emergence of a federated Europe and the dissolution of the present nation-state system will make nationalism itself a thing of the past may be unwarrantedly optimistic. On its more popular levels . . . the movement for a united Europe has recently shown decidedly nationalistic traits. The line between this anti-American Europeanism and the very healthy and necessary efforts to federate the European nations is further confused by the fact that the remnants of European fascism have joined the fight. Their presence reminds everybody that after Briand's futile gestures at the League of Nations it was Hitler who started the war with the promise that he would liquidate Europe's obsolete nation-state system and build a united Europe. The widespread and inarticulate anti-American sentiments find their political crystallization point precisely here. Since Europe is apparently no longer willing to see in America whatever it has to hope or to fear from her own future development, it has a tendency to consider the establishment of a European government an act of emancipation from America.[11]

In this critical reconstruction of contemporary trends about an identity-generating "Europeanism" that is fabricated by using America as a counterimage and that can be traced back ideologically to pan-nationalist forerunners, Arendt is also concisely underlining the difference between this kind of new, anti-American, pan-European nationalism and the political project of a new, genuinely postnational, and postconventional European polity. Arendt, whose own idea of a new European union following the collapse of the nation-state system in Europe is nourished at the outset by the political impulses of European resistance to National Socialism, is criticizing the ideology of pan-European nationalism, which in her view is based primarily on inveterate cultural enemy images instead of on new ways to self-constitute a postnational and liberal-democratic union. Such a construct, in Arendt's opinion, will be absolutely necessary in order to defend the political project of Europe against any kind of cozy anti-American identity that might lead to some sort of populist European nationalism that Arendt labeled Europeanism.

## Fabrications of "America" and "Europeanist" Self-images

Indeed, ever since September 11, 2001, and the "war against terror," the inflationary use of the totalitarian concept by Europeans in reference to America already observed by Arendt has been striking, even among reflective European intellectuals, and therefore in an increasingly undisguised fashion even among politicians. One may observe this, for example, in the popular comparison—disregarding every kind of historical distinction—between Bush and Hitler or between Auschwitz and Guantanamo. As indicated earlier, critical intellectuals like Habermas and Derrida, with an almost mythical-metaphysical sense of urgency on behalf of a "(re)birth of Europe," have been reverting to culturally overarching fabrications about a glaring antagonism between Europe and the United States over the definition of ostensible "norms" and "principles" for the United States in light of the Iraq War. In recent European discussions about "Europe and America," even such features of European history as totalitarianism, the genocide and destructive war perpetrated by Germans and their collaborators, and Europe's colonial crimes are no longer being used as points of reference for self-critical reflection, as Arendt was foresighted enough to indicate. Instead, these things frequently tend to be instrumentalized as "virtues" or "accomplishments" by comparison with the United States, the country—so Europeans claim—that would never know from its own experience "what war and destruction really mean." These references to "totalitarianism" and "utter lawlessness" on the American side of the Atlantic serve, first and foremost, an exculpatory purpose. They are also part of an idealizing self-discourse that one finds, for example, in Europe's predilection increasingly cited with pride in discussions about American politics and culture, and purportedly lending

Europe a special kind of moral qualification in such discussions of this kind for recollecting the "old" continent's crimes, from which Europeans believe they have been able to learn more, and thus mutate into morally superior human beings, than an "inexperienced" America spared the horrors of war and destruction. In this line of argument, it is not just the victims of the brutality of American soldiers in the antifascist war against Nazi Germany who are conjured away, but also that not entirely irrelevant question about the relationship between perpetrators and victims, in other words, between historical actors and subjects. For here the "experience" of war appears as something subjectless and fateful, leveling all differences, presumably affecting all Europeans identically, and ultimately uniting them. The positive reference to war and Holocaust, ennobled into one of Europe's "qualities" along with the ensuing "accomplishments of coming to terms" with the past,[12] that has increasingly proved successful in recent debates about Europe and the United States is just one new parry in a collective psychological repression, or in an instrumental self-reference to history glossing over all the irreconcilable historical breaches, in which history serves the purpose of—or is made fungible for—integrating the past's negative legacy into an idealizing, Euro-nationalist narrative of moral rebirth. There is always a danger here that the history of European civilization's great rupture will be converted into an ideology legitimating the continent's sense of superiority. This new, arrogant way of instrumentalizing the history of European crimes in the discourse about "war and peace," especially vis-à-vis the United States, Europe's continued but waning "occupier," does not, in any event, testify to a self-critical process of understanding and processing Europe's own past, a process that might be able to offer a European public citizenry critical standards for its own conduct; instead, it testifies more to the use of history for the purpose of collective self-idealization.[13]

The new, almost euphoric exuberance in the intellectual discourse about Europe corresponds with both an obvious inclination toward an idealistic self-representation of this emerging polity and its "cultural reservoirs" in the course of which any kind of critical perspective gets completely lost. This extolling of "Europe the good," the virtuous continent that has learned from its past mistakes and has attained a higher moral plateau by dint of this learning process, has to be accompanied by a sharp demarcation vis-à-vis everything that seems to represent "America" in European consciousness today. Indeed, America's role in helping Europe overcome its murderous past has long mutated into a discourse that accuses the United States of retarding, even hindering, European processes of reflection, learning, reckoning, and improving. And such views have long ago departed from the European Left's—and extreme Right's—assessments of America's repressive and evil role in Europe's immediate postwar period and become accepted fare of mainstream European thinking.

One also encounters growing efforts on the part of intellectuals and politicians to filter out, if not silence, all of the European countries' overwhelming problems and challenges for the European Union, often using the increasingly popular technique of defining away and delegating almost all the social, technological, and economic complications and conflicts of globalization (perceived with ever greater frequency as issues of "Americanization") onto America. The United States is handily depicted as the power behind the complex abstract societal processes and changes that move the world today. In Europe, too, the new stage of capitalist development commonly known as "globalization" needs a personification and a face to enter the political realm in any operational sense. "Americanization" does the trick perfectly.[14] Indeed, by equating globalization with Americanization, Europeans score two goals with one kick: First, those that really worry—rightfully—about the ills of this globalization exculpate their conscience by not having to ponder the fact that European companies and countries have been equal agents in this process of capitalism as have their American counterparts and the United States. Second, this gives the European global players an advantage over their American competitors because in the increasingly important court of global public opinion, they and their detrimental activities slide under the radar of scrutiny and opposition since they are not American and thus not the bogeymen of globalization. Nobody in America—or anywhere else for that matter—worries about the "Germanization," "Frenchization," or "Italianization" (indeed "Europeanization") of American or global culture by dint of major multinational companies from these three countries—just as examples—dominating large segments of the American and global markets. Indeed, nobody really knows or cares that according to UNESCO data, the United States is actually a net importer of cultural products and that developing countries and Japan, for example, are net exporters of such.[15]

To the extent that the political, public, and intellectual focus has recently started averting its gaze from the twenty-year-long electoral successes (on the European average) of right-wing extremist and populist parties, from the (in part) dramatic increase in racism in European society, from the growing severity of "Fortress Europe" against people from other countries and asylum seekers since the Maastricht Treaty and Schengen Accord, and from the resolute fight in most of the European countries against a persistently dominant, tenaciously regenerating ethnic national and cultural self-image that is just as hostile toward hyphenated identities as it is toward a lived multiculturalism,[16] a multiculturalism not limited to the preservation of ascribing cultural identities and ethnic tribal reservations— to this extent, the problems of the modern world and of rapid social change over the last few years in this emerging European citizen-public increasingly appear as American problems that, as Arendt critically observed, get transported into Europe from the "outside." This applies to the perception of cultural tensions and societal pluralization of self-images as much as it does to the profound social divisions that are created by the reconstruction (or rather disassembly) of the welfare state, which even those responsible for initiating such reforms portray as a cushioning of "American conditions" (see the extensive illustrations in chapter 3). This also applies to many of the major new transnational challenges, from the power of transnational enterprises, which are all too readily viewed in Europe mainly as "U.S. corporations" or "Wall Street," through the new problem of global terrorism, often perceived as something caused by the United States. Add to these the cross-border ecological dangers by way of the catchword "Kyoto," a treaty (wrongly) not ratified by the United States, thus making America appear as the sole author of this problem, while ignoring European actors' responsibilities for implementing the treaty. Lastly, one should not forget the problems of international law not taking into consideration the once widely discussed subject of how much European countries and the European Union have used this instrument, for example, by way of the International Criminal Court's previous clauses and composition,[17] to push through their particular interests beyond military power.[18]

## Europe the Good as Ur-America

While the Habermas-Derrida essay concentrates almost exclusively on values and is devoid of any mention of political dimensions, some of the essays in an important Habermas anthology are, on first reading, striking for their profound analyses of political problems. In particular the essay "Does the Constitutionalization of International Law Still Have a Chance?" in the third section of the volume (with its characteristic title "The Kantian Project and the Divided West") is a tour de force.[19] But here, too, with regard to the very political answers Habermas attempts offering, it is striking: Europe and the states and political forces operating inside Europe seem to lack any kind of power, any geopolitical interests. They appear as humanistic charitable organizations or Kantian clubs, which are able to defy the powerful in this world (in this case, admittedly, primarily "the USA") only through their kindness and virtues, through universalistic, if not altruistic, motives. In this conceptual and normative framework, universalistic ethical or constitutional norms are placed neither in any kind of relationship to real politics, which is, of course, decisively shaped by interests, nor in relationship to the reality of systems of political order that happen to be undergoing rapid change under transnational pressures. Nor are those Kantian imperatives or cosmopolitan normative orientations and standards for the public use of reason placed in any kind of relationship to contemporary structural problems of global society—such as social antagonisms

and new global power hierarchies, restrictions on law, rights, and
publics, and questions about the institutionalization of democracy
in the transnational realm. We read nary a word about the proliferation of failing states, the continued existence of authoritarian regimes, regional civil wars, and the persecution of minorities in dozens of countries. Finally, the pressing problem of transnational
terrorism receives no attention. In short, the many contradictions
and complexities of contemporary globalization remain unexplored
under the feel-good dichotomy of an idealized core Europe and a
vilified America. The relationship among norms, ethics, and politics
is reduced to a fundamental conflict between Europe and the United
States, a conflict that implicitly reproduces the traditional ideological contrast between the presumed "idealism" of the Old and the
purported "materialism" of the New World: Europe appears in a
way that is different from the postnational constellations Habermas
once used to develop a complex understanding of democratization's
opportunities and problems in the context of globalization. It is now
an inherently peaceful, practically interest-free and social-minded
paradise, a continental Gandhi confronting an American "evil empire" with his pacifist methods and aims.

It was Habermas who, more than any other thinker, always reminded German intellectuals that the great achievement of the
Bonn Republic was its unequivocal acceptance of the political culture of the West across the board. And it was clear to anyone who
kept abreast of these intellectual matters that Habermas not only
included the United States within the "West," but that the United
States occupied an outstanding position in this political-normative
frame of reference.[20] This is now a thing of the past, and if I understand Habermas correctly here, then it seems clear (at least reading
between the lines) that he deems it highly unlikely that America will
ever return—even after the departure of George W. Bush and his
entourage—to the world of rational, enlightened, secular, social-
minded, and democratic values, the world that Habermas and other
like-minded intellectuals now see as solely represented by Europe,
particularly its Franco-German avant-garde core. For Habermas,
one important aspect of this emphasis on the United States as the

counterpart to Europe's current development consists of his citing a strong affinity with the essential character of the "original" United States, which he sees as having gone astray over the last ten years. For progressives and liberals, at least for those among them who share not only Habermas's normative preferences, but also his political attitudes, the new Europe is therefore not simply a "counter-America"; rather, it is simultaneously something like an original "Ur-America" that can be set in opposition to the "Current-America." Thomas Meyer, the Social Democratic intellectual, whom I mentioned in the context of presenting contemporary America as a paragon of a "defective" democracy, also sees present-day Europe as the true heir of a "good" America that has long faded and seems to have no chance of ever appearing again, if one is to give credence to the writings of European intellectuals like Meyer.[21] But in light of this construction, with which Europe is turned into a democratic-universalist and normatively superior "Ur-America," but whereby America's own "return" to democratic universalism is apodictically ruled out after eight years of George W. Bush's regardless how woeful a presidency, one can only suspect that a democratic model once pieced together into a superego is now forcefully and once and for all being pushed off the pedestal by the same people who had placed it there.

There can be no doubt that Europe certainly does pursue clear power interests vis-à-vis the United States—and toward other "players" in world politics—and that, to fulfill its interests on a foundation of relative military weakness, it is especially keen to place its bets on "soft power" and link this stance to corresponding legitimating ideologies that (at least prima facie) are certainly more multilateral and occasionally more "nonviolent" than is the case with the United States. But this hardly means that Europe is a babe in the woods of world politics that frowns on power, a beginner representing global society's universal interests on the world stage. Among most of those speaking up on behalf of European intellectuals, and in the recent writings of Habermas as well, we find virtually nothing about the steely and often hypernationalist pursuit of their country's own interests in the foreign policy of the French, whereby Paris tries to secure its European position of power and—regardless of the issue—to take the opposite side against the United States.[22] That Germany's and Britain's policies in the international arena are also primarily driven by national interest rather than by a European one needs no lengthy elaboration. And if Europe's self-proclaimed post-nationalism were more than a mere veneer—or a useful rallying cry against the United States—surely France and Britain would have volunteered to surrender their permanent seat on the United Nations Security Council for a joint European one, thus making Germany's desire to attain precisely such a seat moot. That France and Britain would ever come around to abandoning their Security Council seats in favor of a European one is remote, to say the least. The much-vaunted postnationalism of the Europeans, positively contrasted with the hypernationalism of the Americans, needs serious rethinking based on real actions rather than self-serving ornamentation. A similar loss of honest, (self-)critical analysis of policy, power, and authority has become such a widespread phenomenon in the course of these European debates that it can sometimes cause the strangest fruit to blossom. Thus, for example, the Italian philosopher Domenico Losurdo has openly and without any contradiction or opposition—at least to my knowledge—talked in academic publications about a "fascistic" "American 'Herrenvolk [master race] democracy.' " Europe, according to Losurdo, is still not in a position to understand the "essence" of American fundamentalism, the "greatest danger to world peace," or to grasp its "mixture of religious and moral fervor" and "open pursuit of political, economic, and military world domination."[23]

## Europeanism and Anti-Americanism as a Political Force: The European "Orientalizing" of America

I think it revealing that neither the fall of the Berlin Wall nor the dissolution of the Communist world, let alone German unification, gave rise to an emotional groundswell of a European common identity anywhere near the degree that the aftermath of 9/11 and the Iraq War did. When Berliners were dancing in the streets and on the hulks of the crumbling Wall in 1989, Londoners and Parisians were sitting at home fretting. Nobody in Western Europe thronged to any public place to support the celebrations occurring in Warsaw and Prague when their repressive regimes were finally vanquished. None of these events triggered anything even approximating the broad enthusiasm that February 15 unleashed across the continent. Only future historians will know whether Strauss-Kahn, Habermas, and their colleagues will be proven right about this day becoming Europe's actual national holiday. One thing, however, is clear: The long tradition of a profound ambivalence toward America set the intellectual stage for this day's powerful symbolic presence. In the context of the sixtieth anniversary of D-Day, the French writer Alexandre Adler offered this pointed characterization for Europe's current drift away from America, against which Arendt had warned, but which she simultaneously did not regard as unavoidable: "D-Day will briefly placate tempers, but it will not alter the fact that the foundation for trans-Atlantic relations are in a process of dissolution. . . . Europe's process of emancipation from America is simply unavoidable. It is a natural phenomenon, the belated fruit of the European continent's unification."[24]

History teaches that every state structure, especially in its initial stages, only achieves self-consciousness when it defines itself in opposition to another state. All nationalisms emerge in opposition to others. This does not mean, however, in Arendt's formulation, that the formation of political communities and associations must necessarily rest upon political-cultural antagonisms, especially since the tendency for the European Union quite beyond the question of its future constitution has been more to develop into a newfangled, post- and multinational "multilevel polity without a state"—and, in the near future, into a "flexible and pragmatic set of arrangements and self-images that allow the member states, both in their internal affairs as well as in the global economy and politics, to keep operating as distinct political entities"—than into a classical nation-state.[25] "Europe" today is neither principally a political goal nor a finished structure, but instead de facto a political process. But now that Europe as a polity is on the agenda and in urgent need of greater legitimacy—and especially since there is still a significant gap between the clear advocacy of European unity among elites and ongoing widespread skepticism among the various European Union countries' populations, as witnessed by the aforementioned events in France and the Netherlands in the spring of 2005—anti-Americanism could admittedly exert a useful mobilization function for the ideational foundation of this new polity: Anti-Americanism might be in a position to help bridge these kinds of discrepancies and legitimacy gaps by using convenient ideological reflexes present both among elites and in significant segments of the population, by means of which obvious structural problems, economic contradictions, and the much-lamented democratic deficit of the European Union could also, at least provisionally, be pushed into the background.

In any event, most of the myths about the "(re-)birth of the European nation" that are enjoying success today (of all times) belong, in the words of Homi K. Bhaba, to "those ideological maneuvers through which 'imagined communities' are given essentialist identities."[26] At the same time, anti-Americanism is a "lazy person's way" of dealing with crises and problems of collective identity, globalization, and modernity[27] that has been rekindled in the course of new public polarizations, though anti-Americanism has also recently induced new critical self-reflection about this counterimage.[28]

Today there is very little that emotionally binds Finns and Greeks or Scots and Italians together. They are not particularly united by a positive identification with a still quite abstract "Europe." For all that, though, a negative, clearly defined, and emotionally omnipresent identification with not being American apparently has increasing binding power, especially as it continues to be more amply formulated in the wake of September 11, 2001. "If one can even speak about a construct called 'Europe,' with a recognizable identity, culture, and view of the world, then most Europeans—especially among the young—would not be able to characterize this except along one very decisive dimension of what Europe is not: America."[29] And then we witness the response of a twenty-six-year-old Prague student who had just completed his master's thesis in "European Studies" at the Charles University on the question of

European identity: "As with all identities, it is always far easier to create an identity by placing it clearly in opposition to one that already exists. The rudimentary European identity I possess is only possible by way of opposition to the United States."[30]

To fill the twofold gap that is plaguing contemporary Europe today—one between people and power, and the other between power and purpose—the young German social scientist Volker Heins argues persuasively that Europe's intellectual as well as professional discourse has created a binary world of "sacred" and "profane" in which the former is Europe and the latter the United States. Public discourse in Europe has, according to Heins, shifted over the past few years "from stressing the 'sameness' of Europeans within the larger family of western nations to highlighting the 'differentness' of Europe vis-à-vis the world in general, and the United States in particular."[31] In so doing, Heins argues that Europeans rely on tropes about America that they used to describe their colonial subjects of yore: brutish, destructive, petulant, disrespectful of international law, in short, behaving like a spoiled child. He labels this process an "orientalizing" of America by Europeans, which might very well help in the construction of a European identity.

"Europe" today, as the empirical world attests, only gets Europeans' hearts to beat a little faster when they hear the word "America." Here, too, the world of sports supplies a good illustration: There is no doubt that by now the European flag has become an important symbol of instrumental authority. It now graces many public buildings in the European Union members' respective capitals alongside each member state's national flag. Yet, I have never seen anybody in Europe wave the European flag with jubilation and pride, and identify with it in an emotional as opposed to an instrumental manner except during the biannual Ryder Cup golf tournament, in which Europe regularly confronts the United States. During this increasingly important event, whose symbolism reaches way beyond the immediate boundaries of sports, we can observe the players and their fans experience a common European identity that is genuinely felt, not intellectually constructed. I will never forget how, during the Ryder Cup tournament in September 2004 at Oakland Hills Coun-

try Club outside of Detroit, a portly fan sporting an England
T-shirt featuring the St. George's Cross jumped up from his seat
near the putting green and yelled from the depth of his soul "Go
Europe" while waving a huge European flag upon an Irish player's
scoring a decisive point against his American opponent. I reckon
with a reasonable amount of certainty that under no other condition
would an English sports fan have behaved anywhere nearly similar
to this occasion. Of course, neither the English fan, nor the Irish
player, nor the German team captain had probably one ounce of
anti-Americanism in their respective bodies. Their behavior had
nothing to do with anti-Americanism, yet everything to do with a
moment of emotionally experienced European identity. Only by opposing the United States did Swedish, Spanish, English, and Irish
players, their German coach, and their many European fans mutate
into emotionally shared Europeans. They arrived as Team Europe,
they spoke as Team Europe, they played as Team Europe, they won
as Team Europe, they celebrated as Team Europe, and they departed
as Team Europe. My point is simple: Only by competing against the
United States did these European players and their fans experience
their primary identity as European—at least for a long weekend.
And that "Europe" forges a much more tangible identity as America's opponent—among both players and their fans—than "the International Team" is best exemplified by the fact that the biannual President's Cup tournament in which the best American golfers play
against the best non-Americans and non-Europeans (hence the "In-
ternationals") does not even come close to creating anywhere near
the excitement and rivalry (bordering on animosity) as has been regularly the case in the Ryder Cup. The sole difference lies in the
European players' feeling an emotional bond in their challenging
the Americans that the world's golfers clearly do not. Put differently,
Spaniards, Germans, Irish, and British feel a closer bond as Europeans when opposing Americans than do South Africans, Australians,
Canadians, and Fijians.

At this time it is completely unclear which direction and what
kind of political and symbolic content this waving of the European
flag will assume: a negative, exclusionary, and therefore arrogant

identity formation that Hannah Arendt labeled "Europeanism"; or a positive and universalistic ideology building on the commonalities of Western values and then forming the basis for further European state and nation building. As with all such historical developments, this choice depends on the discourse and political predispositions of the elites, on the one hand, and then especially on specific decisions on the other. Neither follows from any historically inevitable process but is contingent, in other words, dependent on public and political actors who can determine different directions. But there can be no doubt about one thing: Outfitted with a mass base and the already mentioned congruence between elite and mass opinion, anti-Americanism could, for the first time in its long European history, become a powerful political force going well beyond those ambivalences, antipathies, and resentments that have continuously shaped the intellectual life of Europe since July 5, 1776. "Americanized Europe is not Europe but an alienated Europe. . . . If Europe, in body and soul, wants to reach its unity, it must 'de-Americanize' on every level."[32]

For the time being, there seem to be no visible incentives for Europeans to desist from their continued opposition to the United States for which anti-Americanism will remain a useful discourse: Its tone is popular among European publics; far from harming Europe and its interests, anti-Americanism has helped gain Europeans respect, affection, and—most important—political clout in the rest of the world, as we have seen from data presented in chapter 4. Anti-Americanism has become a currency for Europe whose value fluctuates greatly, but whose existence does represent a chip that Europe will cash in with increasing gusto and to its own advantage. Competition with the United States in the process of globalization will, if anything, become keener, and in that case any discourse to denounce the opponent will come in handy. Since European anti-Americanism—as argued in chapter 1—is a kind of prejudice that is directed at a Mr. Big, and a seemingly retrograde and evil one at that, Europe the good, which—as testimony to progress and tolerance—has rightly dislodged many of its previously held prejudices from acceptable public interaction can indulge in this one free of any guilt, indeed, in its conviction that by being anti-American Europeans act morally, justly, and virtuously. Voicing European discontent with America and putting this discontent into practice via policies will become increasingly practical and "functional" for a Europe that has already emerged as a global player in an era in which the United States and its power will become increasingly contested in every corner of the world.[33] Moreover, unlike in the Cold War era, during which Europeans concealed some of their anti-Americanism because America provided tangible protection at least to the western half of the continent, Europeans experience their alliance with America as a source of instability and threat rather than the previous security and comfort. Lastly, precisely because nationalism in Europe is far from dead and remains a massive emotional and political force in every country, it is not the positive emotion of a European togetherness that creates a bond, but the negative and distancing (i.e., "othering") realization of *not* being American. " 'The big "O," or the big other, can be very useful,' said Jan-Werner Mueller, a Princeton political scientist. 'There's a school of thinking that says if we are building a European identity, we have to build it against something.' "[34] In short, I see few incentives for Europe to divest itself of its current opposition to and antipathy for America and plenty to stay the course.

When in a few decades—perhaps in 2057, commemorating the centennial of the Treaties of Rome, which created what subsequently evolved into the European Union—a stately "Europe Square" will grace Brussels, featuring statues of the Union's founding (and facilitating) giants such as Jean Monnet, Robert Schuman, Alcide De Gasperi, Konrad Adenauer, Paul-Henri Spaak, Francois Mitterand, Helmut Kohl, Jacques Delors, and others, I really believe that a statue of George W. Bush also deserves its honored place in this ornamental setting, thus giving proper tribute to the man who brought Europeans together like nobody before (and perhaps after) him.

Jean Monnet, maybe the most significant of the aforementioned founding fathers, seems also to have believed strongly in the notion that a common adversary and object of antipathy can induce political and emotional coalitions among diverse nations who otherwise would not find their common ground so easily. Monnet wrote in his memoirs that Gamal Abdel Nasser, the charismatic, secular, pan-Arab nationalist dictator of Egypt who successfully challenged the old colonial European powers of Britain and France in the 1950s, deserved a statue as the actual founder of a united Europe (*fédérateur européen*).[35] *Plus ça change, plus c'est la même chose*: The objects of ire, the personages have surely changed; the concept has not.

# NOTES

## Introduction

1. By using the terms "America" and "American" throughout this study to denote the political entity of "The United States of America," I beg the indulgence of all readers who reside north or south of the respective borders of the United States and are thus, of course, "American" though not citizens of the United States. I am using the concepts "America" and "American" not in their wider and more accurate geographic meaning but in their much more commonly used manner as representing one country, the United States of America. But particularly in a work on "anti-Americanism," I feel justified in doing so since the term itself has always applied "exclusively to the United States and not to Canada or Mexico or any other nation of the New World. Many who complain bitterly that the United States has unjustifiably appropriated the label of America have nonetheless gladly allowed that anti-Americanism should refer only to the United States." James W. Ceaser, "A Genealogy of Anti-Americanism," *The Public Interest*, Summer 2003, pp. 3–18. Nobody in Europe, with the exception of German speakers, refers to U.S. citizens regularly as "U.S.-Americans" or has routinely added the qualifier "U.S." to virtually anything American; not even the French talk about "EU-Américains." I will address this particular German neologism when discussing concrete examples of recent anti-Americanism in Germany later in this book.

2. The Pew Research Center for the People & the Press, "Anti-Americanism: Causes and Characteristics," *The Pew Global Attitudes Project* (Washington, DC: Pew Research Center, 2003), p. 1.

3. Glenn Frankel, "Sneers from Across the Atlantic: Anti-Americanism Moves to W. Europe's Political Mainstream," *Washington Post*, February 11, 2003.

4. Austria's entire post–World War II existence has been anchored in its bloc-free neutrality, which means that the country has explicitly not entered into any official political and military alliance with the United States. Still, there can be no question that by dint of its strong cultural ties

to Germany and Western Europe, and—above all—by virtue of its capital-ist economic structure, Austria's neutrality was equidistant from East and West in name only. The realities on the ground placed Austria squarely in the camp of the West and thus the Europe closer to the United States than to Eastern Europe and the Soviet Union.

## Chapter 1
## Anti-Americanism as a European Lingua Franca

1. One of the best recent articles on anti-Americanism is Fouad Ajami's essay "The Falseness of Anti-Americanism," *Foreign Policy*, September 2003. A fine collection of essays is Paul Hollander, ed., *Understanding Anti-Americanism: Its Origins and Impact at Home and Abroad* (Chicago: Ivan R. Dee, 2004).

2. Jon Elster, *Alchemies of the Mind: Rationality and the Emotions* (Cambridge: Cambridge University Press, 1999), p. 65. Elster attributes the distinction between anger and hate to Aristotle's *Nichomachean Ethics*.

3. Joseph Joffe, "What Is Anti-Americanism?" (lecture at Stanford University, November 12, 2005). Emphasis in original.

4. Ibid.

5. For a fine definition and analysis of Anti-Americanism as a prejudice in opposition to its being a tendency or an ideology, see Brendon O'Connor, "What Is Anti-Americanism? Tendency, Prejudice or Ideology" (paper presented to the Anti-Americanism Symposium, Institute for the Study of the Americas, University of London, October 21, 2005).

6. See especially Paul M. Sniderman, Philip E. Tetlock, and Edward G. Carmines, "Prejudice and Politics: An Introduction," in *Prejudice, Politics, and the American Dilemma*, ed. Paul M. Sniderman, Philip E. Tetlock, and Edward G. Carmines (Stanford: Stanford University Press, 1993), pp. 1-31. Also see Paul M. Sniderman and Thomas Piazza, *Black Pride and Black Prejudice* (Princeton: Princeton University Press, 2002).

7. For an excellent article showing how American intellectuals have cultivated anti-American views, see Ian Buruma, "Wielding the Moral Class," *The Financial Times Weekend Magazine*, September 13, 2003.

8. Linda Gordon, "Hating Amerika: Anti-Americanism and the American Left," in *Anti-Americanism*, ed. Andrew Ross and Kristin Ross (New York: New York University Press, 2004), pp. 273–80; and Andrew Ross, "The Domestic Front," in ibid., pp. 281–300.

9. See Andrian Kreye, "Zugpferd des Antiamerikanismus. Schlecht recherchiert, ohne Kontext: Warum ist Michael Moore in Europa so erfolgreich?" *Süddeutsche Zeitung*, October 11, 2003.

10. David Brooks, "All Hail Moore," *New York Times*, June 26, 2004.

11. How often have I heard Europeans say the following: "This cashier's smile, the cab driver's friendliness, the greetings on the street—none of this is authentic. They cannot possibly mean this all." To which I always reply: "No, they don't want to hear your personal story and be your friend, but their sullen European counterparts don't want this either." It has never been clear to me why smiling and friendliness connote stupidity and superficiality while sullenness and arrogance are supposed to signify profundity, cultural erudition, and authenticity.

12. That speaking ill of Americans in progressive circles and among students is far from stigmatized the way speaking about other nationalities certainly—and rightly—is, pertains not only to the discourse in Europe but also to other parts of the world, including Australia. As I was completing the copy-edited stage of this manuscript, I received the following e-mail from my friend and colleague Dr. Brendon O'Connor, senior lecturer at Griffiths University and editor of a four-volume anthology on anti-Americanism in the world. One of his students wrote the following note to him during his sabbatical year in Washington, DC: "There are a whole bunch of University of Michigan students at college at the moment. It is quite amazing how the Australian students talk about 'them.' All of the Australian students are really picking and choosing aspects of their behaviour to confirm stereotypes. If they were doing the same thing about a bunch of students from China they would be racist. It's funny because when some of the Australian girls are saying to me 'Oh, they [the American female students] are all such Barbies' or 'They are all so loud' and then are asking me for my opinion, I have to say I don't think so. Then the Australian girls look at me funny! Maybe I am just a loud Barbie at heart."

13. Paul Hollander, *Anti-Americanism: Critiques at Home and Abroad, 1965–1990* (New York: Oxford University Press, 1992), p. 339 (emphasis in original). In addition to Hollander's key book on this topic, I would like to mention three others that, in my view, offer the most comprehensive analysis on this subject. For Germany, it is clearly Dan Diner's *Feindbild Amerika: Über die Beständigkeit eines Ressentiments* (Munich: Propyläen Verlag, 2002); for France, Philippe Roger's *L'Ennemi américain: Généalogie de l'antiaméricanisme français* (Paris: Editions du Seuil, 2002); and for Canada, Mario Roy's *Pour en finir avec l'antiaméricanisme* (Québec: Boréal, 1993). I have yet to find comparable books for anti-Americanism in Britain and Italy.

14. Alvin Rubinstein and Donald Smith, "Anti-Americanism in the Third World," *Annals (AAPSS)* 97 (1988), p. 35.

15. Todd Gitlin, "Anti-anti-Americanism," *Dissent* 50, no. 1 (Winter 2003), pp. 103–4.

16. Friedrich von Schiller, *Don Carlos, Infante of Spain. A Drama in Five Acts*. Translated by Charles E. Passage (New York: Frederick Ungar Publishing Co., 1959), p. 122.

17. E-mail correspondence from Gerhard Casper, March 30, 2005.

18. Even though the Nazis idolized Schiller (just like they did Goethe), used him shamelessly for their own propagandistic purposes, and continued to extol him as "heroic" and "Nordic" throughout their rule, it is interesting to note that after 1940 all *Don Carlos* productions had to omit the famous line "Geben Sie Gedankenfreiheit," lest any unwanted applause or other manifestations of dissent might occur. On this point, see Paul Michael Lützeler, "Klassik, KZ und Schillers Schreibtisch," *Die Zeit*, May 11, 2005.

19. "A British economist writing in the *Atlantic Monthly* in 1901 used the phrase anti-Americanism explicitly, and made clear what it was about. To a 'despairing (European) envy of her prosperity and success' was coupled a disagreeable new sense of impotence, commercial, diplomatic and moral. 'Cultured Europeans intensely resent the bearing of Americans; they hate the American form of swagger, which is not personal like the British, but national.' Here was a country 'crudely and completely immersed in materialism.' Little wonder that 'anti-Americanism (*sic*) was on the march.' " From David W. Ellwood, "A Brief History of European Anti-Americanism" (paper delivered at the 2003 convention of the Organization of American Historians, Memphis, TN, April 6, 2003).

20. I can just see the perplexed expressions on the faces of the French cultural elite as Woody Allen, on one of his European tours as a jazz clarinetist, responded to the almost imploring questions of journalists by saying how much he loves America and especially New York, and that nothing matters more to him than following a good baseball game on the radio or attending a basketball showdown involving his beloved New York Knickerbockers in Madison Square Garden. There are a few other Americans admired by Europeans, à la Woody Allen and Bill Clinton, who are not counted as genuine Americans by their European fans. How often have I heard it said in Europe that "so and so is not a 'real' American" when the speaker uttering this sentiment is talking about an American he or she happens to admire.

21. Cited by Josef Joffe, "Who's Afraid of Mr. Big?" *The National Interest*, Summer 2001, p. 44. See also his *Überpower: The Imperial Temptation of America* (New York: W. W. Norton, 2006) and his "The Demons of Europe," *Commentary* 117, no. 1 (January 2004), pp. 29–34.

22. In his book *Of Paradise and Power: America and Europe in the New World Order* (New York: Alfred A. Knopf, 2003), Robert Kagan offers a terminologically apt though, on many points, conceptually problematic in-

terpretation of the transatlantic divide as one between Europeans from Venus and Americans from Mars.

23. See, for example, Gret Haller, *Die Grenzen der Solidarität* (Berlin: Aufbau Verlag, 2002), which is her magnum opus on this topic

24. Joffe, "Who's Afraid of Mr. Big?" p. 44.

25. Thomas Meyer, ed., *Die Zukunft der Sozialen Demokratie* (Bonn: Friedrich Ebert Stiftung, 2005).

26. Volker Heins, "Orientalising America? Continental Intellectuals and the Search for Europe's Identity," *Millennium: Journal of International Studies* 34, no. 2 (2006), pp. 433–48.

27. Thomas Meyer, *Die Identität Europas* (Frankfurt a.M.: Suhrkamp, 2004), pp. 144, 145.

28. Klaus Faber, "Reden über Demokratie. Deutsche Debatten über defekte und nicht-defekte Demokratie-Modelle" (Lecture given in Berlin, December 9, 2005).

29. Charles Lane, "The Paradoxes of a Death Penalty Stance," *Washington Post*, June 4, 2005.

30. Eric Frey, *Schwarzbuch USA* (Frankfurt a.M.: Eichborn, 2004). In contrast to the similarly crude *Schwarzbuch des Kommunismus* [Black Book of Communism] published by Stephane Courtois and others in 1997, which Frey's work follows conceptually, there was to my knowledge no protest of any kind against Frey's book as there was all over Europe in the wake of Courtois's.

31. Eckhard Fuhr, *Wo wir uns finden. Die Berliner Republik als Vaterland* (Berlin: Berlin Verlag, 2005), p. 110.

32. Hubert Védrine in his book *Les cartes de la France à l'heure de la mondialisation*, cited by Joffe, "Who's Afraid of Mr. Big?" p. 46.

33. Peter Zadek, "Kulturkampf? Ich bin dabei. Mir ist Amerika zutiefst zuwider," *Der Spiegel*, July 14, 2003. As is typical of so many anti-Americans, Zadek proudly proclaims that he has never set foot in the United States and has no intentions of ever visiting it.

34. As quoted by Alvin H. Rosenfeld, *Anti-Zionism in Great Britain and Beyond: A "Respectable" Anti-Semitism?* (New York: The American Jewish Committee, 2004), p. 41.

35. Russell Berman says: "Anti-Americanism is not a reasoned response to American policies; it is the hysterical surplus that goes beyond reason. That difference is evident in the constant recycling of anti-American images that have a history that long antedates current policy." Berman, *Anti-Americanism in Europe: A Cultural Problem* (Stanford: Hoover Institution Press, 2004), p. 60.

36. Meredith Woo-Cummings, "Unilateralism and Its Discontents: The Passing of the Cold-War Alliance and Changing Public Opinion in

the Republic of Korea" (working paper, University of Michigan, 2003). See, too, James Brooke, "U.S. Soldiers in South Korea Feel Growing Anti-Americanism," *International Herald Tribune*, January 8, 2003.

37. Salman Rushdie, "America and Anti-Americans," *New York Times*, February 4, 2002.

38. Álvaro Delgado-Gal, "Diagnóstico del Antiamericanismo," *ABC*, March 15, 2003.

39. My temporal qualification relates to the intensity that Arab anti-Americanism has assumed for roughly a decade. This anti-Americanism is full of so much hatred and is so extensive, both geographically as well as socially, that it has developed a quality unparalleled anywhere else in the world. This Arab anti-Americanism promotes a public discourse in which television broadcasts of beheadings are not only tolerated by the media and the public but also sanctioned because they are regarded as a legitimate method of resistance in the context of an anti-American hysteria. On this point, see the article by the Arab journalist Marmoun Fandy, "Where's the Arab Media's Sense of Outrage?" *Washington Post*, July 4, 2004. In this article Fandy describes how the glorification of violence in the Arab world is legitimated by the intensity of hatred against Americans and America and either promoted by the media as "cool" or, at best, benevolently passed over in silence.

40. There are, of course, a number of these books and scholarly publications. Here I refer only to the already mentioned book edited by Paul Hollander, *Understanding Anti-Americanism*, and to a special edition of *Annals of the American Academy of Political and Social Science* 97 (May 1988), edited by Thomas Perry Thornton and dedicated to the topic of anti-Americanism.

41. Frank Jansen, "SPD und NPD gemeinsam für den Frieden. Der Vorsteher des Fürstenwalder Stadtparlaments lässt den Chef der Rechtsextremen sprechen," *Der Tagesspiegel*, April 9, 2003.

42. By far the best book on left-wing anti-Americanism, which features precisely the exculpatory phenomenon I am describing, is Michael Hahn, ed., *Nichts gegen Amerika: Linker Antiamerikanismus und seine lange Geschichte* (Hamburg Konkret Literatur Verlag, 2003). Most of the subjects treated by the book's contributing writers apply, of course, not just to Germany but to other European countries as well.

43. For a more detailed breakdown of this Left-Right, culture-political economy scheme pertaining only to Germany, see Andrei S. Markovits, "Anti-Americanism and the Struggle for a West Germany Identity," in *The Federal Republic of Germany at Forty*, ed. Peter H. Merkl (New York: New York University Press, 1989), p. 42 ff.

44. On this point, see Dietrich Schulze-Marmeling, *Die Bayern* (Göttingen: Verlag Die Werkstatt, 1997).

45. There are numerous books that serve the sole purpose of spreading antipathy toward Manchester United. Among the best are *Manchester United Ruined My Life*; *Red Devils: A History of Man United's Rogues and Villains*; and *Yessss!!! United in Defeat*. The latter is an entreaty to pure schadenfreude. As far as parallels to the New York Yankees are concerned, one need only recall the popular musical *Damn Yankees*, in which a player for the Washington Senators, a team always defeated by the Yankees, enters into a pact with the devil so that the Senators can finally beat the hated Yankees.

46. Andrei S. Markovits, "Austrian-German Relations in the New Europe: Predicaments of Political and National Identity Formation" in *German Studies Review* 19, no. 1 (February 1996). In this article I argue that Germans in any form are always a source of irritation for Austrians. To Austrians, Germans and Germany are always an "issue," always some kind of problem, while conversely Germans view Austria as a nice vacation spot where the food is good, the music even better, and where people speak with a charming accent. For the big guy the little guy is simply lovely, at worst occasionally onerous, while for the little guy, conversely, the big guy is always a question of identity. The parallel relationship Germany–Austria and USA–Canada is very nicely treated in Harald von Riekhoff and Hanspeter Neuhold, eds., *Unequal Partners: A Comparative Analysis of Relations between Austria and the Federal Republic of Germany and between Canada and the United States* (Boulder: Westview Press, 1993). This very phenomenon of the threat to the little guy's identity by virtue of the big guy's mere existence is quite vividly reproduced in this volume, in which the editors intentionally kept German and American authors from putting in a word and gave contributors from the small countries—Canadians and Austrians—free play to vent their reflections on the constant threat from their respective big neighbors. The USA-Europe relationship has strong parallels—especially as viewed from Europe—to the USA-Canada or Germany-Austria relationship, with the Europeans feeling like the Canadians or Austrians in this case.

47. Berndt Ostendorf, "The Final Idiocy of the Reversed Baseball Cap: Transatlantische Widersprüche in der Amerikanisierungsdebatte,"*Amerikastudien/American Studies* 44, no. 1 (1999); Ostendorf, "Why Is American Popular Culture So Popular? A View from Europe," *Amerikastudien/American Studies* 46, no. 3 (2001). In this study I will be looking at only the European (and not the American) side of this *folie à deux*.

48. See Gerard Baker, "European Insults Fall on Deaf Ears in America's Heartland," *Financial Times*, February 6, 2003.

49. Timothy Garton Ash, "Anti-Europeanism in America" *New York Review of Books*, February 13, 2003. Although Garton Ash strives to write

about Europe as a whole, his article shows that such an entity hardly exists in the United States. There are indeed strong *ressentiments* against different nations and politicians residing in Europe, but Americans harbor no negative feelings against Europe per se. Garton Ash emphasizes that the French in particular have had to suffer as a target for American *ressentiment* since the controversy over the Gulf War. Jan-Werner Müller concurs when he writes: "It cannot be an accident that American 'Europhobia' puts in an appearance almost exclusively as Francophobia." See Müller, "Das bessere Europa, das schlechtere Amerika? Im Spiegelkabinett transatlantischer Wahrnehmungen," *Neue Zürcher Zeitung*, June 14, 2004.

50. Baker, "European Insults."

51. Herbert J. Spiro, "Anti-Americanism in Western Europe," in *Anti-Americanism: Origins and Context*, special issue of *Annals of the American Academy of Political and Social Science*, ed. Thomas Perry Thornton (Beverly Hills: Sage Publications, 1988), p. 126.

52. "American Anti-Europeanism Does Less Damage Than European Anti-Americanism. But it Is Still Worrying," *Economist*, March 1, 2003.

53. Baker, "European Insults."

54. Cristina Merrill, "Absolutely Fabulous," *American Demographics* 22, no. 1 (January 2000), p. 27.

55. Bernard-Henri Levy, "Wer 'Stoppt den US-Imperialismus' wiehert, hat nichts begriffen," *Frankfurter Allgemeine Zeitung*, January 24, 2006. For the book itself, see Bernard-Henri Levy, *American Vertigo: Traveling America in the Footsteps of Tocqueville* (New York: Random House, 2006).

56. Mary Kenny, "Why Anti-Americanism Divides the Classes," *Sunday Telegraph*, September 30, 2001.

## Chapter 2
### European Anti-Americanism: A Brief Historical Overview

1. Even though I think that the French term *ressentiment* is much more powerful and comprehensive than the English "resentment," I do not see the need to use the former in an English-language text. The French term connotes dimensions of envy, jealousy, and, above all, a sort of lingering hatred arising from a sense of impotence that the English term does not. For Friedrich Nietzsche, for example, ressentiment also includes feelings of impotence and failed (or untried) revenge. Max Scheler's work is absolutely central to the distinction between resentment and ressentiment. See Max Scheler, *Ressentiment*, ed. Lewis A. Coser and trans. William W. Holdheim (New York: The Free Press of Glencoe, 1961).

2. John F. Moffit and Santiago Sebastian, *O Brave New People: The European Invention of the American Indian* (Albuquerque: University of New Mexico Press, 1996).

3. Ira Strauss, "Is it Anti-Americanism or Anti-Westernism?" (manuscript, 2003).

4. Karen Ordahl Kupperman, ed., *America in European Consciousness, 1493–1750* (Chapel Hill: University of North Carolina Press, 1995).

5. Cornelius Jaenen, "'Les Sauvages Amériquains': Persistence into the Eighteenth Century of Traditional French Concepts and Constructs for Comprehending Amerindians," *Ethnohistory*, no. 1 (1982), pp. 43–56. (The citation is from p. 49, in which Jaenen quotes volume 15, pp. 445–46, of the *Oeuvres complètes* by the Comte de Buffon, Georges-Louis Leclerc, 1824–28, published in Paris.)

6. Georges de Buffon, "Of the Varieties in the Human Species," in *Barr's Buffon. Buffon's Natural History Containing A Theory Of The Earth, A General History Of Man, Of The Brute Creation, And Of Vegetables, Minerals, Etc.* (London: T. Gillet, 1807), vol. 4, pp 306–52.

7. Cornelius de Pauw, "Recherches philosophiques sur les Américains, ou Mémoires intéressants pour servir à l'histoire de l'espece humaine par M. de P.," in *Œuvre philosophiques* (Berlin: Decker, 1768), vol. 1, p. II.

8. Susanne Zantop, *Colonial Fantasies: Conquest, Family, and Nation in Precolonial Germany, 1770–1870* (Durham: Duke University Press, 1997), pp. 46–65.

9. Dan Diner discusses de Pauw, Buffon, and other contemporary writers and thinkers in his *America in the Eyes of Germans: An Essay on Anti-Americanism*, trans. Allison Brown (Princeton: Markus Wiener, 1996), p. 6 ff.

10. William Cronon, *Changes in the Land: Indians, Colonists, and the Ecology of New England* (New York: Hill and Wang, 1983), p. 126.

11. Trudy Eden, "Food, Assimilation, and the Malleability of the Human Body in Early Virginia," in *A Centre of Wonders: The Body in Early America*, ed. Janet Lindman and Michele Tarter (Ithaca: Cornell University Press, 2001), p. 30.

12. Martha Finch, " 'Civilized' Bodies and the 'Savage' Environment of Early New Plymouth," in *A Centre of Wonders*, ed. Lindman and Tarter, pp. 43–59.

13. It is interesting that this European anxiety about "going native" was much more pronounced vis-à-vis America than in the case of Africa or Asia, where the threat of "invisible assimilation" seemed relatively minor. In other words, there was, according to colonial rhetoric, little chance of a German or Frenchman being mistaken for an Asian or African native, or vice versa. In contrast, this idea obsessed Europeans in the New World, establishing a crucial aspect of early Anti-Americanism: the nation's ability to attack and destroy European identity from within.

14. Spiro, "Anti-Americanism in Western Europe," p. 124.

15. Philippe Roger, *The American Enemy: A Story of French Anti-Americanism*, trans. Sharon Bowman (Chicago: University of Chicago Press, 2005), p. 157 ff. According to Roger, the South became a sentimental favorite in the right Parisian circles in the era of Napoleon III. The unequivocal partisanship of the London *Times* against the Union is nicely elaborated by Martin Crawford, *The Anglo-American Crisis of the Mid-Nineteenth Century: "The Times" and America, 1850–1862* (Athens: The University of Georgia Press, 1987).

16. Joffe, "Who's Afraid of Mr. Big?" p. 45.

17. The original French refrain goes: "Quelque chose de Tennessee; Cette force, qui nous pousse vers l'infini; Y a peu d'amour avec tell'ment d'envie." To be sure, there is evidence that Hallyday's song is not solely about America as a geographic entity as embodied by the state of Tennessee, but equally about America as a concept, a way of life, as represented by that quintessential American playwright Tennessee Williams, to whom this song is meant as an homage. Indeed, the female voice at the start of the song quotes from Maggie's speech at the end of *Cat on a Hot Tin Roof*.

18. Jean-Francois Revel, *L'obsession anti-americaine. Son fonctionnement, ses causes, ses inconsequences* (Paris: Plon, 2002).

19. Klaus Bade, "German Transatlantic Emigration in the Nineteenth and Twentieth Centuries," in *European Expansion and Migration: Essays on the Intercontinental Migration from Africa, Asia and Europe*, ed. P. C. Emmer and M. Morner (Providence: Berg Publishers, 1992), p. 125.

20. Quoted according to ibid., p. 148. In addition to his undoubtedly brilliant inventions and profound writings, Benjamin Franklin also committed some rather awful anti-German opinions to paper.

21. Ernst Willkomm, *Die Europamüden. Modernes Lebensbild 1. und 2. Teil.* Faksimiledruck nach der 1. Auflage von 1838 (Göttingen: Vandenhoeck & Ruprecht, 1968).

22. Hans-Jürgen Grabbe, "Weary of Germany—Weary of America: Perceptions of the United States in Nineteenth-Century Germany," in *Transatlantic Images and Perceptions: Germany and America since 1776*, ed. David Barclay and Elisabeth Glaser-Schmidt (Cambridge: Cambridge University Press, 1997), pp. 65–86.

23. Wolfgang Helbich, "Different, but Not Out of This World: German Images of the United States between Two Wars, 1871–1914," in *Transatlantic Images*, ed. Barclay and Glaser-Schmidt, p. 115.

24. Rüdiger Steinlein, "Ferdinand Kürnbergers 'Der Amerikamüde.' Ein 'amerikanisches Kulturbild' als Entwurf einer negativen Utopie," in *Amerika in der deutschen Literatur. Neue Welt-Nordamerika-USA*, ed. Sigrid Bauschinger, Horst Denkler, and Wilfried Malsch (Stuttgart: Phillip Reclam jun., 1975), pp. 154–77.

25. Ibid., p. 162.

26. Stefan Ripplinger, "Der Schatz im Silbersee. Mit Karl May und Hegel im Wilden Westen," in *Amerika: Der "War on Terror" und der Aufstand der Alten Welt*, ed. Thomas Uwer, Thomas von der Osten-Sacken, and Andrea Woeldike (Freiburg: ça ira, 2003), p. 38.

27. Ibid.

28. Cited in ibid., p. 43.

29. Karl May, *Winnetou*, trans. David Koblick (Pullman: Washington State University Press, 1999), p. 2.

30. Ibid., p. 174.

31. Richard Cracroft, "The American West of Karl May," *American Quarterly* 19 (Summer 1967), p. 252.

32. May, *Winnetou*, pp. 186, 89, 82.

33. Ibid., p. 23.

34. Cracroft, "The American West," p. 257.

35. Karl May, *Winnetou* (Vienna: Karl May Taschenbücher, 1953) p. 208, my translation. Interestingly, this passage, along with others that are extremely explicit about the European bias of the author, have been either greatly edited or eliminated entirely from the American editions of the book that I consulted.

36. Pascal Grosse, "Turning Native? Anthropology, German Colonialism, and the Paradoxes of the 'Acclimatization Question' 1885–1914," in *Worldly Provincialism: German Anthropology in the Age of Empire*, ed. Matti Bunzl and H. Glenn Penny (Ann Arbor: University of Michigan Press, 2003), p. 189.

37. When American Secretary of Defense Donald Rumsfeld made his provocative remark about "old Europe" in order to strike at the Franco-German alliance against the Bush administration's Iraq campaign, the *Frankfurter Allgemeine Zeitung* asked leading French and German intellectuals to reply to Rumsfeld in its pages. The German artist Jochen Gerz limited his reply to saying that the way in which the United States had mercilessly driven America's original inhabitants to the margins of society was a sure sign for him that the United States was no democracy, and that any and all further commentary was unnecessary. Jochen Gerz, "Not in Our Name," one of several statements collected under the title "Das alte Europa antwortet Herrn Rumsfeld" [Old Europe Replies to Mr. Rumsfeld] in *Frankfurter Allgemeine Zeitung*, January 24, 2003.

38. Katrin Sieg, *Ethnic Drag: Performing Race, Nation, Sexuality in West Germany* (Ann Arbor: University of Michigan Press, 2003).

39. The already-mentioned article by Stefan Ripplinger (see note 26) is also interesting because the author draws parallels between Karl May's and Georg Friedrich Wilhelm Hegel's images of America—the former provid-

ing ordinary German citizens with anti-American prejudices, the latter doing the same for Germany's elites.

40. Three articles have proven particularly useful for my research on the anti-American attitudes of these giants of German culture, politics, literature, and philosophy: Manfred Henningsen, "Das Amerika von Hegel, Marx und Engels," *Zeitschrift für Politik*, vol. 20 (1973), p. 3; Hartmut Wasser, "Die Deutschen und Amerika," *Politik und Zeitgeschichte* (Beilage zur Wochenzeitung *Das Parlament*), June 26, 1976; and Günter Moltmann, "Anti-Americanism in Germany: Historical Perspectives," *Australian Journal of Politics and History* 21, no. 2 (August 1975).

41. Heinrich Heine, "Ludwig Börne: A Memorial (Second Book)," trans. Frederic Ewen and Robert Holub, in *The Romantic School and Other Essays*, ed. Jost Hermand and Robert Holub (New York: Continuum, 1985), p. 263.

42. Wasser, "Die Deutschen und Amerika," p. 10.

43. Moltmann, "Anti-Americanism in Germany," pp. 19–20.

44. Simon Schama, "The Unloved American," *New Yorker*, March 10, 2003.

45. Cited by James W. Ceasar, "A Genealogy of Anti-Americanism," *The Public Interest*, Summer 2003.

46. Cited by ibid.

47. Cited by Peter Gay, *Freud: A Life for Our Time* (New York: W. W. Norton, 1988), pp. 563, 570.

48. James Ceasar, "The Philosophical Origins of Anti-Americanism in Europe," in *Understanding Anti-Americanism*, ed. Hollander, pp. 45–64.

49. Georg Kamphausen, *Die Erfindung Amerikas in der Kulturkritik der Generation von 1890* (Göttingen: Velbrück Wissenschaft, 2002).

50. Ibid., p. 283.

51. Reinhard R. Doerries, "The Unknown Republic: American History at German Universities," *Amerikastudien/American Studies* 50, no. 1/2 (2005), pp. 99–125.

52. On the history of this intriguing development, see Roger, *The American Enemy*, chap. 4, pp. 129–56.

53. One need only recall Helmut Schmidt's arrogant behavior toward President Jimmy Carter, whom the German chancellor at the time regarded as a human rights–preaching moralist, rather than a politician with the ability to lead the Western world. Schmidt was constantly trying to instruct the American president on how he ought to behave. Today the tables have turned. Helmut Schmidt has become a grand moralist and human rights advocate, and in the interim the Americans have become practitioners of power politics.

54. See Doron Rabinovici, "Woodrow Wilson—Zentralfigur im Fremdbild," in *USA und Österreich zwischen altem Reich und neuer Welt. Die Perzeption der USA in Österreich während und nach dem Ende beider Weltkriege* (Vienna: Bundesministerium für Wissenschaft und Forschung, 1993/94), p. 113.

55. Christian Schwaabe, *Antiamerikanismus. Wandlungen eines Feindbildes* (Paderborn: Wilhelm Fink Verlag, 2003).

56. Doron Rabinovici, *Zwischen altem Reich und neuer Welt*, p. 246.

57. Ibid.

58. Quoted by Günter Bischof and Rolf Steininger, "Die Invasion aus der Sicht von Zeitzeugen," in *Die Invasion in der Normandie 1944: Internationale Perspektiven*, ed. Günter Bischof and Wolfgang Krieger (Innsbruck: Studienverlag, 2001), p. 66.

59. Andrei S. Markovits, "Die Helden stehen im Schatten," *Der Tagesspiegel*, June 4, 2004.

60. Cited in Andrew Gimson and Ross Clark, "A Sad Case of Schadenfreude," *Spectator*, September 13, 2003.

61. Tilman Fichter, born in 1937, was the official in charge of schooling and education for the SPD party executive between 1987 and 2001. Fichter's political career began with the Socialist German Student League (Sozialistischer Deutscher Studentenbund, SDS).

62. Gimson and Clark, "A Sad Case of Schadenfreude."

63. "Die Gefahr des Amerikanismus," *Das schwarze Korps*, March 16, 1944, p. 1 ff.

64. Pamela M. Potter, *Most German of the Arts: Musicology and Society from the Weimar Republic to the End of Hitler's Reich* (New Haven: Yale University Press, 1998), p. 24; Nanny Dreschler, *Die Funktion der Musik im deutschen Rundfunk, 1933–1945* (Pfaffenweiler: Centarius, 1998), pp. 24, 33, 42, 131.

65. Thomas Haury, "Von der Demokratie zum Dollarimperialismus. Linke Amerikabilder bei Karl Marx, der KPD der Weimarer Republic und der frühen SED," in *Nichts gegen Amerika. Linker Antiamerikanismus und seine Geschichte*, ed. Michael Hahn (Hamburg: Konkret-Literatur-Verlag, 2003), p. 54.

66. Diner, *America in the Eyes of Germans*, p. 75.

67. Ibid.

68. Brecht, cited by ibid., p. 76. A good description of Brecht's image of America may be found in Russell A. Berman, *Anti-Americanism in Europe: A Cultural Problem* (Stanford: Stanford University Press, 2004), pp. 66–73.

69. Frances Trollope, *Domestic Manners of the Americans* (London: George Routledge and Sons, 1927).

70. History today leaves little doubt that Jefferson had children with some of his slaves. The most famous case is the controversy surrounding Sally Hemmings, whose descendants were able to use DNA methods to prove the paternity of at least one Jefferson. Some who want to defend Thomas Jefferson have pointed out that the father could just as easily have been the president's brother, since the DNA analysis only allows identification of families.

71. Simon Schama, "Them and US: Brash, Vulgar and Absurdly Patriotic—That Was the View of America Held by 19th Century European Visitors," *Guardian*, March 29, 2003. One needs to add that for millions of French, Belgium epitomizes provinciality, irrelevance, and inferiority. The continued proliferation of "Belgium jokes" in France—as well as the Netherlands—testifies to the low regard that the French (and the Dutch) have for Belgium and the Belgians.

72. Charles Dickens, *American Notes* (Gloucester, MA: Peter Smith, 1968); Dickens, *Martin Chuzzlewit* (Oxford: Oxford University Press, 1989).

73. Dickens, *American Notes*, pp. 197, 178.

74. Rudyard Kipling, *American Notes* (Norman: University of Oklahoma Press, 1981), pp. 17, 12.

75. Congress declared war on Austria-Hungary on December 4, 1917, more than eight months after the declaration of war against Germany on April 2, 1917. Despite President Wilson, who drew a distinction before Congress and the American public between the German Empire and the Dual Monarch as enemies and adversaries of the United States, the United States found itself in an official state of war with Austria-Hungary. On this point see Arthur J. May, *The Passing of the Habsburg Monarchy 1914–1918* (Philadelphia: University of Pennsylvania Press, 1966), p. 571 ff. In World War II, Americans fought against Austrians not as representatives of their own country but as members of Nazi Germany's Wehrmacht.

76. There has never been an official declaration of war between the two nations, though the war of 1812 originated out of naval tension between the U.S., British and French shipping policy. The undeclared war with France from 1797 to 1801, again fought on the seas, remains disputed by historians.

77. An excellent case in point was the official "elimination of everything foreign," primarily of the hated "Engländerei" (Englishness) in the early years of German soccer. In this movement of the early decades of the century, at the moment when the sport was becoming a global game, Germans insisted on translating every English sports term into its German equivalent. Arthur Heinrich, *Der Deutsche Fußballbund. Eine politische Geschichte* (Cologne: PapyRossa, 2000), pp. 33–35.

78. Roger, *The American Enemy*, pp. 193–97.

79. These examples cited in ibid., pp. 199, 200, 188–93.

80. Ibid., 185.

81. At that time the front lines were the opposite of today: Clemenceau and other European politicians were the "realists" and power politicians who regarded Wilson's ideas about international institutions and supranational responsibility as phantasms of an American provincial inexperienced in the real world. Today Europeans in their self-proclaimed postnationalism seem to have become adherents of Wilsonian internationalism, while the Bush administration swears by the outdated recipes of "realistic" European power politics.

82. Simon Schama, "The World of Their Own: From Dickens to Kipling to De Beauvoir and Köstler," *Guardian*, April 6, 2003.

83. Knut Hamsun, *Knut Hamsun Remembers America* (Columbia: University of Missouri Press, 2003); and Hamsun, *The Cultural Life of Modern America* (Cambridge: Harvard University Press, 1969).

84. Maxim Gorky, *The City of the Yellow Devil: Pamphlets, Articles and Letters about America* (Moscow: Progress Publishers, 1972); Gorky, *In America* (Honolulu: University of Hawaii Press, 2001).

85. America as a Moloch is a common representation and perception in Europe. On this point, see, for example, Karlheinz Deschner, *Der Moloch. Eine kritische Geschichte der USA* (Munich: Wilhelm Meyne Verlag 2002).

86. Jose Ortega y Gasset, *The Revolt of the Masses* (Notre Dame: University of Notre Dame Press, 1985), p. 126.

## Chapter 3
## The Perceived "Americanization" of All Aspects of European Lives: A Discourse of Irritation and Condescension

1. My selection of sources contains both highbrow and other newspapers and journals from Great Britain, Germany, France, Italy, Spain, Austria, and Portugal. In addition to looking at the periodicals cited in the notes to this chapter, I sifted through and evaluated the following publications for the period 1990–2005, collecting more than 1,500 articles in the process: from Great Britain, *The Guardian*, *The Times*, *The Independent*, *The Daily Telegraph*, *The Sunday Times*, *The Observer*, *The Financial Times*, and *The Scotsman*; from France, *Le Monde*, *Le Figaro*, *Libération*, *Le Temps*, *Les Echos*, *Le Télégramme*, *L'Express*, *Le Point*, *L'Equipe*, and *La Tribune*; from Germany, *Frankfurter Allgemeine Zeitung*, *Frankfurter Rundschau*, *Süddeutsche Zeitung*, *Die Welt*, *Der Tagesspiegel*, *Berliner Zeitung*, *die tageszeitung*, *Die Zeit*, and *Der Spiegel*; from Italy, *Corriere della Sera*, *La Stampa*, *La Repubblica*, and *La Gazetta dello Sport*; from Spain, *El Pais*, *ABC*, *El Mundo*, *5*

*Dias*, and *20 minutos*; from Austria, *Kronen-Zeitung*, *Die Presse*, *Der Standard*, *Salzburger Nachrichten*, and *Tiroler Tageszeitung*; from Portugal, *Expresso*, *Jornal Record*, *Jornal de Noticias*, *Diario de Noticias*, *Publico*, *Jornal Região Sul*, and *Correio da Manhã*.

2. Melvin L. DeFleur and Margaret H. DeFleur, *Learning to Hate Americans: How U.S. Media Shape Negative Attitudes among Teenagers in Twelve Countries* (Spokane, WA: Marquette Books, 2003).

3. Eric T. Hansen, "Typisch deutsch. Die gefühlte Amerikanisierung," *Süddeutsche Zeitung*, July 13, 2004.

4. Valenti Puig, " 'Americanización': entrada y salida del Guiñol," *ABC*, July 14, 2003.

5. Helmut Müller-Sievers, "Der amerikanische Wahlkampf im Zeichen der Kirchen," *Frankfurter Rundschau*, July 9, 2004.

6. The Viennese journalist Michael Freund, a sober and skeptical observer of anything related to "anti-Americanism," looked into the cultural pages of several leading German daily and weekly newspapers between September 2002 and September 2003 with respect to their reporting on America. Among the articles that Freund found in the liberal *Süddeutsche Zeitung* and conservative *Frankfurter Allgemeine Zeitung*, he categorized forty as hostile to America, fourteen as friendly toward America, and twenty-three as balanced. Based on Freund's normative perspective, one can be reasonably sure that his categorizations were selected according to restrictive criteria. Even if, as Freund believes, few of the articles critical of America displayed an "irrational anti-Americanism," the ratio of "anti" to "pro"—almost three to one—is telling for the general tone about America in German periodicals, and in my view this also holds for the entire newspaper landscape in Western Europe. See Freund, "Affinity and Resentment: A Historical Sketch of German Attitudes," in *Understanding Anti-Americanism*, ed. Hollander, p. 118. Of course, there are distinctions: Everywhere left-leaning and radical right-wing newspapers are much more anti-American than newspapers from the political center and center-right; broken down by country, it is striking how France is the only country where an almost unbroken anti-American consensus prevails among all media regardless of size, prominence, or political leanings. This is not the case either in Germany (see the conservative *Die Welt* and the liberal *Die Zeit*) or in Great Britain, where the *Daily Telegraph* and—to a lesser extent—the *Times* take a much more differentiated attitude toward America than the BBC, the *Guardian*, the *Independent*, and the *New Statesman*, for example. In Austria and Italy, the situation more closely resembles the British and German than the French constellation. The Spanish media seem to have been closest to the French uniformity of negatively depicting most things

American and being heavily critical of anything deemed to be "Americanization." Far and away the least hostile to America in their reporting have been the Portuguese media, where a number of voices repeatedly chastised Europe's growing anti-Americanism. But in Portugal, too, the negative tropes about Americans common to Europe remain alive and well.

7. " 'Schneisen durch Bagdad gebombt'—Wie deutsche Medien bei der USA-Berichterstattung aus der Rolle fallen—Gespräch mit dem Antiamerikanismus-Forscher Lutz Erbring," *Die Welt*, February 22, 2005.

8. See Thomas Huetlin, "Showdown in Oklahoma City," *Der Spiegel*, 18/2001. This reissue of the "banality of evil" in the context of America and Americans is not restricted to this German news magazine; it is a Europe-wide media phenomenon.

9. The text of this particular Gerhard Schröder speech of August 5, 2002, in Hanover may be found on the Web site of the Bavarian SPD: http://www.spdbayern.de/servlet/PB/menu/1019445/index.html?view= month&id=1017757. Schröder kept repeating the essence of this speech throughout his political campaigns and the reign of his chancellery.

10. "Demokratisierung statt Amerikanisierung," press statement by the Junge Union from May 22, 2000; see http://www.junge-union.de/ju/news/ pm0072.php3.

11. "Geissler nennt Hartz IV blanken Zynismus," *netzeitung.de*, July 15, 2004, http://www.netzeitung.de/arbeitundberuf/dernuerarbeitsmarkt/295 984.html.

12. "Brauchen wir in der Donaustadt 'amerikanische' Verhältnisse?" http://www.bignot.at.

13. Carlos Lage, "Cultura, cidadania e União Europeia," *Jornal de Noticias*, March 23, 1996.

14. John Simister, "Motoring: Road Test—A Brand New Toy That'll Go the Distance," *Independent*, June 2, 2001.

15. Gary Duncan, "MPs hear emotional plea for gun control," *Independent*, July 17, 1996.

16. Blake Morrison, "Just feel the width . . . ," *Guardian*, June 26, 2003.

17. Ian Aitken, "Rattling the Bars: The Laws of Safety First," *Guardian*, November 20, 1993.

18. Katy Guest, "The Friday Feature: The Scare-the-Rich-Project," *Guardian*, October 31, 2003.

19. Brian Viner, "Should Cricket Be Rocking to a New Tune?" *Independent*, July 1, 2003; see also Marcus Berkmann, "Gladiators of the Green Baize," *Guardian*, January 3, 1993.

20. David Sumner Smith, "Firms Come under Pressure to Ease Mounting Stress at Work," *Sunday Times*, January 7, 2001.

21. Mike Rowbottom, "A Guide to Being 'Nice' and Avoiding 'zzzz' Words," *Independent*, October 24, 1998.

22. Joseph Hanimann, "Wer Kunst hat—Frankreichs Intellektuelle werden plötzlich konservativ," *Frankfurter Allgemeine Zeitung*, December 3, 2005.

23. Laurence Benaim, "Une mode amnésique. Perdant sa mémoire, la haute couture de l'hiver est marquée par une américanisation violente du goût," *Le Monde*, August 1, 1992.

24. The first instance of the term *aus dem Amerikanischen* that I could ascertain was a 1831 translation of James Fennimore Cooper, *Die Wassernixe oder der Tummler der Meere. Eine Erzählung aus dem Amerikanischen übersetzt von W. Irving, Bearbeiter der humoristischen Geschichte New Yorks* (Frankfurt am Main: Gedruckt und verlegt von Johann David Sauerländer, 1831).

25. Josef Joffe, " 'Aus dem Amerikanischen,' " *Die Zeit*, October 23, 2003.

26. Josef Joffe, "Entdeckt: eine neue Fremdsprache," *Süddeutsche Zeitung*, February 23, 1995.

27. Ibid.

28. Ibid.

29. Ibid.

30. Verein Deutsche Sprache e.V., "Sprachpolitische Leitlinien," http://www.vds-ev.de/verein/leitlinine/php.

31. A brief comment on this issue in Italian and Spanish is in order. In Italy, out of the two hundred books written by American authors that I checked, only two featured *Tradotto dall' Americano* and two *Tradotto dall'Inglese*. All others listed the translator's name following a *Tradotto da*. In Spain, too, the overwhelming majority of books written by American authors and translated into Spanish feature the translator's name preceded by *Traducido por*. In the rare instances where this was not the case, I only encountered *traducido del ingles por*; I did not see any case of *Americano* or *Ingles Americano* or any mention of an American language distinct from British English.

32. "English Language," *Independent*, November 25, 2000.

33. Ibid. The allusion here, of course, was a dig at Bill Clinton's infamous and evasive line of defense during his deposition in the Monica Lewinsky affair.

34. The *Oxford Dictionary of English* is the recently introduced companion to the famous *Oxford English Dictionary (OED)*. The former contains only words and expressions used today.

35. Joanna Chung, "Words to Leave Purists Speechless," *Financial Times*, August 21, 2003.

36. Frederic Raphael, "The War of the Worlds, Old and New: Will Britain Sink for Ever in the Ketchup of American Culture?" *New Statesmen*, November 29, 1996.

37. Brian McNair, "Doom-mongers Keep Mum—We're Not So Dumb," *Sunday Herald*, January 9, 2000.

38. Stephen Amidon, "Overlong, Overdone and Over Here," *Times*, May 8, 1994.

39. David Nicholson-Lord, Let's Boycott America," *New Statesman*, December 25, 2000–January 1, 2001.

40. Paul Watzlavick, *Gebrauchsanweisung für Amerika. Ein respektloser Reiseführer* (München: Piper, 1984).

41. As quoted in Andrei S. Markovits, "Reflections on the World Cup '98," *French Politics and Society* 16, no. 3 (Summer 1998), p. 1.

42. Olivier Villepreux, "Crédibilité sportive contre rentabilité économique," *Liberation*, June 9, 1998.

43. Interview with Frank Dell'Apa, soccer reporter for the *Boston Globe*, August 11, 2002.

44. Andrew Buncombe, "Folks Back Home Less Than Overwhelmed by Historic Achievement," *Independent*, June 18, 2002.

45. Sport in Kürze, "Die anhaltende Torwartdebatte," *Frankfurter Allgemeine Zeitung*, August 23, 2004. Oliver Fritsch, "Der Michel mosert gegen Klinsmann," *Frankfurter Rundschau*, March 13, 2006; and Andrei S. Markovits, "Unter der Sonne Kaliforniens," *Der Tagesspiegel*, March 21, 2006.

46. Andrei S. Markovits and Steven L. Hellerman, *Offside: Soccer and American Exceptionalism* (Princeton: Princeton University Press, 2001); and Markovits and Hellerman, *Im Abseits: Fussball in der amerikanischen Sportkultur* (Hamburg: Hamburger Edition, 2002).

47. "Doris im Wunderland," *Der Spiegel*, 24/2001.

48. Mario Rimati, "American and Italian Women's Soccer: A Comparative Study of Its Development, Organization, and Management" (master's thesis, University of Leicester, October 2002).

49. Gofreddo Buccini, "Brandi, piu per spot che per sport," *Corriere della Sera*, July 14, 1999. The title says it all: "Brandi, more for the commercial spot than for the sport."

50. A very good volume on the subject of women's soccer in several countries and different continents is Fan Hong and J. A. Mangan, eds., *Soccer, Women, Sexual Liberation: Kicking Off a New Era* (London: Frank Cass, 2004).

51. See, e.g., Will Buckley's report on the renovated stadium for Nottingham Forest, "Forest's Gateau," *Guardian*, August 27, 1995.

52. Jim White, "White's Week: Highest Bidder Wins as Real Fans Feel the Squeeze in Ticket Fiasco," *Guardian*, November 6, 1999.

53. John Duncan, "Channel 4 Gives US Sport Order of the Boot," *Guardian*, July 25, 1998.

54. Andrew Baker, "The Big Little Picture Show" *Independent*, May 5, 1996.

55. Frank Malley, "Kenneth Wolstenholme; The Voice of English Football's Finest Hour," *Herald*, March 27, 2002.

56. "El Madrid 'Made in Capello' se presenta esta noche al más puro estilo Americano," *ABC*, July 23, 1996.

57. Selena Roberts, one of the *New York Times's* most gifted sports columnists, has repeatedly reported on the antipathy borne by Olympics officials against the United States. See, for example, her "It's Not Cool to Love America at the Games," *New York Times*, February 11, 2006. Roberts also mentions other indignities that have befallen the Americans at the hands of the International Olympic Committee and its officials.

58. Jean-Luc Rossignol, "L'américanisation des nouvelles normes comptables progresse," *La Tribune*, April 22, 2004.

59. Floyd Norris, "Showdown Looms in Europe over Proposals on Accounting," *New York Times*, July 11, 2003.

60. Christoph Keese, "Teuflische Gleichung der Globalisierung," *Berliner Zeitung*, May 8, 1998.

61. Ibid.

62. Torsten Harmsen, "Deutsche Unis vor dem Ruin. Bund Freiheit der Wissenschaft warnt vor weiterer Amerikanisierung," *Berliner Zeitung*, November 12, 2002.

63. Andrei S. Markovits, "Multikultur im Hörsaal," *Der Spiegel: Spiegel Spezial—Welche Uni ist die beste?* May 24, 1993.

64. "Claude Allègre: non à l'uniformisation et l'americanisation de l'enseignement," *Les Echos*, November 24, 1999; and "La France opposée à une americanisation de l'enseignement en Europe," *Agence France Presse*, November 23, 1999.

65. Peter Kingston, "A Whole New Ball Game? Coming Soon, at a Campus Near You, American-Style Semesters and Modules," *Guardian*, November 28, 1994.

66. Richard Reeves, "The Americans Who Are Running Britain," *Observer*, January 23, 2000.

67. Bernard Levin, "All Joe McCarthy's Children Now" *Times*, June 1, 1993.

68. Taki, "The PC Dons Who Blacken Shakespeare," *Times*, January 7, 1996.

69. Suzanne Moore, "Sex Is a Fact of Political Life. Too Much Has Been Revealed Now for President Clinton to Merely Zip Himself Up and Get Back to Business," *Independent*, September 16, 1998.

70. Brian Viner, "Cowardice, Promiscuity and American Presidents," *Independent*, March 2, 2004.

71. Ian Katz, "God Swept Up in PC Crusade," *Guardian*, September 1, 1995.

72. Peter Schönberger, "Durch den Fall Becker amerikanische Verhältnisse," on the web site of the Deutscher Journalistenverband (DJV), reported January 5, 2001. See http://www.djv.de/aktuelles/presse/archiv/2001/05/01/01.shtml.

73. Jan Leeming, "Has the TV World Gone Mad? I Earned Only 23,500," *Daily Mail*, November 11, 1999. The reporter is referring to the more than million-pound annual salary paid to television anchor Kirsty Young by ITV. At the height of her career as anchor for the 9 p.m. news on BBC, Jan Leeming earned exactly 23,500 pounds in 1987.

74. Brian McNair, "Bong, Bong. Seconds Out Round One in the Heavyweight TV News Title Fight," *Sunday Herald*, February 4, 2001.

75. Martin Hoyle, "A Sense of Dyke's Law of Gravity RADIO," *Financial Times*, February 15, 2002.

76. Sally Kinnes, "Is British Too American?" *Scotsman*, June 26, 1998.

77. John Dugdale and James Saynor, "I'm a British Doodle Dandy. Incoming Director-General John Birt Has Promised to Put the British Back into the BBC, Not Least by Reducing Imported Programming," *Guardian*, December 7, 1992.

78. "Pick of the Box: Like Death Warmed Up . . . ," *Daily Record*, December 14, 1999. Incidentally, this article completely predates American reality TV, which did not debut until the summer of 2000, with the surprise hit *Survivor*.

79. Daniel Mugica, "Fumadores," *ABC*, September 16, 1999.

80. See, for example, Esperanza Rabat, "La McDonalización de la vida cotidiana," *El Mundo*, February 24, 1996; Paco Rego, "La Dieta de los españoles se está americanizando," *El Mundo*, December 28, 1997; and Angeles Lopez, "¿Quién es culpable de la obesidad?" *El Mundo*, May 11, 2004.

81. Cristina Odone, "Comment: Cristina Odone's Diary," *Observer*, May 4, 2003.

82. "Amerikanische Verhältnisse drohen," in "Übergewicht: Deutsche immer dicker," http://www.strathmannag.de/sag/public/news/data/20031117.php.

83. "Antidepressivos: dos anos 50 à 'revolução Prozac," *Espresso*, February 4, 2005.

84. Markus Falkner and Gabi Zylla, "Besserer Schutz für Nichtraucher. Politiker und Gesundheitsexperten lehnen amerikanische Verhältnisse ab—Kein generelles Rauchverbot," *Berliner Morgenpost*, August 5, 2003.

85. Vitor Rainho, "Americanos. Fomos proibidos de fumar num café com música dos anos 60," *Expresso*, March 27, 2004.

86. Quico Alsedo, "El 'alijo' diario de nicotina en Barajas," *El Mundo*, April 3, 2002.

87. A good example, from Portugal in this case, can be found in "A 'Lei Seca' do Tabaco," *Correio da Manha*, April 20, 2003; for Spain, see Daniel Mugica, *Fumadores*, September 16, 1999.

88. Mugica, *Fumadores*, September 16, 1999.

89. Ms. Däubler-Gmelin's remarks were first reported by the *Schwä-bisches Tagblatt*. See "Däubler-Gmelin: Bush will ablenken," *Schwäbisches Tagblatt*, September 20, 2002. The occasion in question was a meeting in which the minister (still in Schröder's cabinet at the time) was invited by works councilors and union shop stewards from the Tübingen metal-working firm Walter AG und Flender to talk about "globalization in the world of work." While former Justice Minister Däubler-Gmelin did not compare the persons George W. Bush and Adolf Hitler with each other, she did say their methods were similar. "In other respects as well, the minister was unsparing in her criticism of the U.S.: 'They have a lousy legal system'—just on the basis of the death penalty. And if today's laws against insider trading had been in effect in the 1980s, when the current U.S. President was manager of an oil company, 'then Bush would be sitting in jail.' " Ibid.

90. Ronald Schmid, "Luftfahrt-Großschäden und die Amerikanisierung des Anspruchdenkens. Wider eine unheilvolle Entwicklung durch sog. Opferanwälte" (lecture given on September 13, 2002, at the IAI-Symposium in Frankfurt am Main), http://www.ronald-schmid.de/p2002_Iah.html.

91. Peter Schönberger, "Amerikanische Verhältnisse im Gerichts-saal?—Zur TV–Übertragung von Verhandlungen," May 24, 2001, http://www.rechtpraktisch.de/artikel.html?id=254.

92. Janine Gibson, "Woodward Warns of Trial by TV," *Guardian*, September 1, 1998.

93. Dominic Rushe, "Wanted: Lawyer for Pounds 1m a Year," *Sunday Times*, January 10, 1999.

94. Jonathan Steele and Ian Katz, "The Devil's Advocates," *Guardian*, December 3, 1996.

95. Anna Minton, "Benchmark Drug Courts That Offer Coercive but Supportive Treatment for Addicts Have Been a Big Success in the US. So Will They Work Here?" *Guardian*, June 5, 2002.

96. Maire-Joëlle Gros, "Conseils de discipline à l'école de la justice," *Libération*, June 15, 2004.

97. Delphine de Mallevoüe, "Ces enfants qui traînent leurs parents en justice. Ils étaient plus de 2000 à exiger une pension à leur famille en 2003 contre 30 en 1992; une explosion due à la crise de l'autorité et à l'américanisation des moeurs," *Le Figaro*, April 26, 2005.

98. "Prateleiras de ouro," *Journal de Noticias*, November 14, 2000.

99. Silvia Fagioli, report on National Public Radio's *All Things Considered*, April 11, 2005.

100. C. E., "El Gobierno Catalán quiere privatizar la vigilancia de todas las prisiones y los juzgados," *El Pais*, August 19, 1999.

101. Maria Peral, "El Supremo plantea 'americanizar' los juicios y que el acusado esté junto a su defensor," *El Mundo*, April 29, 2005.

102. Juan Antonio, "Denuncias Exageradas," *20 minutos*, May 24, 2005.

103. Lawrence Donegan, "Drivers Warned after New Car-jack Raids," *Guardian*, October 23, 1993.

104. Richard Williamson, "Should We Fight Fire with Fire? Arming Our Police Would Be Accepting That a Gun Culture Exists," *Sunday Mercury*, December 15, 2002.

105. Duncan Campbell, "Drug Wars: Gangsters Make Another Killing," *Guardian*, November 15, 1997.

106. "Stoiber fordert generelle Reglementierung des Internet," http://www.heise.de./newsticker/meldung/27228.

107. "27. April: Trauer, Entsetzen und Suche nach Konsequenzen," http://www.polozei.bayern.de/schutz/sich_kontr/sicherheit.htm.

108. "Wir wollen keine amerikanischen Verhältnisse," *Die Rheinpfalz*, July 14, 2000.

109. Charles Bremner, "It's Like America Not France—a Pure Nightmare," *Times*, March 28, 2002.

110. For representative articles bemoaning these changes, in this case in Spain, see Carmen De Zulueta, "La Verbena del Carmen," *ABC*, July 16, 2003; and Xavier Marce, "Entre Papá Noel y el Cagatió," *El Mundo*, December 31, 2003.

111. Dale McFeatters, "It's Crass, It's Commercial, It's Ours," *New York Post*, October 31, 2005.

112. "Ausufernde Städte: Amerikanische Verhältnisse bald auch in Europa? Führende Geographen und Stadtplaner konferieren in Heidelberg" (press release from the University of Heidelberg, September 24, 2002); and Ian Katz, "On the Dawn of a New Age in the Evolution of Shopping Ushered in by Wednesday's Court Ruling to Allow Britain's First Out-of-Town 'Warehouse Club'—Yet Another Blow to the Ailing City Centre," *Guardian*, October 30, 1993.

113. Andy Murray, "Over-sized and Over Here," *Herald*, July 3, 1998.

114. Sven H. Waeselmann, "Amerikanisierung im Reich der Tiere," *Hamburger Abendblatt*, February 28, 2003.

115. A brief summary of this argument may be found in Dmitry Shlapentokh, "The New Anti-Americanism: America as an Orwellian Society," *Partisan Review* 49, no. 2 (2002).

116. "We're with you, sort of" is how the *Economist* summarized the mood among the British public. ("We're with You, Sort of," *Economist*, September 22, 2001.) As a survey from the Forsa Institute, which was summarized in the weekly paper *Die Woche*, showed, most Germans felt only "qualified solidarity" with Americans. This and other surveys were exhaustively cited right away (and also later) by right-wing radical newspapers. From their point of view (which is hardly surprising), the surveys testified to a much-welcomed skepticism toward "Americanization" on the part of the German public. See, for example, the Internet article from the *Nationalzeitung* put out by the neo-Nazi DVU at http://www.dsz-verlag.de/Artikel_03/NZ39_3.html.

117. Jean Baudrillard, "L'esprit du terrorisme," *Le Monde*, November 3, 2001 (emphasis in original); see also Baudrillard, *The Spirit of Terrorism* (London: Verso, 2002).

118. Quoted in Geoffrey Wheatcroft, "Two Years of Gibberish: The Garbled Utterances of the Left after 9/11 Merely Flattered the Arguments of Warmongers," *Prospect*, no. 90 (September 2003). Wheatcroft's citation is an accurate rendition of what Stockhausen said in German. See http://www.mdr.de/kultur/musik/872412.html.

119. Cited in ibid. Fo spoke up immediately after 9/11, when many people still assumed that the number of dead was around 20,000. It turned out to be 3,000.

120. Ibid.

121. Andreas Hess, "Intellektuelle Reaktionen auf den 11. September 2001. Versuch einer vorläufigen kritischen Einordnung," *Gewerkschaftliche Monatshefte* 11–12/2001, pp. 642–54; Lars Rensmann, "Hannah Arendt and the Problem of European Anti-Americanism" (manuscript for a lecture at the University of Michigan in Ann Arbor, February 6, 2004); Elliot Neaman, "The War That Took Place in Germany: Intellectuals and September 11," *German Politics and Society* 20, no. 3 (Fall 2002), pp. 56–78; and Henryk Broder, *Kein Krieg, nirgends: Die Deutschen und der Terror* (Berlin: Berlin Verlag, 2002).

122. Peter Schneider, "Moralische Geiselhaft," *Die Zeit*, November 22, 2001.

123. Quoted in Robert N. Bellah, "The New American Empire," *Commonweal*, http://www.commonwealmagazine.org/article.php?id_article=574.

124. Elliot Neaman, "The War That Took Place in Germany," p. 60.

125. Thierry Meyssan, *11 September 2001: L'Éffroyable Imposture* (Paris: Carnot, 2001).

126. Mathias Bröckers, *Verschwörungen, Verschwörungstheorien und die Geheimnisse des 11.9* (Frankfurt: Zweitausendeins, 2002).

127. Tobias Jaecker, *Antisemitische Verschwörungstheorien nach dem 11. September: Neue Varianten eines alten Denkmusters* (Münster: LIT Verlag, 2004).

128. Jochen Bittner, "Umfrage: Blackbox Weißes Haus—Je komplizierter die Weltlage, desto fester glauben die Deutschen an Verschwörungstheorien," *Die Zeit*, July 31, 2003.

129. Brian Viner, "Cowardice, Promiscuity and American Presidents," *Independent*, March 2, 2004.

130. Edgar Reitz, *Liebe zum Kino: Utopien und Gedanken zum Autorenfilm, 1962–1983* (Cologne: Verlag Köln 78, n.d.), p. 102.

## Chapter 4
## The Massive Waning of America's Image in the Eyes of Europe and the World

1. Peter J. Katzenstein and Robert O. Keohane, eds., *Anti-Americanism in World Politics* (forthcoming).

2. Alan Riding, "U.S. Stands Alone on Unesco Cultural Issue," *New York Times*, October 13, 2005; and Riding, "Unesco Adopts New Plan Against Cultural Invasion," *New York Times*, October 21, 2005. The only country to have voted with the United States was Israel. Australia, Nicaragua, Honduras, and Liberia abstained.

3. Gaetan de Capcle, "Une ligne de défense très politique," *Le Figaro*, July 20, 2005. The sentence reads as follows: "Manipulation or preventive defense of a cathedral of French industry menaced by an American ogre?"

4. Steven Lukes, *Power: A Radical View*, 2d ed. (New York: Palgrave Macmillan, 2004).

5. Roger Cohen, "Anti-Americanism Is One 'ism' That Thrives," *International Herald Tribune*, November 26, 2005.

6. Ibid.

7. DeFleur and DeFleur, *Learning to Hate Americans*.

8. Nina Bernstein, "Young Germans Ask: Thanks For What?" *New York Times*, March 9, 2003.

9. Barbara Lefebvre and Ève Bonnivard, *Élèves sous influence* (Paris: Editions Audibert, 2005).

10. Ibid., p. 348.

11. James Graff, "Book Learning: A Controversial New Work Says French School Textbooks Are Just Plain Anti-American," *Time Europe*, http://www.time.com/time/europe/eu/printout/0,9869,1118296,00.html.

12. GlobeScan and the Program on International Policy and Attitudes (PIPA), the University of Maryland, "In 20 of 23 Countries Polled Citizens Want Europe to Be More Influential than the US."

13. Ibid., pp. 4, 5.

14. Ibid., p. 4.

15. Ibid., p. 2.

16. Pew Global Attitudes Project, *American Character Gets Mixed Reviews: U.S. Image Up Slightly, but Still Negative* (Washington, DC: Pew Research Center, 2005), p. 11. Also, Stephen Brooks, *As Others See Us: The Causes and Consequences of Foreign Perceptions of America* (Peterborough, Ontario: Broadview Press, 2006).

17. Ibid., p. 15.

18. Simon Anholt, "The Anholt-GMI Nation Brands Index," http://www.nationbrandindex.com.

19. Andrian Kreye, "Nationalbrand Index," *Süddeutsche Zeitung*, August 2, 2005.

20. Pew Global Attitudes Project, p. 1.

21. Tom Brown, "A Common Language Should Not Blind Us to the Reality of a Deepening Transatlantic Gulf," *Financial Times*, May 29, 2004.

22. Pew Global Attitudes Project, p. 30.

23. Robert Wright, "They Hate Us, They Really Hate Us: Two books about the roots of current anti-Americanism," *The New York Times Book Review*, May 14, 2006.

24. Andrew Kohut and Bruce Stokes, *America Against the World: How We Are Different and Why We Are Disliked* (New York: Times Books/Henry Holt & Company, 2006).

25. Julia E. Sweig, *Friendly Fire: Losing Friends and Making Enemies in the Anti-American Century* (New York: Council on Foreign Relations Book/Public Affairs, 2006).

## Chapter 5
## "Twin Brothers": European Anti-Semitism and Anti-Americanism

1. Although the term "anti-Semitism," just like "America," ought to be unmistakably clear to all concerned, the former requires (as did "anti-Americanism" in the opening to this book) a brief explanatory footnote, since there are always people who, for whatever reason, attempt to relativize and alter the concept. Ever since Wilhelm Marr (in his 1879 anti-Jewish pamphlet "The Victory of Jewry over Germanism") introduced the expression "anti-Semitism" into the public sphere and common usage of every European country as a negative attitude toward the collectivity of "Jews" and everything Jewish, this is precisely what this generic term has meant: a general negative prejudice against Jews that can coagulate into an ideo-

logical explanation of the world attributing all kinds of social phenomena to the impact of Jews. In the course of the Jewish-Arab conflict during the twentieth century, Arabs and (later) Europeans developed the stubborn ideology that their attitude toward Jews could not possibly be anti-Semitic, since Arabs themselves are "Semites." Quite apart from the fact that Arabs can also be anti-Arabic—and, according to this logic, also "anti-Semitic" (since, as I said at the beginning of this book, prejudices are spiritual, intellectual, and emotional constructs not tied to the birthplace or "peoplehood" of anyone holding them)—this argument only serves as an exculpation and disguise of modern Arab hatred of Jews. In discussing the phenomenon that is generally characterized as anti-Semitism, it ought to be clear that this has nothing to do with any kind of "Semitic" linguistic regions or "ethnic groups," but with modern hostility to Jews. Some authors—in order to evade this pseudo-problem—have reverted to using the term "anti-Judaism" (in place of "anti-Semitism"). I find this superfluous and politically unacceptable. For a precise definition of terms like anti-Semitism, the German *Judenfeindschaft* (hostility or animosity toward Jews), and Judaeophobia in current social science discussions, and for more on the debate about new symbolic forms of these phenomena, cf. Lars Rensmann, *Demokratie und Judenbild: Antisemitismus in der politischen Kultur der Bundesrepublik Deutschland* (Wiesbaden: Verlag für Sozialwissenschaften, 2004), pp. 71–95; see also Joseph Joffe, "Nations We Love to Hate: Israel, America and the New Anti-Semitism" (http://sicsa.huji.ac.il/ppjoffe.pdf).

2. Glucksmann develops this link in his impressive analysis of the existence of hatred. See André Glucksmann, *Le Discours de la Haine* (Paris: Plon, 2004).

3. André Glucksmann, "Scharons Irrtum," *Frankfurter Allgemeine Zeitung*, July 23, 2004.

4. I have been impressed by the research of Richard Landes, who dates the start of acute and ultimately lethal European anti-Semitism to the winter of 1010. As a response to the destruction of the Holy Sepulcher by the Muslim Caliph al-Hakim, anti-Semitism brought the first organized massacres of Jews to Europe (especially to France). This systematic, politically motivated mass murder occurred in connection with new efforts at state building in Christendom and with mobilization measures helping to raise armies in order to fight the Muslims in the Holy Land. There had, of course, also been violent actions against Jews heretofore, though they had not (according to Landes) gone beyond the usual, vendetta-like acts of revenge that characterize rival communities and cultures living side by side all over the world. Cf. Richard Landes, "What Happens When Jesus Doesn't Come: Jewish and Christian Relations in Apocalyptic Time" (manuscript, Center for Millennial Studies, Boston University, 2000), p. 1 ff.

5. Hannah Arendt, *Eichmann in Jersualem* (New York: Viking, 1965).

6. On this important difference between the United States and Europe, see the work by Ronald Inglehart and his World Value Survey at the University of Michigan, Ann Arbor.

7. Of course there was the infamous lynching of Leo Frank in August 1915 in Marietta, Georgia, when an anti-Semitic mob abducted Leo Frank from his jail cell and hanged him from an oak tree. And there was the stabbing of Yankel Rosenbaum in August 1991 in the Borough Park section of Brooklyn, when an angry mob attacked Jews indiscriminately. In both cases chants of "Kill the Jew" filled the air. But the mere fact that I can list individual cases with names in America's 230-year history proves my point: These were exceptional cases. It would be well-nigh impossible to do so listing the bevy of anti-Semitic atrocities in most European countries, East and West.

8. David Klinghoffer, "Hate Thy Neighbor," *New York Times Book Review*, April 17, 1994.

9. Peter Pulzer, *The Rise of Political Anti-Semitism in Germany and Austria* (London: Peter Halban, 1988).

10. Jean-Claude Milner, *Les penchants criminels de l'Europe démocratique* (Paris: Verdier, 2003).

11. Attac Österreich, *Blinde Flecken der Globalisierungskritik. Gegen antisemitische Tendenzen und rechtsextreme Vereinnahmung* (Vienna: attac, 2005).

12. Marcus Hammerschmitt, "Ein Sheriffstern mit sechs Zacken. Globalisierungskritik am Abgrund?" http://www.heise.de/tp/deutsch/inhalt/co/14065/1.html.

13. David Landau, "Davos Chair Apologizes for Magazine's Israel Boycott Call," *Haaretz*, January 27, 2006.

14. Manfred Gerstenfeld, "Rewriting Germany's Nazi Past: A Society in Moral Decline," *Jerusalem Viewpoints*, no. 530 (May 1, 2005), pp. 1–2.

15. "U.S. Firmen in Deutschland: Die Aussauger—Die Plünderer sind da," *metall* 57, no. 5 (May 2005), pp. 14–17.

16. Europäische Stelle zur Beobachtung von Rassismus und Fremdenfeindlichkeit EUMC, *EUMC Report on Anti-Semitism*, http://www.crif.org/index.php?menu=5&dossier=33.

17. Ibid., p. 13.

18. Mitchell Cohen, "Auto-Emancipation and Anti-Semitism: Homage to Bernard Lazare," in *Jewish Social Studies* (Bloomington: Indiana University Press, 2004).

19. Europäische Stelle zur Beobachtung von Rassismus und Fremdenfeindlichkeit EUMC, *EUMC Report on Anti-Semitism*, p. 13.

20. Andreas Zick and Beate Küpper, " 'Die sind doch selbst schuld, wenn man was gegen sie hat!' oder Wie man sich seiner Vorurteile entledigt," in Wilhelm Heitmeyer, *Deutsche Zustände* (Frankfurt: Suhrkamp, 2005), pp. 129–43. See also the authors' English-language article "Old

Myths, New Stories—A Report on Anti-Semitism in Germany," *Journal für Konflikt- und Gewaltforschung,* 1/2005.

21. Thomas Friedman, "Campus Hypocrisy," *New York Times,* October 16, 2002.

22. Reverend King's words are quoted in an op-ed article by Congressman John Lewis, " 'I Have a Dream' for Peace in the Middle East: King's Special Bond with Israel," *San Francisco Chronicle,* January 21, 2002.

23. For a fine treatment of these ideas in the context of the different approaches to the Nazi past taken by Germany and Austria, see David Art, *The Politics of the Nazi Past in Germany and Austria* (Cambridge: Cambridge University Press, 2006).

24. Pulzer, *The Rise of Political Anti-Semitism.*

25. See http://www.ynet.co.il/articles/1,7340,L-1790529,FF.html. One of the best articles treating the cases of Theodorakis and Saramago within the larger context of the old and new anti-Semitism in Europe and the role of intellectuals is Pilar Raholas, "Los Protocolos de los Sabios de la Información. El Ojo Tuerto de Europa," http://www.harrymagazine.com/2003/los_-protocolos_de_los_sabios_de_html.

26. It would go beyond the scope of this book, both conceptually and physically, to review the anti-Semitic themes and depictions that are omnipresent in the Arab media. Suffice it to mention briefly that today, as never before, a radical anti-Semitic discourse dominates most media in all the Arab (and, increasingly, Islamic) countries. In Egypt, a soap opera based on "Protocols of the Elders of Zion" running for several weeks became a major hit. This triumph was then repeated in other Arab countries. In the Arab media over the last several years, any distinction between Jews and Israelis has ceased to exist. Jews/Israelis are routinely depicted as wild beasts, monsters, and devils. The classic personifications of European anti-Semitism are, of course, fully applied: murdering Arab children for Jewish ritual purposes, the Jew with the hooked nose and the hunched-over posture, the avaricious gaze, the skullcap, the demonic disposition. Mel Gibson's *The Passion of the Christ* was not only a major hit in the Arab world; the film was also used to depict the "crucifixion" of contemporary Arabs. And, of course, the swastika is repeatedly used. Jews are constantly portrayed as Nazis. See Anti-Defamation League, *Arab Media Review: Anti-Semitism and Other Trends* (New York: Anti-Defamation League, 2004). The fact that anti-Semitism, with all of its traditional (and even Nazi) symbols and content, has a long history in the Arab world is demonstrated by Matthias Küntzel, *Djihad und Judenhass. Über den neuen antijüdischen Krieg* (Freiburg: Ça ira Verlag, 2002).

27. See Europäische Stelle zur Beobachtung von Rassismus und Fremdenfeindlichkeit EUMC, "EUMC Report on Anti-Semitism," p. 14.

28. This, for example, is the line of argument advanced by the German and Franco-Italian left-wing intellectuals Elfriede Müller, Klaus Holz, and Enzo Traverso when they write: "An arson attack on a synagogue is an anti-Semitic act that needs to be condemned and sanctioned. But it is useful to know if it was committed by skinheads, those nostalgic for Vichy France, by Islamic fundamentalists, or by youths with a Maghreb background who wanted to show their support for the Palestinian Intifada." And the struggle against Israel is construed as legitimate, a reaction against state terrorism, for ultimately Israel is an "apartheid system," the product of a "colonization process," and practicing a "policy of suppression exercised with brutal force." Therefore, it is important to pull down the "Auschwitz blinder," and the solidarity that still exists among portions of the Left toward "Jewry . . . generally" needs to be withdrawn, because these are the "oppressors of today," and the Palestinians should not be "instructed about the ways and means of their struggle" in reaction to this oppression. Klaus Holz, Elfriede Müller, and Enzo Traverso, "Schuld und Erinnerung," *Jungle World* 47 (2002), cited by Lars Rensmann, *Demokratie und Judenbild*, pp. 113, 319.

29. Martin Klocke, *Die deutsche Linke, Israel und Antisemitismus: Zur Geschichte eines schwierigen Verhältnisses* (Frankfurt a.M: Haag und Herchen, 1990); and Wolfgang Kraushaar, *Die Bombe im jüdischen Gemeindehaus* (Hamburg: Hamburger Edition, 2005).

30. This anti-Semitic kind of hostility toward Israel is conspicuous for its "double standards"—always reliable indicators of this phenomenon— which are aimed at Israel as a Jewish state in toto and are obviously distinguishable from legitimate criticisms of the way the government is acting at any particular time. Israeli military actions are vastly exaggerated and stylized as singular crimes against humanity, while acts of terror against the Israeli civilian population are idealized as "resistance" or mere "reaction to the occupation." As part of this anti-Israeli double standard and manner of perception, the crimes of Arab dictatorships against civilian populations, such as the massive Jordanian massacre of Palestinians during "Black September," are routinely downplayed, or else they simply drop out of consciousness, since they have limited usefulness for demonizing "Zionism" or as a political cipher that can be mobilized. The reaction of the European Left to the persecution and murder of black Muslims by the Sudanese in Darfur, for which neither Israel nor the United States could be held responsible, has been correspondingly minimal. Indeed, some have tried to explain away the genocide commited by Muslims of Muslims in Dafur as an American and Zionist cabal.

31. I remember distinctly how at the beginning of the Gulf War in 1991, a prominent German television anchorman interviewed the Israeli ambassador to Germany and asked him in an irritated voice how he felt about the whole world becoming engulfed in the Armageddon of World War

III on account of Israel, which—as will be remembered—was not even a contestant in this war and whose civilian population was indeed a target of Iraqi Scud missiles.

32. David Hirsh, draft defining statement for ENGAGE, http://liberoblog,com/2005/06/23/draft-defining-statement-for-engage-please-read-and-comment.

33. Mark Lilla, "The End of Politics," *The New Republic*, June 23, 2003.

34. Daniel Jonah Goldhagen, "The Globalization of Anti-Semitism," *The Forward*, May 2, 2003. The concept of the "tough Jew" is nothing new, of course. Particularly in the United States, there is an entire literature on "tough Jews," mainly gangsters and boxers among whom Jews played a prominent role, often to the delight—even pride—of other Jews, especially Jewish men. See, for example, Rich Cohen's *Tough Jews: Fathers, Sons, and Gangster Dreams* (New York: Simon and Schuster, 1998), an excellent account of the life and world of Jewish gangsters. Paul Breines offers a very different study under the same main title, *Tough Jews: Political Fantasies and the Moral Dilemma of American Jewry* (New York: Basic Books, 1990).

35. Salomon Korn, "NS- und Sowjetverbrechen. Sandra Kalietes falsche Gleichsetzung," *Süddeutsche Zeitung*, March 31, 2004.

36. I desist from discussing Islamic anti-Semitism, about which I know next to nothing.

37. André Glucksmann, "Scharons Irrtum," *Frankfurter Allgemeine Zeitung*, July 23, 2004. It is interesting how translations can decisively influence both nuance and content. This quote comes from the just-cited publication in the *FAZ*. On July 24, 2004, the *Scotsman* published the same article by Glucksmann in an English translation. The Scottish paper used the word "people" instead of "country" (as reported by the Frankfurt paper). At issue was whether the world ought to risk a Third World War because of this "people/country." Furthermore, the *FAZ* translation talked about an "important and reputable posting" for Bernard as ambassador in Algeria. For the *Scotsman* this was "a choice posting and a strategic one," which, given France's pro-Arab policy, indicates a clearly strategic move for an ambassador who openly utters these kinds of words about Israel. Even the English title of the article is much more telling than the German one. See André Glucksmann, "Potent Ingredients Stirred into a Dangerous Anti-Semitic Cocktail," *Scotsman*, July 24, 2004. Bernard's indignation about Israel's being the cause of a possible World War III harkens to the identical sentiment expressed by the German television anchor mentioned in Note 31.

38. Simon Schama, as cited in Alvin H. Rosenfeld, *Anti-Zionism in Great Britain and Beyond: A "Respectable" Anti-Semitism?* (New York: The American Jewish Committee, 2004), p. 8.

39. Ibid.

40. Melanie Phillips, "Return of the Old Hatreds," *Observer*, February 22, 2004. In the article she identifies herself as Jewish.

41. Marie Woolf, "Anti-Semitism Is 'Infecting' British Politics, MPs Warn," *Independent*, April 21, 2004.

42. For an amazingly stark demonstration of this, see the *New Statesman*'s cover story, "The Kosher Connection." Also see Peter Beaumont's article in the *Observer* of Sunday, February 24, 2002. Peter Pulzer's reply was not published by this newspaper.

43. Antje Kraschinski, "Wenn der Präventivschlag zur Vergeltung wird," *Frankfurter Rundschau*, July 2, 2003. The following e-mail message from a German student of mine whom I taught at St. Gallen University in Switzerland in 2004 and with whom I have remained in touch is quite revealing. Christian Erk wrote: "During my very first trip to Israel, I experienced the following incident: Our group of European tourists and students who were in the Holy Land for the Christmas season was accompanied on our bus trip to Bethlehem by a group of journalists from the German television station RTL. I sat next to their leader and we got to chatting. In the course of our conversation, he told me that he was really hoping to have the Israeli border guards undress us, preferably down to our shorts, at the border crossing, and that it would be better still if they even roughed up some folks on the bus. That would be great copy and film footage. When nothing transpired, the man was visibly disappointed and clearly upset." (E-mail message from Christian Erk, December 30, 2005.)

44. For a fine statement on the inextricable relationship between recent anti-Americanism and and anti-Semitism, see Yossi Klein Halevi's paper, "Entwined Hatreds: Anti-Americanism," delivered to a conference on Anti-Americanism at the Gloria Center, Herzliya, Israel, September 17, 2003.

45. Ibid.

46. Quite apart from the fact that this figment conjured up in attempts to ward off the "anti-Semitism accusation" is itself replete with anti-Semitic features from the realm of conspiracy theory, scholarly investigations show that it really makes no sense to talk about a "taboo" on discussing Israel's policies critically. Nor do any European country's media take the side of Israel in any significant way. On the contrary: Reporting on politics in the Near East is overwhelmingly preformed by the construct of an oppressed Palestinian David struggling against a ruthless Israeli Goliath. The preponderant image is one of media-staged productions showing the deceptive picture of a conflict between stone-throwing children and murderous soldiers in tanks; cf. inter alia Rolf Behrens, *Raketen gegen Steinewerfer: Das Bild Israels im "Spiegel"* (Münster: Unrast-Verlag, 2003); Duisburger Institut für Sprach- und Sozialforschung, *Die Nahost-Berichterstattung zur Zweiten Intifada in deutschen Printmedien unter besonderer Berücksichtigung*

*des Israel-Bildes: Analyse diskursiver Ereignisse im Zeitraum von September 2000 bis August 2001* (Münster: Unrast-Verlag, 2002).

47. "Our Dulled Nerve," *Guardian*, November 18, 2003.

48. The original "Berlin anti-Semitism dispute" was triggered in 1879 when the historian Heinrich von Treitschke published an article accusing Germany's Jews of insufficient willingness to assimilate.

49. Martin Walser, *Der Augenblick der Liebe* (Reinbek: Rowohlt, 2004).

50. Hellmuth Karasek, "Der ewige Antisemit? Der Germanist Matthias Lorenz behauptet, Martin Walser sei schon immer ein Feind der Juden gewesen. Stimmt das?" *Die Welt*, July 30, 2005.

51. Holger Kulick, "Schröder, Walser und eine verplauderte Chance," *Der Spiegel*, May 9, 2002.

52. This view of Auschwitz as instrumentalized extends beyond Germany; a recent ADL survey found 42 percent of Europeans saying the statement that "Jews still talk too much about what happened to them in the Holocaust" is probably true.

53. For the text of Walser's speech, see "Die Banalität des Guten," *Frankfurter Allgemeine Zeitung*, October 12, 1998.

54. On this point, see the study by Lars Rensmann, *Demokratie und Judenbild*, p. 123 ff.

55. Jörg Friedrich, *Der Brand* (Berlin: Propyläen, 2002); and *Brandstätten* (Berlin: Propyläen, 2003).

56. See, e.g., Jörg Friedrich, *Die kalte Amnestie* (Munich: Piper, 1994).

57. Lucy Ward, "Oxford Suspends Don Who Rejected Student for Being Israeli," *Guardian*, October 28, 2003.

58. The Mona Baker affair was discussed for months in the media of Great Britain, Israel, the United States, and other English-speaking countries. Scholars from numerous countries and in diverse forums took positions on this case in a variety of articles in newspapers, and journals, at conferences, and on the Internet. The two best summaries are Ori Golan, "Boycott by Passport," *Jerusalem Post*, January 17, 2003; and Andy Beckett, " 'It's Water on Stone—In the End the Stone Wears Out,' " *Guardian*, December 12, 2002.

59. As quoted in Alvin Rosenfeld, *Anti-Zionism in Great Britain and Beyond*, p. 16.

60. For a detailed presentation of the initial resolution by the AUT and the responses against it, see the work of Jeff Weintraub, particularly his appeal to oppose the boycott, which was accepted by a number of American academic associations. http://www.PetitionOnline.com/j141789/petition.html.

61. Mark Steyn, "We Are Falling under the Imam's Spell," *Daily Telegraph*, January 13, 2004.

62. The Tom Paulin affair produced dozens of articles. A good summary of the entire story is Piper Fogg, "Harvard Reverses Decision and Reinvites Poet Who Made Incendiary Comments," *Chronicle of Higher Education* 49, no. 16 (December 13, 2002). It was interesting to follow the reactions to the Paulin and Baker cases on either side of the Atlantic. The materials confirmed my long-held opinion that (unfortunately) intellectuals also—or perhaps especially—have political convictions and normative preferences, creating an ethic that is used to legitimate these very preferences and then sold as a rationalization disguised in universalistic terms. The people who defended Tom Paulin almost always used arguments based on freedom of speech and opinion. But when it came to supporting Mona Baker, many said that the editor of a scholarly journal has the right to fire people from the editorial board at her discretion without commentary. Freedom of speech and opinion did not matter in this case. It was overridden by the logic of guilt by association. Sometimes it was the very same people who used these fundamentally different and clearly contradictory arguments to advocate on behalf of their ideologically like-minded colleagues.

63. For a fine article on how anti-Americanism migrated from the British Right to the British Left, see Geoffrey Wheatcroft, "Dickens to Le Carré: Smiley's (Anti-American) People," *New York Times*, January 11, 2004.

64. European Commission, "Flash Eurobarometer 151," November 2003, p. 81.

65. Anti-Defamation League, "Attitudes toward Jews," April 2004, p. 23.

66. For a solid treatment of this issue, see John Zaller, *The Nature and Origins of Mass Opinion* (New York: Cambridge University Press, 1992).

67. "Anti-Semitism in Greece: Embedded in Society—An Interview with Moses Altsech," *Post-Holocaust and Anti-Semitism*, no. 23 (July 11, 2004), p. 1.

68. Even in Ireland, where there are very few Jews, and where attacks on Jews or Jewish institutions have been practically nonexistent for decades, Jews are not viewed as genuinely Irish. See Jonathan Wilson, "The Fading World of Leopold Bloom," *New York Times Magazine*, June 13, 2004.

69. Ari Shavit, "The Jewish Problem, According to Theodorakis," *Haaretz*, August 27, 2004, http://www.haaretz.com/hasen/spages/469781.html.

70. Ibid.

71. This information comes from Moses Altsech, who teaches at Edgewood College in Madison, Wisconsin, and has been doing research and writing on anti-Semitism in Greece for decades.

72. Simon Wiesenthal Center, "Spirit of Olympic Games Must Inspire Greece to Deal with Its Antisemitism," http://www.wiesenthal.com/ed.cfm?m=20117L26945810.

73. Max Horkheimer, *Gesammelte Schriften* (Frankfurt a.M: S. Fischer, 1985), p. 288.

74. Emanuele Ottolenghi, "Europas 'gute Juden,' " *Die Welt*, January 21, 2006.

75. Raday Eszter, " 'Oneletrajzi regenynek' alcazott tiszta fikciok' Kertes Imrevel beszelgetett Raday Eszter," *Elet es Irodalom* 50, no. 30 (July 2006), pp. 6, 7.

## Chapter 6
## Anti-Americanism: A Necessary and Welcomed Spark to Jump-start a European Identity?

1. Dominique Strauss-Kahn, "Die Geburt einer Nation," *Frankfurter Rundschau*, March 11, 2003.

2. Jürgen Habermas and Jacques Derrida, "Unsere Erneuerung. Nach dem Krieg: Die Wiedergeburt Europas," *Frankfurter Allgemeine Zeitung*, May 31, 2003. A French version appeared in *Libération*. On the same day the *Süddeutsche Zeitung* published a supportive essay by the American intellectual and Habermas friend Richard Rorty. Adolf Muschg wrote in the *Neue Zürcher Zeitung*, Umberto Eco in *La Repubblica*, Gianni Vattimo in *La Stampa*, and Fernando Savater in *El Pais*. With the exception of the Habermas-Derrida article, all the others were completely independent contributions to their respective papers, tied together only by a common theme: the Iraq War as the occasion for separating Europe from the United States and the fortunate birth of a European nation. Umberto Eco was the only one who made an effort not to depict the United States as a completely alien "Other" worthy of rejection, but simply as different from Europe (something America always was and always would be). It was disappointing that intellectuals from Great Britain, Scandinavia and smaller countries, and especially Eastern Europe, were apparently deliberately excluded. Even a fleeting perusal of the Habermas-Derrida text (primarily written by Habermas, as both authors conceded) reveals that this purportedly pan-European vision was shaped above all by a commitment to a Franco-German duo that is intended to lead Europe out of being patronized by the United States. Instead of the "joint practice" of a democratic, pan-European process of self-agreement and decision making, for which Habermas had been admonishing in earlier writings and which he had viewed as something that ought to precede a European constitution (see *Die postnationale Konstellation* [Frankfurt am Main: Suhrkamp, 1998]), he proceeded to talk openly of an "avant-gardist" core Europe (by which he clearly meant

the Franco-German axis) that the other European countries are meant to follow. For an excellent English-language collection of all the articles authored by these intellectuals and a fine selection of the many responses that the original pieces engendered, see Daniel Levy, Max Pensky, and John Torpey, eds., *Old Europe, New Europe, Core Europe: Transatlantic Relations after the Iraq War* (London: Verso, 2005).

3. Jürgen Habermas, "Ein Interview über Krieg und Frieden" in *Der gespaltene Westen* (Frankfurt: Suhrkamp Verlag, 2004), p. 88.

4. Hannah Arendt, *Essays in Understanding 1930–1954*, ed. by Jerome Kohn (New York: Harcourt, Brace & Co., 1994). The three chapters are entitled "Dream and Nightmare," "Europe and the Atom Bomb," and "The Threat of Conformism." For more on Arendt's views of America and her trenchant insights into anti-Americanism and its relations to European identity formation, see Lars Rensmann, *European Political Identity, the Problem of anti-Americanism, and the Future of Transatlantic relations: An Arendtian view* (New Haven: Yale University International Security Studies Occasional Papers Series, 2004); and Rensmann, "Hannah Arendt and the Problem of European Anti-Americanism" (lecture given at the University of Michigan, February 6, 2004).

5. Arendt, *Essays in Understanding*, p. 410.

6. Ibid., p. 412.

7. Ibid.

8. Ibid., p. 413.

9. Ibid., pp. 413, 414.

10. Ibid., p. 415.

11. Ibid., pp. 416, 417.

12. On the discussion about the idea of "processing" and "overcoming" the Shoah, cf. Theodor W. Adorno, "Was bedeutet: Aufarbeitung der Vergangenheit," in *Gesammelte Schriften 10.2* (Frankfurt a. M: Suhrkamp, 1987), pp. 555–72; also Jürgen Habermas, "Was bedeutet 'Aufarbeitung der Vergangenheit' heute?" in *Die Normalität einer Berliner Republik* (Frankfurt am Main: Suhrkamp, 1995), pp. 21–45.

13. An especially significant example of this new intellectual anti-Americanism, which has been enjoying success in the wake of the debate on the war in Iraq, is the recently published work by the young scholars Nicole Schley and Sabine Busse, *Die Kriege der USA: Chronik einer aggressiven Nation* (Kreuzlingen: Hugendubel Verlag, 2003). Busse and Schley, still active in managing the project on "transatlantic relations" for the Bertelsmann Foundation, maintain that all of America's wars, from the War of Independence through the two world wars until the recent Gulf War, spring from the aspirations of an essentially "aggressive nation" as they accuse the United States of being.

14. Many important thinkers, particularly on the left, have equated Americanization with globalization and see the latter merely as a linguistic euphemism for the former. The late Pierre Bourdieu was perhaps most prominent among those holding this view. See Paula Izquierdo, "Pierre Bourdieu, 'Europa está dominada por Estados Unidos,' " *El Mundo*, July 4, 2000.

15. Andrés Ortega, "La Globalización de las Diferencias," *El Pais*, July 9, 2001.

16. For the tenacity of one-dimensional, exclusionary self-images in "white" Europe, the opportunities for upward social and political mobility are an especially good indicator. While France and Great Britain, owing to their democratic traditions and the legacy of colonialism, have developed more multicultural, pluralist self-images, it would be unimaginable in today's Germany (as in the rest of Europe) that new immigrants might assume leading political positions. It is, for example, unthinkable that somebody speaking German poorly, or with a strong foreign accent, might marry into a high-status family and become premier of one of the most important state governments (say, North Rhine-Westphalia). That would be the German equivalent of Arnold Schwarzenegger's political success story in the United States. This culturally based exclusion applies not only to Germany, but to all European countries, all of whom continue to have trouble with the political and social integration of immigrants. In no single European country would immigrants like Henry Kissinger, Zbigniew Brzezinski, Madeleine Albright, or John Shalikashvili (chairman of the Joint Chiefs of Staff of the U.S. Armed Forces, and it should be noted that the military is the most nationalist and conservative structure in most societies) be likely to achieve success and recognition.

17. As praiseworthy as it may seem, prima facie, for the EU to have pushed so emphatically for the internationalization of the legal system, an effort crystallized (among other things) by strong support for the International Criminal Court (ICC), which the United States has refused to back for various reasons, seldom have the limits of and concrete interests involved in this pro-ICC policy become a subject for discussion. Nor has there been any discussion about the problematic structural principles presented by this court, which simply reproduces all the problems of the UN General Assembly: Here representatives of authoritarian states have a majority (in the case of the ICC, this includes Malaysia, Morocco, and Egypt), states whose countries consequently will either seldom or never be indicted for human rights violations.

18. It should be noted that the previous practice and geopolitical goals of European foreign policy, which have recently been construed as a "countermodel" to "unilateralism" and American "particularism" as guided

by U.S. national interests, have not exactly provided an occasion for excessive confidence or enthusiasm, especially from a human rights and multilateral (as well as normatively cosmopolitan) perspective—this quite independently of military resources and the question of how critically one evaluates U.S. foreign policy. This applies to the EU's extraordinarily good relations with brachial dictators in China and the Near and Middle East, including Iran and Syria, or the joint conferences of EU member states with terrorist organizations like Hezbollah early in 2004, or the EU's enormous caution about confronting today's mass persecutions and genocidal murder in the Sudan.

19. Jürgen Habermas, "Hat die Konstitutionalisierung des Völkerrechts noch eine Chance?" in *Der gespaltene Westen*, pp. 113–93.

20. Habermas was constantly and vehemently criticized from the Right and Left for his unambiguous avowal of a normative-universalistic commitment to Western liberal democracy.

21. Volker Heins, "Orientalising America?" Heins discusses the writings of Habermas, Meyer, and Ulrich Beck about Europe and America as he forges the argument that there is an "othering" of America afoot in contemporary Europe that he calls "orientalising."

22. As in the genocide in Rwanda, where France, by supporting the putsch that triggered the genocide, at least benevolently tolerated the murderous Hutu militias (the Interahamwe), today France also opposes any international action that clearly labels the systematic genocidal murder of the Janjaweed militias in the Dafur region of the Sudan and might thereby enable the international community to have the legitimacy it needs to intervene, if only with a peacekeeping force. This, too, hardly testifies to the much-praised "postnational" phase—with its purportedly cosmopolitan normative orientation—in which European policy, guided by an avantgarde (core) European consciousness, supposedly finds itself. See BBC News, "France Opposes UN Sudan Sanctions," July 8, 2004. France led the opposition to any action by the U.N. As in Iraq, France has important oil interests in the Sudan. France has also been supporting every Arab dictatorship since 1967. In the meantime: No European demonstrators who might have been mindful of their heightened cosmopolitan consciousness with regard to mass crimes in the "global village" have yet been sighted doing anything about the crimes of Arab militias in the Sudan. The United States, admittedly, has also not been involved there to a degree that would truly end the atrocities against black Africans.

23. Domenico Losurdo, "Preemptive War, Americanism, and Anti-Americanism," *Metaphilosophy* 35 (2004), p. 366 ff.

24. Roger Cohen, "On Omaha Beach Today. Where's the Comradeship?" *New York Times*, February 5, 2004.

25. Roger Morgan, "What Kind of Europe? The Need for a 'Grand Debate,' " *Government & Opposition* 35 (2000), p. 558.

26. Homi K. Bhabha, *The Location of Culture* (London: Routledge, 1994), p. 12.

27. James W. Ceasar, "A Genealogy of Anti-Americanism," *Public Interest* 152 (2003), p. 18.

28. For recent perspectives, see, inter alia, Jean-Francois Revel, *Anti-Americanism* (San Francisco: Encoumer Books, 2003); and Philippe Roger, *L'Ennemi américain.*

29. Sarah Lyall, "Newest 'Europeans' Struggle to Define That Label," *New York Times*, May 1, 2004.

30. Ibid.

31. Volker Heins, "Orientalising America?" p. 434. See also his "Crusaders and Snobs: Moralizing Foreign Policy in Britain and Germany, 1999–2005," in David Chandler and Volker Heins, eds. *Rethinking Ethical Foreign Policy: Pitfalls, Paradoxes and Possibilities* (London: Routledge, 2006), pp. 50–69.

32. Eliseo Álvarez-Arenas, "La Europa Americana," *El Pais*, March 3, 1992.

33. For a collection of essays of how European discontent can, should and will contest American power, see Sergio Fabbrini, ed., *The United States Contested: American unilateralism and European Discontent* (London: Routledge, 2006).

34. As quoted in Roger Cohen, "Anti-Americanism Is One 'ism' That Thrives," *International Herald Tribune*, November 28, 2005.

35. Jean Monnet, *Memoires* (Paris: Fayard, 1976), p. 495.

# INDEX

------------------------------------------------

With Thanks to the Donors of the Public Square

President William P. Kelly, the CUNY Graduate Center
President Jermey Travis, John Jay College of Criminal Justice
Myron S. Gluckman
Caroline Urvater